Cover, Title Page Photo Credits: Escalator ©Rodrigo Apolaya/APU Imagenes/Getty Images. All Other Photos ©HMH

Escalate  English

4

Dear Student,

Welcome to *Escalate English*! This program is designed to help you take the final steps to becoming fully proficient in English. You will practice and master the skills you need to listen, speak, read, and write English at home, in your community, and at school. This is your opportunity to fine tune your skills so that your English is great in both social and academic situations. You will be ready to conquer the next phase of your education.

Escalate English and your teachers will help you, but you also have a job to do. As you work through this program, ask questions, share what you are learning, and discuss your ideas. The more you practice, the faster your skills will improve. Being an active partner in your learning will ensure that you reach your goals—one step at a time!

What is

Escalate English is a program designed to help you quickly increase your English skills so that you can fully participate in all of your classes. You will master the academic language you need to excel—now and in the future.

escalate *verb*
1. to increase rapidly
2. to rise quickly
synonyms: soar, climb, accelerate

Escalate English?

You are ready.

Ready to increase
your English skills.

Ready to achieve more in
school, in life, in a career.

Ready to tackle the language
you need to succeed.

You are ready to Escalate!

UNIT 1 Reaching Out

Tell Me More

UNIT 3   Inside Nature

(tl) ©Siede Preis/Photodisc/Getty Images; (tr) ©Candy Rodó

Unbreakable Spirit

UNIT 5 Change It Up

Paths to Discovery

Student Resources

Connecting to Your World

Every time you read something, view something, write to someone, or react to what you've read or seen, you're participating in a world of ideas. You do this every day, inside the classroom and out. These skills will serve you not only at home and at school, but eventually (if you can think that far ahead!), in your career.

The digital tools in this program will tap into the skills you already use and help you sharpen those skills for the future.

Start your exploration at my.hrw.com.

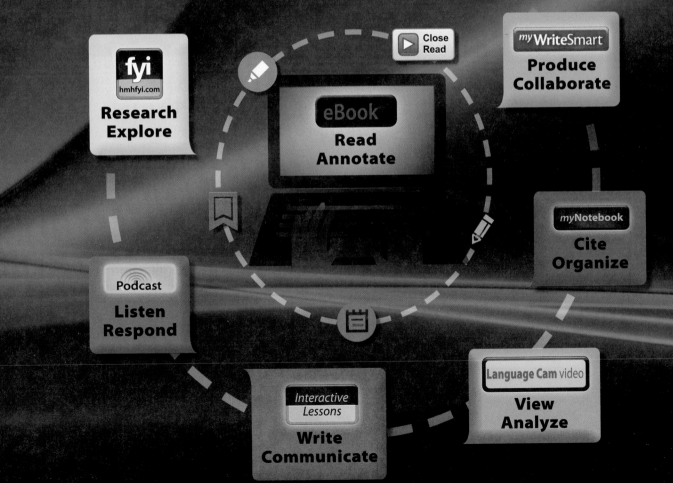

Interacting in Meaningful Ways

Every day you interact with people in many different situations. You text with friends, make plans with family, give directions to your siblings, talk with people in your community, and participate in discussions at school. You have probably noticed that the language you use in one situation might not work in another. In *Escalate English*, you will see and hear examples of English used in meaningful ways. You will have opportunities to practice using words, phrases, and structures so that you are able to successfully interact in every situation.

Collaborating

You have a lot of knowledge to share with others and there is a lot you can learn from others. Whether at home, at school, or in the workplace, it is important to learn the language you need to participate in collaborative discussions. You will be successful if you are prepared for discussions, listen carefully to what others say, and can ask questions and provide feedback.

It is also important to pay attention to the rules of conversation, such as knowing when to take your turn.

Sometimes your interactions are spoken and sometimes they are written. Either way, it is important to understand your purpose and your audience. It is different to exchange social texts and emails with friends than it is to exchange information for school or work. In *Escalate English*, you will practice writing and responding to blogs as well as collaborating with your classmates on a variety of academic topics. The more you practice, the more you will be able to express what you know.

In *Escalate English,* you will learn about many topics and you will have an opinion about what you hear, view, and read. You may need to support your opinion and persuade others. It is important to provide facts and examples to support your opinion. In *Escalate English*, you will learn the language you need to clearly make claims and to persuade others. You will know what language to use in every situation.

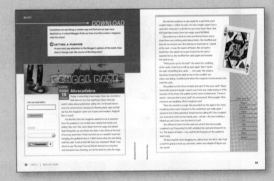

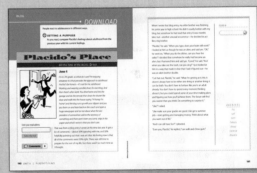

Interacting in Meaningful Ways

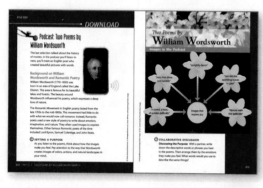

To effectively communicate, it is important to listen and read as carefully as you speak and write. Sometimes it is easy to understand what we hear and read and other times the language and the topic may be less familiar and more challenging. In *Escalate English*, you will learn many strategies for listening, viewing, and reading.

Interpreting

It is important to know how to ask questions when you do not understand or when you want more information. In *Escalate English*, you will learn when and how to ask questions effectively.

Even when what you are viewing or reading seems difficult, it is important not to give up. In *Escalate English*, you will learn to view and read closely. The skills you learn will help you figure out what unfamiliar words and phrases mean and explain what you understand.

You will see that some words and phrases have different meanings in different contexts. As you learn more about language choices, you will be able to impress people with your ability to use language accurately.

Language Cam video

Watch the video to find out more about ways people can reach out and help others.

Language Cam video

Watch the video to find out more about kids making discoveries.

Language Cam video

Want to learn more about revolution? Watch the video.

Language Cam video

Watch this video to learn about nature at work.

Producing the Right Language

One of the most important skills you will develop in school is the ability to talk to a group of people in a formal situation. You will be asked to do this frequently in *Escalate English*. At first, it can be frightening to prepare and present to a group of people, but, with practice, you will find it gets easier. Learning to present formal oral presentations on a variety of topics is a skill you will need throughout your life.

Producing

Sometimes, instead of expressing your ideas orally, you will be asked to write them. You will learn a variety of formats and will practice using different technology tools to organize your thoughts and to write. Being able to explain your ideas and opinions, to present your argument, and to share information with others clearly will prepare you for college and for your future career.

©Kamira/Shutterstock

at the Right Time

In *Escalate English,* you will learn that "one size does not fit all." The way you write will change if you are communicating with friends via social media, completing homework or a test, or doing a writing assignment for class. You will learn to select the most appropriate vocabulary and language structures to effectively convey ideas depending on the situation.

Understanding How English Works

Have you ever noticed that texts look different depending upon where you see them? Some texts might be easier for you to read and some might be more difficult. Is it easier for you to read a magazine, a story, or something from your science or social studies text? That is because texts are put together differently for different purposes. In *Escalate English,* you will practice reading varied texts. As you do, you will also learn how these texts are put together and why. You will practice writing using these texts as models. Soon, you will be able to write accurately for multiple purposes.

Some texts are harder to follow than others. Sometimes readers get lost in a story or article and have to use strategies to find their way. In *Escalate English,* you will learn how to identify words and phrases that help you, as a reader, understand how the text is glued together. This will help you read more fluently and, with practice, reading and understanding will become much easier.

You will also learn to watch for language that tells you the important details in a text. You will begin to notice language that indicates when something happened. You will begin to tune into the language that describes what is going on in the text. You may be surprised how exciting it can be when you understand all the details.

Understanding How English Works

The more you read and listen to English for different purposes, the more you will be able to express yourself in many ways. As you prepare for your future college and career experiences, you will want to be sure you are able to write and speak fluently and efficiently.

In *Escalate English*, you will learn the language you need to connect your thoughts together. You will practice this orally and, with enough practice, you will be able to use the language in writing. The people who listen to what you say and read what you write will be able to understand exactly what you mean.

You will also learn words and phrases that will help you become more efficient with your language. Learning how to condense your ideas will enable you to say what you mean and mean what you say!

This is your opportunity to become
academically proficient in English.
Work hard, practice, and prepare
for your successful future!

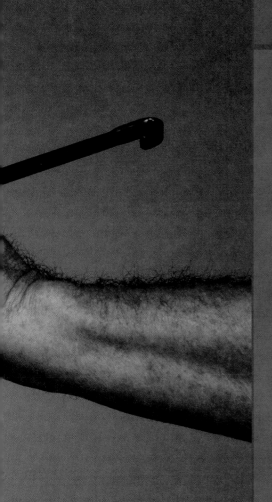

Reaching Out

*Those who are happiest
are those who do the
most for others.*

**— Booker T. Washington,
educator**

Essential Question

How can we help each
other every day?

The Language of Reaching Out

There are many ways of reaching out to other people.
Whether carrying groceries for a neighbor, working to clean a local park, or sharing a sandwich with a friend who forgot her lunch, people help one another every day. When you help someone, you do something to make that person's life a little easier or a little nicer.

We can help people in our local community. Your local community is made up of all the people who live and work in your neighborhood. Giving directions, checking in on elderly neighbors, and taking care of a neighbor's pet are ways we can help in our community.

Business owners, teachers, scientists, doctors, and many others help people as part of their work. Sometimes people choose careers that allow them to help other people while also earning a living. Doctors, for example, help keep us healthy. Teachers help us to learn.

In this unit, you will learn about some of the ways people help one another. First, you will find out about a boy who volunteered at a local senior center. Then you will learn about engineers and the work they do to solve problems and help people around the world. You will also read a story that tells about how one act of kindness changed an entire family's life.

> **In what ways do you try to help others? In what ways do others help you?**

Lending a Hand: Context Clues

Often when we read stories or articles, we come across words we don't know. Sometimes we can figure out the meaning of an unfamiliar word by using clues in the words or sentences around it. Here's an example.

> Stella stared at the stars above. As an astronomer, she was always thinking about stars.
>
> The word *astronomer* may be unfamiliar, but context clues can help you define this word.
>
> > Stella stared at the stars above.
> >
> > As an astronomer she was always thinking about stars.
>
> You can guess from the clues that an astronomer is someone who studies or does work related to stars.

These sentences have context clues. Try to figure out the meaning of each word using the clues.

> Michael is in a great **mood** because today is his birthday.
>
> I was so sure that I had finished my homework that I told my mom I was **positive** that it was done.
>
> Our family has a **nourishing** diet because we eat fruits and vegetables every day.

↻ Performance Task

Choose an example of a way in which people help one another.
You may select one of the examples on page 2, one in **Browse** magazine, or another example that interests you. Write a short speech about your chosen example. Why is it important to help others in this way? Don't forget to use your **Activity Book**, too.

→ *Browse* magazine

DOWNLOAD

Have you ever volunteered or offered to help someone? How did it make you feel? Read on to find out what this blogger discovered while volunteering at a senior center.

⏻ SETTING A PURPOSE

As you read, think about how the blogger's feelings about visiting the senior center change.

Clarinet and Cupcakes

Enter your email address:

Subscribe me!

SEARCH

September 16, 5:19 p.m.—Not What I Expected!

I just got back from a visit to the senior center. It was not at all what I expected!

Each kid in my class had to choose a volunteer project this week. We could:

◊ read in a pre-K classroom,
◊ help with the recycling, or
◊ visit the senior center across the road.

OK, so, going to the senior center was not my first choice, or my second choice. All the slots for the other choices were filled when I went to sign up. I groaned and rolled my eyes. I was not in a great mood. But actually, it turns out I was lucky.

Six of us went over together, with a teacher. I brought my clarinet. I've started playing in band, and I know a couple of tunes. I guess I thought it would be kind of sad and boring over there. OK, so the "day

room" where they hang out is nothing fancy, and some of the seniors were dozing in their chairs. But the others were so happy to see us! They made such a fuss. This lady named Ida introduced herself and asked if I wanted to play cards. We played "War" (I love that game), then she taught me a game called "Kings in the Corners." I think she knew about a hundred different games.

Ida's buddy Murray came over and said, "So, you gonna play that thing or is it just decoration?" I took out my clarinet and played the tunes I know. A few of the seniors clapped and smiled. Murray said, "Not bad, kid. Practice every day for the next twenty years and you might get somewhere."

Then Murray sat down at the piano and started to play. My brain almost exploded! His hands whizzed up and down the keyboard. Ida started to sing, and the rest of the seniors joined in. They knew ALL the words! Murray showed me how to play along with the song, switching between three notes on my clarinet. Then he taught my classmates the words to the chorus, and they joined in every time it came around. It was the best thing ever.

When I got home and thought about what had just happened, it felt like a dream. I was the "volunteer" but they helped me, too. Well, maybe when I go back I can help them with something I know about—like computers and blogging!

💬 **Comments** | 2

8:19 p.m. **Clarinet and Cupcakes gets Schooled.**

6:57 p.m. **Thanks for the visit, Clarinet and Cupcakes. It wasn't a dream. FYI, some of US know about blogging, too! Your New Friend, Ida**

ARCHIVES

September

August

July

June

May

April

March

February

January

UPLOAD

⏻ COLLABORATIVE DISCUSSION

Discussing the Purpose In a small group, discuss how Clarinet and Cupcakes felt at the beginning of the blog about visiting the senior center. How did Clarinet and Cupcakes's feelings change during the visit? What caused the blogger's feelings to change?

Staying Safe How can bloggers stay safe when they communicate online? Work in a group to make a list of safety rules that bloggers should follow.

Write On!

Like many blogs, "Clarinet and Cupcakes" gives readers the opportunity to post a comment. Usually when people comment, they share their opinion about the blog post or share a similar story. Write a short comment in response to this post. Then trade comments with a classmate. 🗨 **Comments**

⟳ Performance Task

Writing Activity: Start a Blog People write blogs about all kinds of things. Some blogs are about a hobby. Other blogs are about the blogger's day-to-day experiences. Do you blog?

1 Start and keep a blog as you complete this unit. First decide what you want to write about. Be sure to pick a topic that you care about.

2 Next, decide what website you'll use to host your blog. There are many free blogging websites out there. Using one of these sites is a good idea because you don't have to pay anything to get started.

③ Then, decide what your blog will look like. There are many free themes on the Internet to choose from. Free blogging websites often have themes that are built-in. Pick a catchy title for your blog. You can also add some art at the top or in the background. For safety's sake, you should use a nickname when you are blogging.

④ Finally, it is time to start writing! Share your blog posts with people you know. If you use a free blogging website, you can often follow other users of that website. These users can also follow you back. You can keep a "blogroll" that lists all of the other blogs you enjoy reading. It is common for bloggers that you add to your blogroll to add you back, which lets you reach even more readers.

Language Cam video

Watch the video to find out more about ways people can reach out and help others.

DOWNLOAD

SOLVING PROBLEMS AROUND THE WORLD

Think about ways in which Sam and the seniors at the center helped each other. Then read on to find out ways people work together to help solve problems.

Background on Engineers

An engineer is a person who uses science, math, and creativity to find solutions to problems. Some engineers help to build or design physical spaces, such as buildings or roads. Other engineers work to build or design machines and technology. Still others think of ways for people to work together better, or to work more safely.

READING TOOLBOX

Author's Purpose

An author often has many reasons, or purposes, for writing. You can read the details in informational texts to help you figure out the **author's purpose**. Some authors include their opinion about a subject. The author may express her or his opinion with the words she has chosen to describe something or someone. She may also support her opinion with facts and examples. Facts and examples help explain why the author feels the way she does.

⏻ SETTING A PURPOSE

As you read, pay attention to words the author uses to describe engineers and their work. How do these words help you know the author's opinion about engineers?

Solving Problems Around the World

by Paloma Barranco

Engineers like to solve problems. The problem could be fixing a dangerous **intersection** in Sacramento, California, or bringing water to a village in Bangladesh. Many engineers spend their lives helping people.

intersection: a place where two paths meet; a junction or crossroads

ENGINEERS know a lot about things like design and construction. But before they can start a project, they have to learn more. Before they can solve a problem, they have to learn all they can about the problem. They also have to learn about the people affected by the problem.

▲ The Buriganga Riverside in Dhaka, Bangladesh

This is a **long sentence**. How could you break up this sentence so it is easier to understand?

Before you can fix a dangerous intersection, you have to study how the traffic moves through the area. You have to learn how people drive there, you have to know what

10 routes they tend to take, and you have to find out what they want from the new intersection.

If you want to bring water to a village in Bangladesh, you have to study the land. Where is the nearest source of water? How can you get it to the village? You also have to find out how the people in the village use water. They drink it and wash in it, sure. Do they water crops?

Give it to animals? Clean machinery? Is the best idea to dig wells or catch rainwater? Should they purify the water that they have? The answers to these questions can come only
20 from the people who live there.

Engineers often **team up with** the people they are working to assist. These people have knowledge and skills the engineers don't have. Often, the best plan is to improve people's methods, not replace them.

Another example comes from southern India. People gather many agricultural products in the forests there. Some of these products, such as fruit, need to be dried before they are eaten or sold at market. The traditional method of drying fruit is to set the fruit out in the sun.
30 This takes a while, and the quality of the fruit can **degrade**.

▲ Merchants sell fruit at a food market in Kolkata, India.

A group called The Keystone Foundation is working with these people. In other parts of the world, produce is dried by machines, but that won't work here. Keystone's T. Balachander says, "Half of technology is the people that use it. If you have a fancy machine that nobody knows how to operate, then it won't be used. And if you bring in a machine that requires … electricity [or] flowing water, or needs to be carried by vehicle, then it won't even get there in the first place."

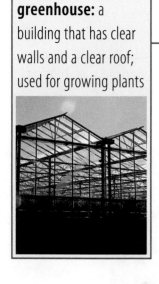

greenhouse: a building that has clear walls and a clear roof; used for growing plants

40 Instead, Keystone worked with the local people to build drying stages. They have roofs of clear plastic, which increases the sunlight's heat, like in a **greenhouse**. The sides are open so air can circulate. The fruit stays clean and dries more quickly. And that means the farmers have more product to sell.

Good engineers learn about local conditions. Then they decide what the next steps should be. Some engineering schools even offer courses in community feedback. That's how important helping the community is to the 50 engineer's job.

This is a **long sentence**. Read the sentence again to be sure you understand its meaning.

⏻ COLLABORATIVE DISCUSSION

Discussing the Purpose In a small group, talk about the words or sentences that helped you understand the author's opinion about engineers. Did her examples help you believe that engineers are helpful people?

Analyzing the Text [Cite Text Evidence]

1. Which examples did the author use to show ways engineers help people?

2. Why do you think the author states that it is often better to improve people's current methods than to change them?

Speak Out! Which example that the author uses do you think is the most helpful or important to a community? Share your opinion with a partner. Do you and your partner agree?

⟳ Performance Task

Speaking Activity: Sharing Opinions In a small group, review the selection, "Solving Problems Around the World."

What examples does the author use to describe how engineers are helpful to a community?

Which example do you think is the most important or the most helpful?

Take turns sharing your opinions.

Do the students in the group agree or disagree?

What words can you use to try to change your classmates' opinions?

DOWNLOAD

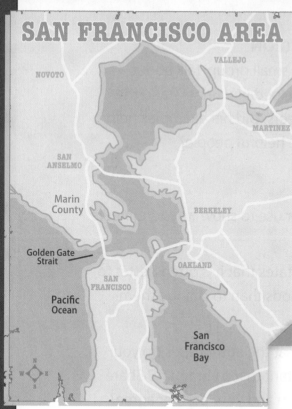

SAN FRANCISCO AREA

VALLEJO

NOVOTO

MARTINEZ

SAN
ANSELMO

Marin
County

BERKELEY

Golden Gate
Strait

OAKLAND

SAN
FRANCISCO

Pacific
Ocean

San
Francisco
Bay

The Birth of the Golden Gate Bridge

In the last selection, you read about how engineers help people. Many engineers were involved in building the Golden Gate Bridge. Find out how the building of the bridge helped the people of California.

READING TOOLBOX

Finding Facts

Informational texts give information about a topic. They usually include many facts. A **fact** is a true statement. The date or time that something happened is a fact. How you feel about something is an **opinion**. Opinions are different from facts.

Fact	Opinion
The Golden Gate Bridge opened in 1937.	The Golden Gate Bridge is beautiful.
San Francisco is a city in California.	San Francisco is the nicest city in which to live.

⏻ SETTING A PURPOSE

As you read, pay attention to the facts that the author includes.

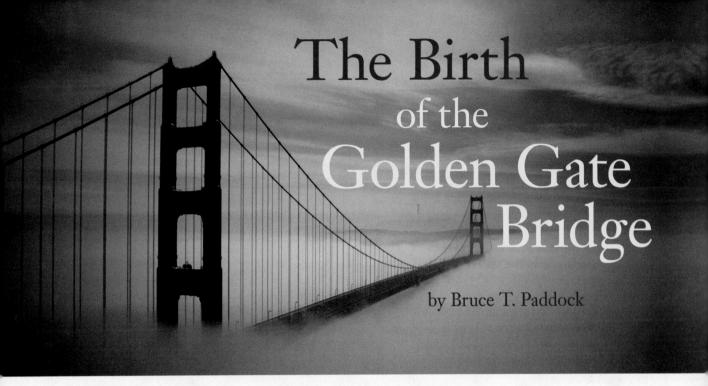

The Birth
of the
Golden Gate
Bridge

by Bruce T. Paddock

Hold one finger in front of your face, pointing straight up. Now hold up another finger, pointing down, so the tips almost touch. You can think of this as a map of San Francisco.

Your lower finger is the land that San Francisco sits on. Your upper finger is an area called Marin County. To the left of your fingers is the Pacific Ocean. To the right is San Francisco Bay, which stretches miles from north to south. The space between your fingers is a narrow stretch of water
10 called the Golden Gate **Strait**.

Use Context Clues
What words give you a clue about the meaning of the word *strait*?

You can put your hands down now.

One hundred years ago, getting from Marin County to San Francisco wasn't easy. Driving around the bay took hours. Ferries ran across the strait, but ferries take time. You would have to drive to the pier and wait for a boat. Then all the cars and people had to be loaded on board. The trip was short, but **unloading** the boat on the other side took time, too.

The **prefix *un-*** changes a word to mean its opposite. To *load* means "to put things onto something." To *unload* means "to take things off of something."

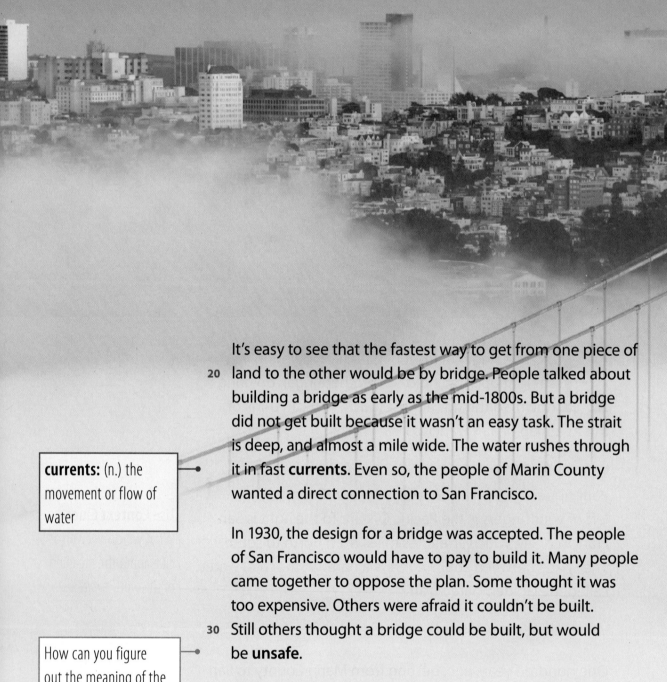

It's easy to see that the fastest way to get from one piece of
20 land to the other would be by bridge. People talked about
building a bridge as early as the mid-1800s. But a bridge
did not get built because it wasn't an easy task. The strait
is deep, and almost a mile wide. The water rushes through
it in fast **currents**. Even so, the people of Marin County
wanted a direct connection to San Francisco.

currents: (n.) the
movement or flow of
water

In 1930, the design for a bridge was accepted. The people
of San Francisco would have to pay to build it. Many people
came together to oppose the plan. Some thought it was
too expensive. Others were afraid it couldn't be built.
30 Still others thought a bridge could be built, but would
be **unsafe.**

How can you figure
out the meaning of the
word *unsafe*? Do you
know what the **prefix
un-** means?

Other groups came together to support the project. The
California Chamber of Commerce said it would provide
jobs. The State Automobile Association thought more
people would buy cars if there were a bridge. Other groups
wanted to increase tourism in northern California.

©Francesco Carucci/Shutterstock

These workers are building the Golden Gate Bridge.

On November 4, 1930, voters in San
Francisco County and five neighboring
counties voted. More than three-
40 quarters of voters wanted to build the
bridge. Construction on the Golden
Gate Bridge began in 1933 and took
four years to complete. The chief
engineer insisted on more safety
precautions than on any previous
work. New safety systems included
hard hats and a safety net. This
attention to safety for the workers
made the bridge possible, and with
50 fewer injuries than anyone expected.

The day the bridge opened, May 27,
1937, no cars were allowed. Instead,
200,000 people from all over the area
crossed the span on foot. Cars started
making the crossing the next day.
People were delighted to make the trip
from Marin County to San Francisco so
quickly. Since then, billions of drivers
and walkers have taken advantage of
60 the fast, easy connection between the
two places.

> Break down the
> word **precautions**
> into two parts to
> help you figure out
> what it means.

⏻ COLLABORATIVE DISCUSSION

Discussing the Purpose In a small group, talk about the facts you found in the article. Did the author include any opinions? Talk about these, too.

Speak Out! In this selection, you read that some people were in favor of building the Golden Gate Bridge, while other people were against it. Both groups supported their opinion with reasons. Imagine you lived in San Francisco in the early 1800s. Would you be in favor of a bridge spanning the Golden Gate Strait? What reasons would you use to support your opinion? The best arguments are supported by facts. Which facts might support your opinion? Work with a partner to debate the building of the Golden Gate Bridge.

Vocabulary Strategy: Using Prefixes

A **prefix** is a word part that may be added to the beginning of a word. Knowing common prefixes can help you understand the meaning of unfamiliar words. The chart below shows three common prefixes.

Prefix	Meaning
re-	again
un-	not; the opposite of
dis-	not

Copy the words below in your notebook. Draw a box around the prefix in each word and underline the root, or base, word. How does the prefix change the meaning of the base word?

reschedule   untie   disappear   retry   unable

DOWNLOAD

Podcast: The Grateful Beasts

The last selection told how the Golden Gate Bridge connected people in San Francisco and Marin County. In this podcast, you'll hear how the way someone acts toward others can make important connections, too.

Background on Folktales

This podcast is a folktale. Folktales are stories that have been passed down over many years through people telling and retelling them. Folktales begin as stories told out loud, and are only later written down. Usually, no one knows who the author is. Folktales often explain something in nature or teach a lesson.

This story, "The Grateful Beasts," was first told in Hungary. One of the first English-language versions of it is from the 1890s. It was published in a folktale collection called *The Yellow Fairy Book*. Older versions of folktales are often changed to fit modern audiences.

Hungary

⏻ SETTING A PURPOSE

As you listen to this podcast, think about how Franci acts toward the animals she meets. What effects do her actions have later?

The Grateful Beasts

Cause and Effect in the Folktale

Cause	Effect
1. Franci feeds the hungry wolf.	The wolf helps Franci drive the king and Franci's sisters out of the kingdom.
2. Franci protects the bees' broken hive with her coat.	The bees build a beautiful palace of honeycomb and flowers.
3. Franci gives the hungry mouse the last of her food.	The mice carry the corn into the barn.
4. Franci is kind to the animals even when it means that she has to give something up.	Franci and the animals live happily ever after.

⏻ COLLABORATIVE DISCUSSION

Discussing the Purpose With a partner, think about what Franci did when she met each animal. How did this help Franci later in the story? How were Franci's actions different from those of her sisters?

How to Get Rich

You heard a folktale about a girl who lives happily ever after when she helps the animals in a forest. Now read about a kind act that changed everything for one family.

Know Before You Go

The Year of the Dog is a novel about growing up in a Chinese American family. The narrator is a young girl. In this section she and her family celebrate the Chinese New Year. This holiday celebrates the end of the old lunar year and the beginning of a new one. Many of the traditions associated with this special time are intended to attract good luck and wealth in the coming year.

In this chapter, the narrator's mother tells a story about how Grandpa helped someone and how that act of reaching out changed his family's life.

⏻ SETTING A PURPOSE

As you read, think about what Grandpa did, and why it was so important.

How to Get Rich

from *The Year of the Dog*

by Grace Lin

"TIME TO EAT!" MOM CALLED.

In the dining room, there was so much food. There was a whole fried fish—crispy and brown, meat dumplings fried golden, vegetables shining with oil, **steamed buns that looked like puffy clouds**, shrimp in a milky sauce, and pork colored a brilliant ruby pink. The fish's eyes stared at me. I didn't like it, so I turned that plate around so it would look at Lissy instead. She turned it back toward me. And I turned it again. Finally we had

10 it look at Ki-Ki. She didn't notice.

> Can you **imagine** what this image would look like?

"Everything we eat tonight has a special meaning," Dad said. "These vegetables mean wealth."

"How about the shrimp?" I asked.

"That means wealth, too," Dad said.

"What does the pork mean?" Lissy asked.

"Wealth, too!" Dad said.

"Everything means wealth," Lissy said. "All we care about is money!"

"Well, don't you want to be rich?" Mom asked.

20 "Yes!" Lissy and I said at the same time. Ki-Ki nodded her head.

"I want to be a millionaire," I said.

"I want to be a **gazillionaire**," Lissy said.

"Me, too," Ki-Ki said. "Me, too."

"Well, eat these," Mom told us, passing us the fried dumplings. "They say these symbolize gold coins, so if you eat them you'll be rich."

"I don't know how they're going to make me rich," I said. "They don't look like gold coins to me."

30 "Maybe that's what coins looked like in the olden days," Lissy whispered to me.

"I'm going to eat all of them," Dad teased, "then I'll have all of the money and you'll have none."

"That's not fair," I said, trying to grab some dumplings off his plate. "Give me some."

"I'll sell you one for a dollar," Dad said. "That's how you get rich!"

The phone rang again and this time it was Grandpa calling to say Happy New Year.

40 "I bet Grandpa ate a lot of these dumplings," Lissy said. "Grandpa's rich."

"Maybe he charged two dollars for each dumpling!" I joked.

"Actually," Mom said, "Grandpa got rich by doing a job for free. Did I ever tell you the story about Grandpa's first patient?"

We all shook our heads and Mom started the story.

The word **gazillionaire** comes from *zillion*, a very large number. What word in the previous sentence gives you a clue about its meaning?

HOW GRANDPA GOT RICH

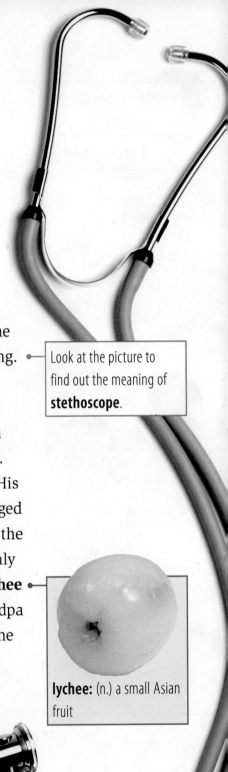

When Grandpa graduated from medical school and was officially a doctor, he was so proud! But he had a
50 problem. He had no patients. It seemed like whenever people were sick, they went to someone else. No one wanted to go and see Grandpa, a young doctor with no experience.

Still, with the help of his parents he opened a small clinic in the neighborhood. Sometimes his mother would come over saying she had back pains so he could cure her. Sometimes Grandpa would use the **stethoscope** on himself just to make sure it was working. But most of the time, Grandpa just sat there alone, like
60 the last dumpling on a plate.

> Look at the picture to find out the meaning of **stethoscope**.

Then, one night, just when the sky began to darken with shadows, there was a frantic banging on the door. A street vendor had been robbed and was badly hurt. His clothes looked like dishrags of blood, and his wife begged for help. Grandpa jumped up and worked hard to save the vendor's life. He worked deep into the night, and he only stopped when the moon hung like a freshly peeled **lychee** in the sky. Finally, the patient was out of danger. Grandpa left him with his wife in the clinic and told them that he
70 would check up on them in the morning.

lychee: (n.) a small Asian fruit

But, when Grandpa woke up the next morning and went to check on his patient at the clinic, there was no one there. The bed was made and the room was as clean as an empty rice bowl. Had he dreamed it all?

sneaked away: left quietly and secretly

Later, Grandpa found out that his patient was very poor. He and his wife had **sneaked away** after Grandpa had left because they knew they could not pay him. In fact, right after the accident the wife had brought the 80 vendor to two other doctors before Grandpa; the other doctors had refused to operate because they knew he couldn't pay. Grandpa, on the other hand, didn't even think about asking for payment and had just hurried to save his life.

So it looked like Grandpa's first patient was going to be free of charge. Grandpa worried because he thought that it didn't look like a good start for his business. He had his family to support and they were counting on him to make money as a doctor. Was this first patient a sign 90 of his future?

But he shouldn't have worried. Like the smell of roast pork, the news of Grandpa's good work spread around the village. People were warmed by the fact that Grandpa cared more for their lives than their money. They stopped seeing their other doctors and came to him instead. Soon he had more patients than he could handle.

"And that is how Grandpa became rich," Mom finished. Then she looked at the empty table. "Ai-you! There's no food left for me!"

⏻ COLLABORATIVE DISCUSSION

Discussing the Purpose In a small group, discuss Grandpa's act of reaching out to someone in need. How did this generous act change everything for Grandpa and his family?

↻ Performance Task

Speaking Activity: Different Kinds of Language Work in a small group to explore the different kinds of language used in this story. Talk about how the following quotes make you feel.

- "... steamed buns that looked like puffy clouds ..."

- "Grandpa just sat there alone, like the last dumpling on a plate."

- "Then, one night, just when the sky began to darken with shadows, there was a frantic banging on the door."

- "... and he only stopped when the moon hung like a freshly peeled lychee in the sky."

- "The bed was made and the room was as clean as an empty rice bowl."

Can you describe what you imagine when you read the words?

DOWNLOAD

Helping people seems like the right thing to do. But sometimes the best way to help someone is unclear. What happens when someone doesn't want help? Is it best to just leave them alone?

⏻ SETTING A PURPOSE

As you read, look for arguments that support the idea of helping people even if they don't want to be helped. Look for arguments that support not helping, too.

WHAT IS THE BEST WAY TO
Help Homeless People?

❖

by Susan Buckley

---

huddled: curled up or hunched over

The **wind picked up** is an **idiom**. It means that it became more windy.

The man sat **huddled** against the wall of the office building. As the temperature dropped below freezing, **the wind picked up**. It was getting dark, and people were heading home from school or work. Most people walked right past the man. They didn't stop to talk or even to look at him. But when Paula and Ann saw him, they were upset. *What could they do to help?* they wondered.

©Nella/Shutterstock

10 Paula wanted to help the man herself. *I could buy him a cup of soup*, she thought. *Or perhaps I could get him a blanket from home.* Ann had a different idea. She wanted to find a police officer. She would ask him to take the man to a shelter to get out of the cold. "What if he doesn't want to go?" Paula asked. Ann was positive that the police officer should force the man to go, for his own good.

The U. S. Department of Housing and Urban Development estimates that more than 610,000 Americans are homeless on any given day. Nearly a quarter of them are children.
20 And more than a third of the total do not spend the night in a shelter. Especially in the winter, this can be a dangerous problem. But it is not an easy one to solve.

Organizations like the National Coalition for the Homeless publish lists of ways to help the homeless. They use CARE as an acronym. It stands for Contribute, Advocate, Reach Out, and Educate. These are ways in which you can help people who are experiencing **homelessness**. Whether you are buying someone food, giving them a blanket, or working to fund new shelters—you can help.

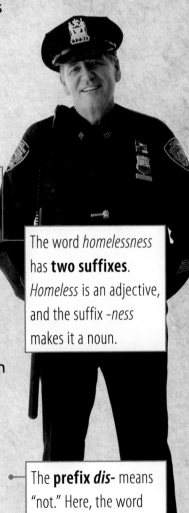

The word *homelessness* has **two suffixes**. *Homeless* is an adjective, and the suffix *-ness* makes it a noun.

30 Another problem occurs, however, when people who are homeless refuse your help. What should you do then? This is the question Paula and Ann discussed.

Ann believes that society has a responsibility to watch out for people who have serious problems. If the homeless man is not able to find a shelter or not willing to go to a shelter or other safe place, Ann thinks the police or other officials should make the decision for him.

Paula **disagrees**. She believes that forcing the homeless man to protect himself would violate his civil rights. If he
40 wants to stay out, he should be allowed to, she thinks.

The **prefix dis-** means "not." Here, the word *disagrees* means "does not agree."

What do you think?

⏻ **COLLABORATIVE DISCUSSION**

Discussing the Purpose Talk with a small group about ways you can help people in need. Discuss the reasons mentioned in the article that tell why you should help. Then discuss the reasons mentioned for why you should not force help. What is your opinion?

SPEAKING TOOLBOX

Persuasive Speaking

Present your argument without lecturing or bullying your listeners.

▶ **Make your argument.** Explain the position you take, and state your points clearly.

▶ **Support your argument.** Give facts and details that support your position.

▶ **Be convincing.** Make your argument evenly, but with enthusiasm.

©Houghton Mifflin Harcourt

Idioms

An **idiom** is a group of words in which the words together have a meaning that is different from the dictionary definitions of the individual words. Here are some sentences with idioms. Can you figure out what they mean?

- I had butterflies in my stomach before the big test.

- That test was a piece of cake because I studied hard the night before.

- When I told my family how well I did on the test they were on top of the world.

- Maurice got the hang of riding a scooter after falling once or twice.

- We had a field day riding our scooters all around the schoolyard.

- Maurice and I rode our scooters all day on Saturday until we finally ran out of steam.

Write On! Do you think it's better to help someone who doesn't want help or to leave people alone? Choose a side to argue. Then write a short paragraph telling why you feel the way you do. Remember, the best arguments are supported with facts.

DOWNLOAD

Balto's Story

You have just read a selection about helping homeless people. Now you will read about a brave dog who helped to save many lives.

Know Before You Go

Balto was a Siberian husky who became known as a hero all over the world. Balto completed the last lap of a mission that brought medicine to the children of Nome, Alaska. This medicine saved many lives.

SAVED! After the mission was over, Balto and his team ended up in a vaudeville act in Los Angeles, unhealthy and badly treated. Enter George Kimble, a businessman visiting from Cleveland. Working with the newspaper *The Plain Dealer*, Kimble brought the dogs to Ohio. On March 19, 1927, Balto and six companions marched into Cleveland, where they were given a hero's welcome.

STAR HOUND Balto has long been a favorite subject of writers, artists, and animators. In 1965, the American cartoonist Carl Barks created a dog-hero character named Barko for his *Uncle Scrooge* series. People think that the character was created to honor Balto. An animated film of Balto's life, *Balto*, was made in 1995. It starred Kevin Bacon as the voice of Balto.

⏻ SETTING A PURPOSE

As you read, think about why Balto is considered a hero.

Balto's Story

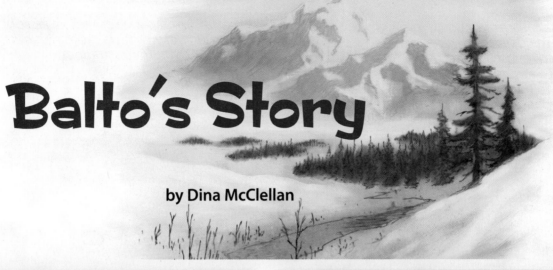

by Dina McClellan

DECEMBER, 1924: NOME, ALASKA. A TWO-YEAR OLD INUIT BOY BECOMES THE FIRST PERSON TO DIE OF DIPHTHERIA. DR. WELCH, NOME'S ONLY PHYSICIAN, THINKS IT IS TONSILLITIS — UNTIL OTHER CHILDREN BEGIN TO DIE OF THE SAME THING . . .

MID-JANUARY, 1925: DR. WELCH CORRECTLY IDENTIFIES THE DISEASE AS DIPHTHERIA.

There is only one cure for diphtheria —a special serum. Unfortunately there's none of it in Nome . . .

JANUARY 22, 1925: DR. WELCH SENDS A FRANTIC TELEGRAM TO THE U.S. PUBLIC HEALTH SERVICE EXPLAINING THE NEED FOR SERUM— AND FINDS OUT THAT THE CLOSEST SOURCE IS 1,000 MILES AWAY, IN ANCHORAGE! IMMEDIATELY, A TRAIN LOADED WITH THE SERUM IS ON ITS WAY.

Don't worry folks! We'll be back in no time!

THE TRAIN DOES NOT GO ALL THE WAY TO NOME, SO THE ONLY WAY TO DELIVER THE SERUM IS OVER LAND —AND THE ONLY WAY TO DO THAT IS BY DOGSLED.

Bring in the mushers!*

MUSHERS FROM MILES AROUND RESPOND, BRINGING WITH THEM THEIR STRONGEST AND MOST INTELLIGENT DOGS.

*Mushers are the people who drive the dog teams.

TWENTY TEAMS OF OVER 200 DOGS WOULD PARTICIPATE IN A RELAY: ONE TEAM WOULD PULL INTO AN OUTPOST, UNLOAD THE SERUM, AND PASS IT ON TO THE NEXT TEAM, WHO WOULD DO THE SAME THING—FOR THE REMAINING 667 MILES.

JANUARY 27, 1925: THE RELAY TO THE STRICKEN CITY BEGINS. THE TEMPERATURE IS DROPPING FAST.

THE SERUM GOES FROM HAND TO FROZEN HAND.

Good luck, mate . . .

ESKIMO, INDIAN, AND EUROPEAN MUSHERS FIGHT THEIR WAY THROUGH THE ARCTIC DARKNESS. SOMETIMES THE SERUM FREEZES, AND HAS TO BE THAWED AT THE OUTPOSTS.

THEN THE SERUM IS PASSED TO LEONHARD SEPPALA, THE GREATEST MUSHER OF ALL, AND TOGO, HIS MOST EXPERIENCED SLED DOG.

AT NORTON SOUND, SEPPALA IS FACED WITH AN AWFUL DECISION: TO GO AROUND IT, WHICH ADDS TIME, OR CUT ACROSS IT, WHICH IS RISKY, AS THE ICE COULD BREAK AT ANY TIME.

Over the ice, boys!

BUT SEPPALA KNOWS THAT TIME IS SHORT: THE CHILDREN OF NOME ARE DESPERATE FOR SERUM. HE HAS TOTAL CONFIDENCE IN HIS TEAM. HE CHOOSES THE SHORTCUT.

SEPPALA EXPERTLY LEADS THE DOGS ACROSS THE JAGGED ICE FLOES. BY THE TIME THE ICE BREAKS IN NORTON SOUND, THE LIFE-SAVING SERUM IS WELL ON ITS WAY. AT THE NEXT OUTPOST, SEPPALA PASSES IT TO CHARLIE OLSON, WHO GIVES IT TO THE LAST MUSHER, GUNNAR KAASEN.

THE LEAD DOG ON KAASEN'S TEAM IS BALTO. BALTO IS STRONG, AND SMART, AND VERY, VERY STUBBORN.

BALTO HAS NEVER BEEN LEAD DOG MATERIAL, BECAUSE OF HIS BULKINESS. BUT IT'S HIS BULKINESS THAT MAKES HIM STRONGER THAN THE OTHERS. THIS TIME, KAASEN CHOOSES HIM TO LEAD THE TEAM.

BALTO'S TEAM FACES THE WORST OF A WICKED BLIZZARD THAT'S BEEN POUNDING THE REGION FOR DAYS. AND THEY DO IT ALMOST ENTIRELY IN THE DARK.

You are entering Nome

FEBRUARY 2, 1925: KAASEN AND HIS TEAM ARRIVE AT THEIR DESTINATION AFTER COMPLETING THE 53-MILE ORDEAL— THE LAST LAP OF THE THOUSAND-MILE, FIVE-AND-A-HALF DAY RACE TO SAVE THE CHILDREN OF NOME.

KAASEN HANDS THE SERUM OVER TO THE AUTHORITIES, WHO MAKE SURE IT GETS TO THE CHILDREN AS QUICKLY AS POSSIBLE. COUNTLESS LIVES ARE SAVED!

Thank you! Thank you!

KAASEN HALTS THE TEAM IN FRONT OF MERCHANTS BANK ON FRONT STREET, WHERE HE STUMBLES UP TO THE FRONT OF THE TEAM.

WITNESSES SEE HIM DROP TO THE GROUND, HIS ARMS AROUND HIS LEAD DOG, BALTO.

IN HIS OLD AGE BALTO LIVES IN COMFORT AND IS LOVINGLY CARED FOR BY DR. POWELL IN HIS ANIMAL HOSPITAL.

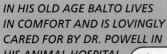

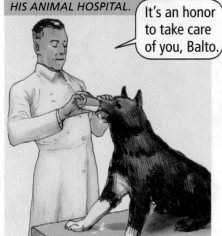

It's an honor to take care of you, Balto.

BALTO'S MEMORY LIVES ON TO THIS DAY. HE HAS BECOME A TRUE SYMBOL OF STRENGTH, DETERMINATION, AND COURAGE UNDER FIRE.

UPLOAD

⏻ **COLLABORATIVE DISCUSSION**

Discussing the Purpose In a small group, talk about Balto. Do you think he was a hero? Why, or why not?

LISTENING TOOLBOX

Agree or Disagree

When you share your opinion, it's easy to get excited. Sometimes you want to jump in when someone else is speaking. Be sure to respect other students. Don't interrupt, and give them a chance to say what they think. When you disagree, be sure to be respectful and polite.

The useful phrases below are some suggestions that you can use when you disagree or don't understand what someone else is trying to say.

Useful Phrases

▷ I'm not sure what you mean by ____ .

▷ I understand what you mean, but ____ .

▷ That sounds right, but I still think ____ .

⟳ Performance Task

Writing Activity: Write a Scene from a Play Work in a group to write your own play using "Balto's Story" as inspiration to get started. You can write a scene about the children in Nome, or imagine what happened when the dogs finally arrived in Nome. You can write a script for the dogs by imagining what they might have said.

Remember that a play is a form of literature. Plays are written down in books, and also performed by actors in front of an audience. In their written form, plays usually include:

- **Cast of characters**—a list of the characters in the play. The list appears at the beginning of the play.

- **Dialogue**—the words that the characters say. The character's name comes before his or her lines of dialogue.

- **Stage directions**—instructions for how the play should be performed in front of an audience. The instructions are often set in parentheses and italic type. They usually say what the character is doing or how the lines should be read.

Speaking Activity: Perform a Scene from a Play Now that you have written your scene from a play, assign roles and perform your scene. Be sure to use emotion in your voice, and speak loudly and clearly so that everyone can hear and enjoy the performance.

If you have time, exchange roles so that you get a chance to play different parts in your play.

Performance Task

Writing Activity: Opinion Piece

In this unit, you have read about the different ways people help their families and communities. You have read about how people use their skills to solve problems. You have even read about a famous dog that helped out. Your task is to write an opinion piece on the theme of reaching out and helping others.

Planning and Prewriting

Connect to the Theme

People help out their communities in different ways. Whether it's through volunteer work, their job, or simply by being a good neighbor, reaching out to others is an important part of life. But what's the best way to reach out? How important is it? How can you get others to join in? In this activity you will be writing an opinion piece stating your views on the theme of reaching out. But first you need a topic. What will it be?

Write Down Some Possible Topics

In an opinion piece, you give your opinion on a topic. Think about the topics covered in the selections you read. Jot down several statements that express your opinion on one of these topics. You can also choose your own topic. Choose the one that's most promising to write about. Here are some examples:

- Small acts of kindness are just as important as big ones.

- People should choose jobs that allow them to help others.

- Volunteering is better than getting paid to do the job.

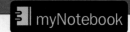

Decide the Basics

Now that you have chosen an issue you have a definite opinion about, you'll have to back up your opinion with reasons. You'll need to organize your thoughts and decide how to express yourself.

State Your Opinion

In an opinion piece, you take a position on an issue.

- Write your opinion in the form of a statement.
- Make sure your opinion is clearly stated at the beginning of your piece.
- Begin your opinion piece with a fact or a question that will make readers curious.

Find Reasons

Reasons are examples from the text that back up your opinion.

- Use only those examples that relate to your position.
- Look for more than one example. This makes your case stronger!
- Make sure the reasons you choose are factual, and not just opinion.
- Make sure you present your reasons in logical order.

Vocabulary

Think about vocabulary and word choice.

- Use a formal tone. (But don't lecture the reader!)
- Explain words a reader may not be familiar with.
- Include enough connecting words, phrases, and clauses (*first/next; for example; however*) to link opinion and reasons and ensure a smooth flow of ideas.

Performance Task

Present the Information

You've got the basics down. You have an opinion based on the selections you read; you know which facts, examples, and details you'll use to support your position on the issue. All you need is a way to present the information. Use the diagram in the Writing Toolbox to help you.

WRITING TOOLBOX

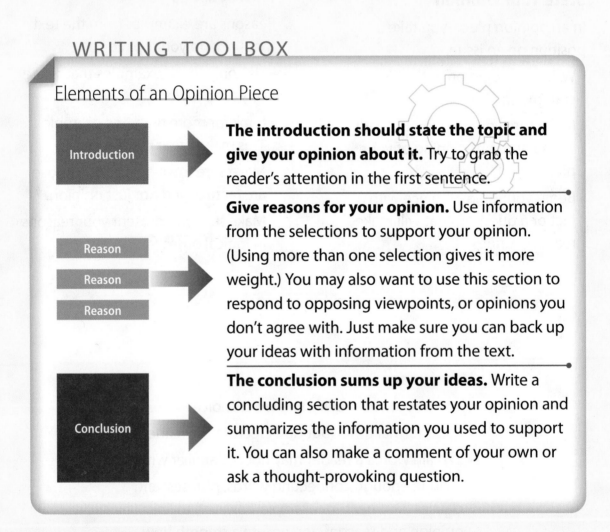

Elements of an Opinion Piece

Introduction → **The introduction should state the topic and give your opinion about it.** Try to grab the reader's attention in the first sentence.

Reason
Reason
Reason → **Give reasons for your opinion.** Use information from the selections to support your opinion. (Using more than one selection gives it more weight.) You may also want to use this section to respond to opposing viewpoints, or opinions you don't agree with. Just make sure you can back up your ideas with information from the text.

Conclusion → **The conclusion sums up your ideas.** Write a concluding section that restates your opinion and summarizes the information you used to support it. You can also make a comment of your own or ask a thought-provoking question.

Draft Your Essay

You have your topic and opinion. You know which examples you'll use. You have a way to organize your ideas. Now it's time to start writing! As you write, ask yourself:

- **What's my point?** Make sure you state your topic and opinion at the beginning, so that readers can follow the rest of what you have to say.

- **Can I come up with the right examples?** Make sure you include only meaningful examples from the text, and that you've included enough of them to make your case.

- **Is my opinion my own?** Not everyone sees things the same way. Your opinion doesn't have to be shared by everyone—it just has to be supported by the facts. It might be a good idea to mention a viewpoint you don't agree with and why you disagree.

- **Do my ideas flow?** Make sure that your ideas are linked together in a way that makes sense and that they appear in logical order.

- **Does the conclusion tie my ideas together?** The conclusion should summarize and tie up your ideas. Remember to refer to the opinion statement you made in the introduction. You may want to add some new thoughts based on information you found in the selections.

Revise

Self Evaluation

Use the checklist and rubric to guide your analysis.

Peer Review

Exchange your opinion piece with a classmate. Use the checklist to comment on your classmate's work.

Edit

Edit your opinion piece to correct spelling, grammar, and punctuation errors.

Publish

Finalize your opinion piece and choose a way to share it with your audience.

Tell Me More

Life has been your art. You have set yourself to music. Your days are your sonnets.

— **Oscar Wilde,** *author*

Essential Question

What are some of the ways that we can express ourselves?

The Language of Communication

People communicate in many ways. People use their bodies and facial expressions to show emotions. They may use paintings or dance to tell a story. Words are another way people communicate thoughts and ideas. When you communicate, you share information or ideas.

People use words in speaking and writing to share information and tell how they feel. Often, information is shared through words. In literature and plays, we use words to tell a story. In reports, we use words to explain something. In poetry, we use words to express thoughts or feelings. Words and language help us express ourselves.

People use art and other creative forms of expression to communicate. Sometimes people find it is easiest to express themselves without words. Music, dance, sculpture, and photography can convey emotion, meaning, and information without using words at all.

In this unit, you will find out about some of the ways we communicate. In the blog on pages 50–51, you will discover how a young blogger, SkoolGrl, feels when attending a poetry slam. You will read a poem and learn how poetry can be effective at expressing deep feelings. You will also explore ways in which animals may communicate, and much more.

> **How does communication help people put ideas into effect?**

Easy as Pie: Talking About Similes

People use similes to express themselves in imaginative ways. A **simile** compares two things, often with the word *like* or *as*. The phrase *easy as pie* is a simile we use when we want to say that something is very simple. See if you can figure out the meanings of these similes.

Simile	Meaning
soar like an eagle	fly high; to excel at something
work like a dog	put in a lot of effort and time; to work hard
like watching grass grow	slow or boring
like a lead balloon	very unsuccessful
as hard as nails	tough
as smooth as silk	without obstacles
as strong as an ox	
as steady as a rock	
as sharp as a razor	
as clear as mud	

↻ Performance Task

Choose a way that people communicate or express themselves. Select one of the examples listed on page 48, such as painting, dancing, or writing. You can also choose an example from **Browse** magazine or any other means of communication that interests you. Write a short speech about the example you chose. Why do people communicate or express themselves in this way? Why is it effective?

Don't forget to use your **Activity Book**, too.

→ *Browse magazine*

DOWNLOAD

A blog can communicate ideas online. This blog tells about another form of communication, poetry.

⏻ SETTING A PURPOSE

As you read, pay attention to the blogger's choice of words. How does the blogger show her feelings about the Poetry Slam at the beginning of the blog? How does she communicate her feelings at the end of the blog?

SkoolDayz

Enter your email address:

Subscribe me!

SEARCH

Poetry Slam, Here I Come!

Posted by SkoolGrl at 10:26 a.m.

Yesterday my friend Doug said he wouldn't be walking home with me as usual because he was going to a poetry slam. "Poetry slam?" I asked. "What's that?" Doug said it's when kids read their poems out loud to an audience, like they're performing in a play or a concert. OK …

When Doug asked me if I wanted to go with him I choked back a laugh. "Me? Listen to a bunch of kids read poems out loud? No thank you!" I thought I knew exactly how deadly dull the whole thing would be. I thought I knew. I was *sure* I knew. But it turns out I was *wrong*!

Doug was so excited about the slam he didn't care that I didn't want to go with him. He just nodded and said, "OK, see you tomorrow." Then he headed off like he was on a mission. That made me curious, so I turned around and followed him into the auditorium. I slipped into a seat at the back, and a few minutes later the first "slammer" was on stage, doing her thing.

From her opening lines, I knew this was like nothing I had ever heard before. It was more like rap, but not really—less boasting, more opening up, more scary for the performer, more tense for the audience. I was in awe. The poets performed like their lives depended on it. Some talked about personal stuff, the kind of things that really hurt—you know, the stuff you hide because you think you're the ONLY one who is going through it, then it turns out that other people are facing that same thing too. They were so *brave*, sharing all that, but you could tell the sharing made them feel stronger, like nothing could touch them, like they could *fly*.

The poems filled me with so many ideas, images, and feelings. I was almost dizzy. My heart was beating like a drum, and my palms were sweating. I was picturing myself up there on stage, using words to *soar* over the audience. I knew without a doubt I wanted to write a poem and *slam* it!

Later Doug and I walked home together. This was for middle school, but Doug said that even elementary schools have poetry slams. First you have to write poems, then you have to learn to speak them from the heart.

Doug's teacher is working on organizing a slam for 4th and 5th grade. All I know is, when my class is invited, I'm going to be there, with a poem, ready to *fly*.

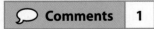 **Comments** 1

Posted by Dougie Douglas at 3:45 p.m.

And I'll be right there with you, cheering you on, every step of the way!

ARCHIVES

September

August

July

June

May

April

March

February

January

⏻ COLLABORATIVE DISCUSSION

Discussing the Purpose Talk with a partner about the language the blogger used. Was her tone casual as if she were talking to a friend, or formal as if she were presenting a class report? How did her choice of words make you understand her feelings? Could she have told this story another way?

Exploring Communication Think about how the slammers used poetry to communicate difficult feelings. Why was reciting their poems out loud important? How did this form of communication help them?

Write On! Add a short comment to SkoolDayz. You can share your opinion, send a poem, or tell about a similar experience. Remember to be respectful in your response.

↻ Performance Task

Writing Activity: Brainstorm Topics for Your Blog Now that you have successfully started a blog, what do you write about when you are stuck for ideas? If you don't blog about your day-to-day experiences, brainstorming topics for your blog can be overwhelming. You can write about any interests, hobbies, your favorite subject at school—use your imagination.

- If you are interested in animals and are knowledgeable about them, you can share new and exciting facts that your friends may not know.

- You can write about a new place that you may have visited recently or a location that you want to see in the future.

- You may wish to discuss your favorite bands. If so, you can upload audio files or links to music videos.

- Other ideas for topics can include writing a review about a new book, movie, or food; giving step-by-step directions for a craft project; or sharing your opinion about a current event at school or in your town.

Language Cam video

Do you want to find out about another way people can express themselves? Watch the video.

DOWNLOAD

THE WILD BOOK

You read how the blogger SkoolGrl loved the ideas, images, and feelings she experienced at the poetry slam. Now it's your turn to experience poetry.

Know Before You Go

The Wild Book is a collection of poems that tell the story of Fefa, the narrator. She has dyslexia, a condition the doctor in the poem describes as *word-blindness*. Dyslexia makes reading difficult. However, people with dyslexia can learn to read, even though it is a struggle. Pay attention to Fefa's determination, and how she describes her challenges, in these poems.

READING TOOLBOX

Poetry is a type of writing in which words are carefully chosen and arranged to create certain effects. Poetry emphasizes rhythm and sound as well as meaning, and the words and phrases are chosen for that. To help understand the poetry, ask yourself these questions:

- How does this poem make you feel?
- How do the words sound together?
- What do you picture while you read the poems?

⏻ SETTING A PURPOSE

While you read the poems, pay attention to the way the poet expresses herself through words and phrases that express ideas in an imaginative way.

from

The Wild Book

by Margarita Engle

➤ ⬅

Word-Blindness

Word-blindness.
The doctor hisses it
like a curse.
Word-blindness,
he repeats—some children
can see everything
except words.
They are only blind
on paper.
10 Fefa will never be able
to read, or write,
or be happy
in school.

Word-blindness.
It sounds like an evil wizard's
prophecy, dangerous
and dreadful,
but Mamá does not listen

What does the word **hissing** sound like?

to the serpent voice
20 of the hissing doctor.
She climbs in the wagon,
clucks to the horse,
and carries us home
to our beautiful green farm,
where she tells me to follow
the good example of Santa Mónica,
patron saint of patience.

Word-blindness,
Mamá murmurs
30 with a suffering sigh—who
ever heard of such an impossible
burden?

She refuses to accept
the hissing doctor's verdict.
Seeds of learning grow slowly,
she assures me.
Then she lights a tall,
slender candle,
and gives me
40 a book.

I grow anxious.
I pretend that my eyes hurt.
I pretend that my head hurts,
and pretty soon
it is true.

I know that the words
want to trick me.
The letters will jumble
and spill off the page,
50 leaping and hopping,
jumping far away,
like slimy
bullfrogs.

Think of this little book
as a garden,
Mamá suggests.
She says it so calmly
that I promise I will try.

Throw wildflower seeds
60 all over each page, she advises.
Let the words sprout
like seedlings,
then relax and watch
as your wild diary
grows.

I open the book.
Word-blindness.
The pages are white!
Is this really a blank diary,
70 or just an ordinary
schoolbook
filled with frog-slippery
tricky letters
that know how to leap
and escape?

> Why does the author compare the letters on the page to **bullfrogs**?

> Why do you think the author says the schoolbook is filled with **tricky letters**?

School

The others laugh.
They always laugh.
When I am forced to read
OUT LOUD,
they mock
my stumbling voice,
and when I have to practice
my horrible
handwriting,
10 they make fun
of the twisted
tilted
tormented
letters.

My fingers fall away
from the page.
I lose the courage
to try.

> This is a **very long sentence**, stretched over many lines. Try to identify smaller phrases to understand the meaning better.

(bn) ©R-studio/Shutterstock; (b) ©Sergei Razvodovskii/Shutterstock

Word Hunger

Is it possible that I am
no longer completely
discouraged?

I do still dread reading,
but I dread it a little bit less
each day.

When 1 consider
the happy possibility
that maybe someday
10   I will feel smart,
I grow a little bit hungry
for small, tasty bites
of easy words.

What do you think the author means when she says she is **hungry**?

Magic

When I finally
climb back down
from the tower,
I sip a bit of water
from the well.

I don't really feel
any different, but it's easy
to imagine that today
I have grown
10   just a little bit
stronger
and wiser.

The word **well** has multiple meanings. Here, it is a noun that refers to a source of water.

UPLOAD

COLLABORATIVE DISCUSSION

Discussing the Purpose In a small group, talk about the language that the poet used and how it made the poems come to life.

SPEAKING TOOLBOX

Reading Aloud with Expression

When reading poetry and other text out loud, it is important to use your voice to convey the meaning of the words you are saying. Pay attention to the meanings of the words in the poem, the way the words are written on the page, and the punctuation used. Read the words carefully, picking which syllables to emphasize.

Pay attention to the way you read the words. Decide whether you will make your voice:

- fast or slow

- high or low

- loud or soft

- emotional or without emotion

Speak Out! Choose a part of one of the poems and recite it out loud.

Explore Figurative Language

In a small group, talk about the figurative language in these poems.

Onomatopoeia is a word that sounds like what it means. These lines from the poem are an example of onomatopoeia: **Can you think of or make up other words like *hissing*?**	. . . the serpent voice of the hissing doctor. . . .
This sentence is a *simile* because the poet is comparing letters on the page with bullfrogs: **What other *similes* can you make up?**	The letters will jumble . . . leaping and hopping, . . . like slimy bullfrogs.
In *alliteration* writers use the same letter or sound for effect. This phrase is an alliteration: **Make up some other phrases that include *alliteration*.**	they make fun of the twisted, tilted, tormented, letters.

↻ Performance Task

Writing Activity: Rewrite Poetry as Prose In a small group, talk about what you think makes poetry and prose different. Then choose the poem from the selection that you liked best. Retell the poem as if it were a short story. You can add dialogue and descriptions to your story, if you want.

Podcast: Alex and Me

The poems you just read described a girl's problem in learning how to read. Now find out what happens when you try to teach human language to a parrot.

Background on Scientific Research

In this podcast, Dr. Irene Pepperberg must work hard to get funding for her scientific research with Alex the Parrot. Funding is money given to scientists so that they can do experiments. Most of this funding comes in the form of grants—small amounts of money given by a government organization. Dr. Pepperberg was funded by grants from the National Science Foundation. Dr. Pepperberg attended scientific conferences about Alex. Many scientists gather at these conferences to discuss their findings.

⏻ SETTING A PURPOSE

As you listen, pay attention to Dr. Pepperberg's relationship with Alex the Parrot. Think about what she says about Alex. How does she feel about Alex? Does she care more about Alex as a pet or as a lab subject? Do you think Dr. Pepperberg and Alex were able to communicate with each other?

Alex and Me

Alex: Research Subject or Friend?

Research Subject

The reason Dr. Pepperburg bought Alex was to do experiments with him.

Dr. Pepperburg took Alex to a scientific conference.

Dr. Pepperberg taught Alex to speak as part of her research.

Alex lived in the lab, not with Dr. Pepperberg.

Dr. Pepperberg gave Alex a name.

Alex and Dr. Pepperberg argue and Alex apologizes.

Dr. Pepperberg was very sad when Alex passed away.

Dr. Pepperberg was proud of Alex.

Friend

⏻ **COLLABORATIVE DISCUSSION**

Discussing the Purpose In a small group, discuss Dr. Pepperberg's relationship with Alex. Do you think Alex was more of a friend or a research subject? Do you think they really understood each other?

Pam Muñoz Ryan: Storyteller

People usually communicate informally in blogs, such as SkoolGrl's. But writers share information more formally in informational texts, such as in the next selection. Informational texts are pieces of nonfiction that tell you factual information about someone or something.

READING TOOLBOX

Analyze Structure: Text Features

Text features are the parts of a text that help organize and call attention to important information. Informational texts often have these features:

▶ **Title** The title is the name of a book or article. In nonfiction texts, the title often tells what the text will be about.

▶ **Subheadings** Smaller headings that appear at the beginning of sections within the text. They help the reader understand what each section of a text is about.

▶ **Bold Words** Important words are often highlighted with color or thick type to grab your attention.

▶ **Photographs and Captions** Nonfiction texts often include photographs with captions to help you understand the information.

⏻ SETTING A PURPOSE

As you read, pay attention to the text features included in the selection.

Pam Muñoz Ryan:
STORYTELLER

by Nura Mustafa

Two Grandmothers, Two Traditions

Pam Muñoz Ryan is an author who is proud of her ancestry. One of her grandmothers was from Mexico, and the other from Oklahoma. At one house Ryan often ate enchiladas, rice, and beans. At the other she had black-eyed peas, fried okra, and peach cobblers. With one grandmother she spoke Spanish, with the other, English. Ryan is inspired by both parts of her **heritage**.

10 Her love of family and family history is a strong part of her writing.

❧❧❧

▲ Pam Muñoz Ryan enjoys writing about spirited and courageous girls and women.

heritage: (n.) traditions and beliefs that are part of a group

When Ryan was growing up, she spent a large part of her time reading. Reading was a way to escape into a world of enchantment and possibility. In college she studied to become a teacher. She thought that would be a good way to keep books and stories in her life.

Teacher, Mother, Student, Writer

After college Ryan worked as a teacher. When she had her own children, she stayed home to look after
20 them. Eventually she went back to work, but she also decided to go back to school. After being a teacher and a mother, now she was a student again.

One day, one of her professors asked her to stay after class. She asked Ryan a question: "Have you ever thought about being a writer?" The question **planted a seed** in Ryan's mind.

Soon Ryan started to write. At first she wrote for adults. Then she tried writing a picture book for children. More picture books followed, and finally
30 she expanded her range and tried her first novel.

What do you think **"planted a seed** in Ryan's mind" means? Read on to get clues and figure out the meaning.

©LanKS/Shutterstock

The Esperanza Behind *Esperanza Rising*

One of Ryan's most popular books is *Esperanza Rising*. The story is based on the life of Ryan's own grandmother, whose name is also Esperanza. When she was a little girl in Mexico, Ryan's grandmother was wealthy. Her family had servants and property. But after her father died, everything changed. Esperanza ended up living and working at a company farm camp in California. Using her imagination, Ryan gave her grandmother's
40   extraordinary story a new life, adding people, events, and **twists and turns**.

Did you know? In Spanish, **esperanza** means "hope."

twists and turns: an expression that means "unexpected changes"

▲ On a short flight to and from Baltimore, aviator Amelia Earhart points out the White House to resident, First Lady Eleanor Roosevelt.

Strong Women, Strong Stories

Ryan has done something similar in other books. She starts with a true story, and then uses her imagination to add more. For example, *Amelia and Eleanor Take a Ride* is based on real people, Amelia Earhart and Eleanor Roosevelt. It's about an event that really happened. But Ryan has imagined all the details that have been lost to time—what they said, how they felt, what they saw. She **brings the story** 50 **to life** in a way that makes us feel we were there ourselves.

> What other phrases in the paragraph helps you understand the meaning of the expression **brings the story to life**?

Ryan loves to write about strong and determined women who aren't afraid to chart their own path. It's something she has done in her own life. When asked what **motivates** her as a writer, she says that she simply wants the reader to turn the page!

motivates: (v.) gives a reason for an action

⏻ **COLLABORATIVE DISCUSSION**

Discussing the Purpose In a small group, review the text features used in this text. How did they help you as you read?

Exploring Language Talk about the language the author uses to tell about Pam Muñoz Ryan. How is the tone of this text different from that of the blog? Why do you think the author wrote this piece the way she did?

Vocabulary Strategy: Identify Suffixes

A suffix is a word part added to the end of a word. Knowing the meaning of common suffixes can help you figure out the meaning of unfamiliar words. The author states that Pam Muñoz Ryan was a teacher and a writer. These words have the suffix -er at the end of their root words.

Suffix	Meaning	Examples
-er and **-or**	someone who	actor, painter, sculptor, designer
-y	made up of	windy, sunny, creamy, rocky
-ous	full of	wondrous, nervous, glorious

♻ Performance Task

Writing Activity: Informational Paragraph The author describes the extraordinary life of Pam Muñoz Ryan's grandmother in this selection. Write a paragraph about someone you think is extraordinary.

- Think of an extraordinary person you admire. It could be someone from your local community, someone you've read about, or someone you've seen and heard about.

- Make a list of the things that make this person extraordinary.

- Choose the most important things from your list to include in your paragraph.

- Use your list to write a paragraph that explains why this person is extraordinary.

©Shutterstock

DOWNLOAD

Do You Speak Animal?

You read about a wonderful writer who uses her imagination to tell fascinating stories. Now read about some amazing animals and how they communicate with humans.

READING TOOLBOX

Main Idea and Details

Most informational texts have a main idea. The main idea is the most important idea that the selection discusses. It tells what the selection is mostly about.

Details are the examples, definitions, facts, quotations, and other pieces of information that support the main idea.

As you read, use the graphic organizer below to help you organize your main idea and details for "Do You Speak Animal?"

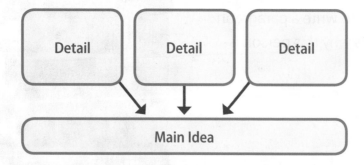

⏻ SETTING A PURPOSE

As you read, think about the main idea and details that the author uses to explain the ways in which scientists try to communicate with animals.

Do You Speak Animal?

by Dmitri Lubov

If you have a pet in your home, you've probably talked to it at some point. Maybe you talk to it all the time. You probably don't expect it to answer you. But are there animals that can talk to people? The answer is definitely "maybe."

Scientists have been testing animal intelligence for over a century. One way is to try to communicate with animals. Monkeys and apes would seem to be a good place to start because
10 they are the closest relatives of humans, but early attempts failed. Chimps' tongues and mouths and vocal cords are different from those of humans, so they can't form words. If they can't form words, how can they talk?

American Sign Language

American Sign Language (ASL) is a language used by **hearing-impaired** people. ASL users form words with their hands. In 1966, scientists began working with a chimp
20 named Washoe. The scientists raised Washoe as they would a hearing-impaired human baby.

> To understand the meaning of the **compound word** *hearing-impaired*, check the meaning of the two words separately.

They communicated with Washoe using ASL and, at age four, Washoe could sign 132 words.

In 1972, other scientists taught ASL to a baby gorilla named Koko. Today, this extraordinary gorilla has a vocabulary of over 1,000 words. A chimp named Kanzi uses a computer instead of ASL. It has a special keyboard with many keys, each key

30 marked with a **symbol** that represents a word. Kanzi uses almost 400 words, and his humans say he understands about 3,000 words when he hears them spoken.

Other Types of Communication

Scientists are trying to communicate with other species as well. Dolphins can be taught to recognize simple sentences. And, of course, there is one entertaining kind of non-human that can produce words. In 1977, a scientist started working with a parrot named Alex.

40 Alex learned to recognize colors and shapes, and to use the words that describe them.

But is it really communication? The scientists working with the animals often say "Yes," but many critics say "No." Most people just aren't sure.

> Use context clues to help you figure out the meaning of the word **symbol**.

©Nancy Nehring/PhotoDisc/Getty Images

You tell a dog, "Sit," and it sits, but it probably doesn't understand the concept of sitting. It knows
50 that when it hears that word, it will probably get a treat if it sits down. You could just as easily train a dog to sit when it hears the word "tennis."

What Do Animals Understand?

It's impossible to know what an animal is thinking, so it's very hard to know whether the animal is really communicating or not. It could just be pressing the keys or making the signs the humans want it to. Does it understand the meaning that the words **convey**? How can we tell?

One reporter for *The New York Times* was
60 convinced. This reporter could hear, but his parents were both hearing-impaired. He learned ASL before he learned English. The reporter spent some time with Washoe. The reporter was amazed that he could communicate with Washoe. After the interview with Washoe, the reporter said:

> **"** I realized I was conversing with a member of another species in my native [language]. **"**

Use context clues in this paragraph to help you figure out the meaning of the word **convey**.

⏻ COLLABORATIVE DISCUSSION

Discussing the Purpose Talk with a small group about the main idea and details that you entered in the graphic organizer in your **Activity Book**.

↻ Performance Task

Writing Activity: Main Idea and Details Work in a small group to write about the main idea and details in "Do You Speak Animal?"

- What is the main idea of this selection?

- What details support the main idea of this selection?

Use your graphic organizer to help you write a paragraph that tells about "Do You Speak Animal?" Try to answer the questions above when you write your paragraph.

Write On! Choose one detail from the text and explain it in your own words.

↻ Performance Task

Speaking Activity: Conversation Imagine that you and an animal you know are having a conversation. The animal can be a dog, a cat, a goldfish, or any other animal that you would like to talk to. What would you say to the animal? What do you suppose the animal would say to you?

With a partner, have a conversation with any animal that you choose.

Take turns playing the person and the animal.

Speak Out! Do you think animals and humans can communicate? Why or why not? Share your opinion with a partner.

DOWNLOAD

You just read about ways in which animals communicate. Read on to find out how people use both pictures and words to communicate information and ideas.

⏻ **SETTING A PURPOSE**

As you read, pay attention to the arguments and points that the author makes.

Is a Picture Worth a Thousand Words?

by James Pitt

The expression "a picture is worth a thousand words" is something people say a lot. It's also more or less true. A picture can present information more vividly than words can. But there are some kinds of information that
10 words express better than pictures do.

© Gary Russ/Houghton Mifflin Harcourt

Of course, it's easy to **quibble** about the details of a statement as vague as "a picture is worth a thousand words." A thousand words by a good writer can tell you much more than a thousand words by a not-so-good writer. And how big a picture are we talking about? A thousand words fills about two pages. Surely a picture the size of two pages can tell you more

20 than a smaller picture.

quibble: (v.) to argue about unimportant things

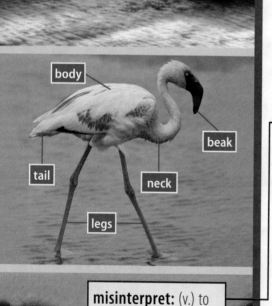

It's faster and easier to look at a picture than to read the same amount of text. Also, it's easier to show small details in a picture than to explain them in words. Charts, diagrams, and maps show information in a visual way. They can show in one picture what it would take paragraphs to say. Imagine describing the roads on a map in words!

30 On the other hand, there are some ideas that can be expressed in words more clearly. A picture can show an *example* of an abstract idea like love or bravery, but there's no way to draw love or bravery. Words can explain ideas in ways that a picture can't. I could never have made this argument just using pictures.

It is usually easier to express a clear meaning with text than with a picture. No matter what you illustrate, viewers will interpret it in different ways. Suppose you love dogs and

40 draw a picture of one that you think is cute. Someone who is afraid of dogs might not think the picture is cute at all.

It is usually more difficult to **misinterpret** words, but it still happens. This is especially true if the writer is using difficult words or a complicated writing style.

Often, words and pictures can be used together. A picture of something complicated might not make any sense if the parts aren't

50 labeled. A picture of an unfamiliar animal can't tell you much about its habits or behavior, but a description of it will be easier to remember if it comes with a picture.

misinterpret: (v.) to understand something incorrectly

So, is a picture worth a thousand (or so) words? Depends on what you're trying to say. See what you think. Here is a description of a sunset.

▼ Mark Twain

" *I still keep in mind a certain wonderful sunset which I witnessed when steamboating was new to me. A broad expanse of the river was turned to blood; in the middle distance the red hue brightened into gold, through which a solitary log came floating, black and* **conspicuous** ... "

conspicuous: (adj.) very easy to see or notice

And here is a picture of a sunset. Now you decide.

UPLOAD

⏻ COLLABORATIVE DISCUSSION

Discussing the Purpose In this selection, the author argues that both words and pictures are useful forms of communication. What examples did the author use to support the opinion that a picture can express ideas more easily than words? How did he support the idea that words are sometimes more useful? Talk about it with a small group.

Exploring the Theme Which form of communication do you think is better, pictures or words? Choose one side to argue with a partner.

Vocabulary Strategy: Antonyms

big (line 16)   **small** (line 23)

easy (line 12)   **difficult** (line 43)

Words that have opposite meanings are *antonyms*. The word pairs above are examples of antonyms. Knowing a word's antonym can sometimes help you understand the meaning of a word. Knowing the word *hot* can help you understand the meaning of *cold*, for example. Here are some other useful antonyms to know:

vague	clear
same	different
complicated	simple

Practice and Apply Think of antonyms for the following words from the text. Use a dictionary to help you.

unfamiliar (line 50)   **abstract** (line 31)   **complicated** (line 48)

⟲ Performance Task

Writing Activity : Words or Pictures? In this selection, you learned that things can be described in more than one way. Now it's your turn.

- Write a paragraph that describes something you find beautiful or interesting or even strange. Then draw a picture of that thing.

- In a small group, share your paragraph and your drawing with your classmates. Which form of communication do you think is better, pictures or words?

- Finally, decide for yourself: Is a picture worth a thousand words?

SPEAKING TOOLBOX

Using Academic Language

Even when participating in a class discussion, you should be aware of the differences between the expressions that you use every day among your friends and the academic language that is appropriate for the classroom. Here are some examples of academic language that you can use when contributing your opinions or when asking for clarification of someone else's.

Everyday Language	Academic Language
What?	Will you please restate your idea?
What do you mean?	Can you explain what you mean by ____?
I don't get it.	I don't understand your (response/ suggestion/example).
That's not true.	I don't agree.

DOWNLOAD

The Lion's Whisker

You just read a selection that asks whether a picture is worth a thousand words. Now read this graphic novel that has both words and pictures.

Know Before You Go

This story was adapted from a folktale. Folktales are stories that people around the world have been telling for years. Sometimes they are written down and illustrated, like this one. But folktales began with people telling stories out loud. These stories were passed on from one family member to another for years and years. Many folktales involve talking animals or magic spells, while others are about things that could have actually happened. Folktales often have a lesson at the end.

CAST OF CHARACTERS

Sister One

Sister Two

Father

Village Healer

Lion

⏻ SETTING A PURPOSE

As you read, think about the sisters and what they finally realized.

The Lion's Whisker

Retold by Mercedes Roffé

IN A BEAUTIFUL AFRICAN VILLAGE, THERE WERE TWO SISTERS WHO HAD ALWAYS BEEN VERY CLOSE.

My turn!

THEY ALWAYS PLAYED TOGETHER.

I like these too!

These fit us very well!

THEY EVEN LIKED TO DRESS ALIKE.

THEY WERE GOOD AT THE SAME THINGS AND LOVED TO DO THINGS TOGETHER.

I love this spot.

It's my favorite place in the whole world!

ONE DAY, THEIR FATHER TOLD THEM SOMETHING IMPORTANT.

My girls, it's time for you to choose good and kind husbands.

A FEW WEEKS LATER, THE FAMILY THREW A HUGE PARTY.

ALL THE YOUNG MEN AND WOMEN OF THE OTHER VILLAGES WERE INVITED, EVEN SOME FROM FAR AWAY.

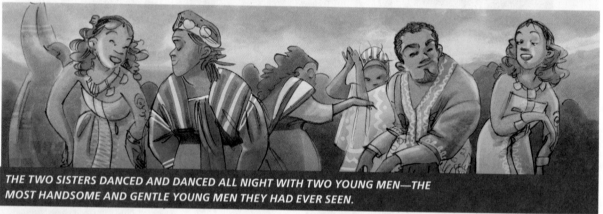

THE TWO SISTERS DANCED AND DANCED ALL NIGHT WITH TWO YOUNG MEN—THE MOST HANDSOME AND GENTLE YOUNG MEN THEY HAD EVER SEEN.

Isn't he wonderful?

Isn't he kind?

SOON ENOUGH THE TWO SISTERS REALIZED THAT THEY WERE THINKING AND TALKING ABOUT THEIR NEW FRIENDS ALL THE TIME. THEY HAD FALLEN IN LOVE! AS FOR THE YOUNG MEN, THEY HAD FALLEN IN LOVE WITH THE TWO GIRLS AS WELL.

BUT SOON THE TWO SISTERS HAD TO CONFRONT A BIG PROBLEM.

Once we get married, we'll be living so far away from each other!

I have never spent a single day of my life without you!

What are we going to do?

©Escletxa

SO THE TWO SISTERS DECIDED TO GO SEE THE VILLAGE HEALER.

. . . forever.

We want you to give us a potion that would preserve our close bond . . .

THE HEALER LOOKED AT THE GIRLS. THEN HE TOLD THEM:

There is a special potion which I can make. When both of you drink it, your bond will be cemented forever.

Please . . .

. . . make it for us.

It is difficult to make. It requires the whisker of a living lion.

THE SISTERS FELT THEIR HEARTS POUND IN THEIR CHESTS. WHAT A TERRIFYING TASK! THEN, THEY LOOKED AT EACH OTHER AND SAID:

We will get this whisker.

No matter what!

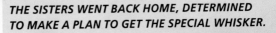

THE SISTERS WENT BACK HOME, DETERMINED TO MAKE A PLAN TO GET THE SPECIAL WHISKER.

First we'll try this . . .

. . . and if that doesn't work we'll try something else.

87

THE NEXT AFTERNOON, THEY TOOK SOME MEAT TO A POND WHERE THEY HAD SEEN A LION'S TRACK. THEY PUT THE MEAT BY THE WATER AND HID BEHIND A TREE.

We will watch what he does.

Yes, we need to stay hidden.

SOON AFTERWARDS, A LION CAME. THE LION SNIFFED THE AIR AND KNEW THAT THERE WERE PEOPLE AROUND. BUT HE ATE THE MEAT AND DID NOT CARE ABOUT THE GIRLS.

THE NEXT EVENING THE SISTERS DID THE SAME THING. THE LION SNIFFED THE AIR, BUT DID NOT APPROACH THEM. HE WAS VERY HAPPY ABOUT THE MEAT THEY BROUGHT HIM.

That lion certainly was hungry!

THE NEXT EVENING, THEY LEFT THE MEAT BY THE POND ONCE AGAIN AND WAITED FOR THE LION TO APPROACH. THEY DID NOT HIDE BEHIND THE TREE. THE LION LOOKED AT THEM, THEN LOOKED AT THE MEAT AND STARTED TO EAT.

That lion is so hungry he does not seem to notice us!

ONE EVENING, THE SISTERS PUT THE MEAT ON THE GROUND AND STAYED RIGHT THERE. THE LION APPROACHED, SNIFFED THEM, AND LOOKED AT THE MEAT. AS HE LOWERED HIS HEAD TO START EATING, THE SISTERS REACHED OUT, AND PLUCKED ONE WHISKER FROM HIS CHEEK.

We got it!

THE FOLLOWING DAY, THE SISTERS WENT BACK TO THE HEALER TO GIVE HIM THE LION'S WHISKER. THE HEALER WAS ASTONISHED WHEN HE SAW THE WHISKER.

Here is the lion's whisker . . .

. . . for the potion. Could you make it right now?

SO THE HEALER GOT UP FROM HIS CHAIR, AND SMILING, PUT HIS ARMS AROUND THE GIRLS.

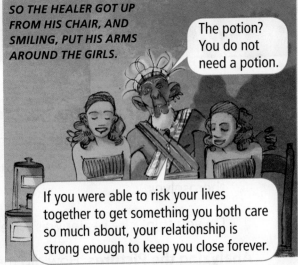

The potion? You do not need a potion.

If you were able to risk your lives together to get something you both care so much about, your relationship is strong enough to keep you close forever.

WHEN THE GIRLS ARRIVED BACK HOME, THEY REALIZED IT WAS HIGH TIME TO START PREPARING FOR THE WEDDINGS.

You will be a beautiful bride!

And you will always be my beautiful sister.

THE TWO SISTERS WENT TO LIVE IN TWO DIFFERENT, DISTANT VILLAGES.

THEY WERE VERY HAPPY WITH THEIR NEW FAMILIES.

THEY KNEW THAT NO MATTER HOW FAR AWAY THEY WERE FROM EACH OTHER, THEIR LOVE WOULD BE AS STRONG AS EVER.

©Escletxa

⏻ COLLABORATIVE DISCUSSION

Discussing the Purpose In a small group, talk about "The Lion's Whisker" and what the sisters learned about themselves.

Do you think the healer was wise? Why or why not?

Analyzing the Pictures How did the pictures help you to understand the story?
Did the pictures make you enjoy the story more?
Do you think that the pictures were necessary to understand the story?

↻ Performance Task

Writing Activity: Write a scene from the graphic novel
In a group, talk about which scene from "The Lion's Whisker" was your favorite and why.

Then write your favorite scene in the form of a story. Don't forget that you will have to describe what is happening because your reader will not have any pictures to look at. Share your story with the students in your group.

↻ Performance Task

Speaking Activity: Perform a Skit Use the dialogue from "The Lion's Whisker" to create a skit.

Pretend that the graphic novel is a script. Choose a narrator to read the words that are not in the speech balloons. Choose other actors to read the words that are in the speech balloons. Decide how the lines should be read. Should they be read in a happy voice or in a serious voice?

Let the performance begin!

LISTENING TOOLBOX

Listening to a Performance

▶ When you are listening to other students perform, it is important to be respectful.

▶ Do not speak during the performance.

▶ Pay careful attention to what is being said and shown.

▶ Applaud when the performance is over.

▶ If you are asked for your opinion, say what you think without hurting anyone's feelings.

Performance Task

Writing Activity: Informative Essay

You have been reading about the different ways that people express themselves. Now it is your turn to write an informative essay about this subject.

Planning and Prewriting

Connect to the Theme

All over the world, in every culture, people communicate. They are talking to each other, writing, making art, and telling stories. They are learning each other's languages and reading each other's writings. Even when communication is a struggle— especially when it's a struggle—they are coming up with unusual and creative ways to express themselves. In this activity you will write an informative essay on the theme of how we communicate. But first you need a main idea. What will it be?

Write Down Some Possible Main Ideas

Your main idea is the most important idea about your topic. It is a statement that expresses and summarizes your thoughts. Write down several possible main ideas, and choose the one that seems most promising. You can use an idea from the list below or use your own. Here are examples of main ideas taken from the selections you read:

- Animals communicate with humans in different ways.

- People often express themselves through their actions.

- Self-expression comes in many different forms.

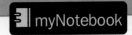

Decide the Basics

Now that you have a main idea that reflects the theme of the unit, you'll need to figure out how to support your idea with examples and details. Use the notes below to help guide your decision making.

Main Idea

The main idea is the "big idea" of your essay.

- Write your main idea in the form of a sentence.
- Think about the most important point you're making.
- Present your main idea in the first sentence. Grab your readers' interest by presenting a fact that will surprise them or make them curious.
- You might also ask a question that readers can relate to.

Supporting Details

Supporting details are facts or examples that support the main idea.

- Find details in the selections that tell more about your main idea.
- Use enough details to support your main idea.
- Include only evidence that is connected to your topic.

Vocabulary

Think about vocabulary and word choice.

- Explain any proper nouns that a reader may not be familiar with.
- Make sure you include transitional words and phrases (*another, for example, also, because*) to help readers connect one idea to the next.

Text Features

Text features organize information.

- **Title:** The title of your essay should identify the topic in a way that catches the reader's interest.
- **Opening sentence:** The first sentence in your essay should refer to the overall main idea.
- **Subheadings:** If your supporting details can be grouped together, use a subheading for each grouping.

Performance Task

Finalize Your Plan

You know the basics of your essay. You have a main idea based on the theme of how we communicate. You know which facts, examples, and details from the selections you'll use to support this main idea. You may even have your title picked out.

Now you need to decide how you will present your information. Follow the structure in the Writing Toolbox.

WRITING TOOLBOX

Elements of an Informative Essay

Opening Paragraph	Present your main idea. "Hook" your audience with an interesting detail, question, or quotation that relates to your main idea.
Supporting Details	Each of these paragraphs should include a supporting detail for your main idea, or a group of examples that have a common thread. If your supporting details can be grouped together, use a subheading for each grouping.
Conclusion	The conclusion should follow and sum up how the details support your main idea. You may want to include another idea about the topic or ask a question that will make the reader think.

Draft Your Essay

You have the basics of your informative essay. Start writing! As you write, think about:

- **Purpose and Audience** What effect do you want your essay to have on readers? Try to present your information in such a way that your audience understands and learns from what you've written.

- **Point of View** Establish your main idea quickly so that the reader can follow the points you are making.

- **Structure** Use the diagram to help you organize the information you are presenting. Use subheadings where necessary. Be sure to link your ideas together in a way that makes sense.

- **Conclusion** Use a concluding paragraph to tie your ideas together. You may want to restate your main idea, which will have more weight now that you have supported it with examples.

Revise

Self Evaluation

Use the checklist and rubric to guide your analysis.

Peer Review

Exchange your essay with a classmate. Use the checklist to comment on your classmate's essay.

Edit

Edit your essay to correct spelling, grammar, and punctuation errors.

Publish

Finalize your essay and choose a way to share it with your audience.

Inside Nature

The creation of a thousand

forests is in one acorn.

— **Ralph Waldo Emerson, poet**

Essential Question

How can we enjoy nature anywhere and everywhere?

©Candy Rodo

The Language of Nature

Earth is full of fascinating, sometimes dangerous, natural wonders. From mountains and streams to deserts and plains, nature is everywhere.

People interact with nature in some way almost every day. Whether we live in cities or wide-open spaces, nature is around us. Whether we tend to a huge garden or a lonely plant on a windowsill, we can enjoy nature. We share our environment with plants, animals, and other living things.

People get useful materials from nature. We use rocks, wood, and metal to build homes, buildings, furniture, and many other things. These materials come from nature. We also farm the land and fish in lakes and oceans. Nearly all of our food comes from nature.

It is important to take care of nature. Nature is beautiful. It also provides us with things we need to live. For these reasons, we need to take care of our Earth. We should only use the things we really need and recycle materials so that they can be used again.

In this unit, you will learn about ways people interact with nature. You will read about a boy's discovery of nature in both a blog and a story called "Mama Goose and Jonathan." You will discover ways in which people struggled across challenging natural terrain to reach California nearly 200 years ago, and find out how the gold they were looking for was actually formed.

> **What are some of Earth's natural wonders?**
> **How can we appreciate them?**

What's in a Word? Descriptive Language

Words help us tell stories and communicate about the world around us. Just how well we use words can have a big impact on the story we tell. Here are two sentences about Earth's natural features.

> The mountains were tall behind the plains.
>
> The tall mountains rose majestically above the endless, amber-colored plains.

Which of these sentences paints a more vivid picture in your mind? Why? The second one, of course. And the reason is adjectives and adverbs! **Adjectives** are words we use to describe nouns—people, places, or things. **Adverbs** are used to describe verbs—or action words.

What adjectives and adverbs could you add to these sentences so that they paint a picture in the reader's mind?

> The girl sat at her desk.
>
> The man stood next to his car.
>
> The woman waited for the bus.

When describing things or actions, ask yourself: What color was it? How big was it? How fast was it going?

○ Performance Task

Explain why it is important to take care of nature. Use the information on page 98 to help you. You can also use information from **Browse** magazine. Write a short speech to communicate your ideas. Why is nature important? Why should we protect and enjoy nature? Don't forget to use your **Activity Book**, too.

➜ *Browse magazine*

DOWNLOAD

There are many ways to explore nature. Read ahead to find out how Citrus10 discovers nature right in a city park.

⏻ SETTING A PURPOSE

As you read, pay attention to Citrus10's words. What do the words tell you about the blogger?

Daily Juice

A Walk in the Park

Posted by Citrus10 5:12 p.m.

Enter your email address:

Subscribe me!

SEARCH

💬 Comments 14

I live in a city, but even in the city there are parks, and in the parks there is a variety of animal habitats. When my friend Beni went to the park with his science class, he saw a mother deer with a fawn. That's a baby deer. He even got a picture before they disappeared into the trees. Cool!

I was excited when our turn to go to the park rolled around. I wanted to find those same deer and get a picture just like Beni's. Our class split into groups and walked around for an hour before meeting up to share what we'd found. Mrs. Romero came with my group. She's Selina's mom.

At first I was really in a hurry to find those deer. The more time I spent looking, the more frustrated I got. "There's no deer here!" I said. "There's nothing here! This is a big waste of time!" I was so annoyed and impatient I didn't notice much of anything around me. Mrs. Romero encouraged me to walk more slowly. She said to stop and look longer and listen to the noises from the woods. She pointed things out: a tiny purple flower; a pair of grasshoppers on a piece of grass; a spider's web . . .

It took a while for me to slow down, but when I did, I was glad. I looked more, and I saw more, too. We all did. Jake pointed out a pair of metal-blue dragonflies. Lucy found an old bird's nest. Selina showed us deer tracks in the mud—big tracks and little ones. My deer were out there somewhere! We all stared into a small pond. At first we saw nothing, but after a while we noticed little brown fish and water bugs on the surface. It was too bad because there was trash in the pond: plastic water bottles, cans, plastic bags . . . Actually, there was trash throughout the park—stuff people had left or that had blown in. Yuck.

ARCHIVES

September

August

July

June

May

April

March

February

January

The best part was when, just before we got back to the meeting point, a big hawk flew up over the path in front of us. We could practically hear its wings swooshing. It turned its head back for a quick glance as it flew up and away. It all happened too fast for a photo, but I didn't care. That look gave me goose bumps.

Between all the groups, we'd seen a lot! No deer, but someone saw a skunk, and Mike found three porcupine quills. One thing we had all seen too much of was trash. That's why, next weekend, some of us are going back to take part in the "Clean Our Parks" trash pick-up day. I'm excited. You never know—maybe I'll see my deer after all . . .

UPLOAD

⏻ COLLABORATIVE DISCUSSION

Discussing the Purpose Citrus10 shared an experience in his blog entry, "A Walk in the Park." Although the blogger wasn't writing about himself, his words can give you an idea about his personality. With a partner, discuss words or phrases the blogger used that tell you what he's like.

Exploring the Theme What are some things you would like to do to find out about nature?

Write On! Citrus10 gives readers the opportunity to post comments about the blog. Write a short comment to Citrus10. State your opinion about what he wrote. You can also share information you know about the animals he saw, or share a similar experience.

↻ Performance Task

Writing Activity: Designing Your Blog Use your blog design to show people what your personality is like. Your blog software should have different settings to help you design your blog. You can choose among different templates or themes. These templates have different colors and styles. You can choose how many columns you need, and how wide they should be. You might have a blogroll in the sidebar, where you can keep a list of website links that you visit often. You can then upload photos and art images to your template. NOTE: If you are using a photo or an image that is not yours, you must be sure to give proper credit. You must give the person or organization's name as well as the date of the photo or image.

1 Write a blog post describing why you chose this particular template and any art or images. You may use a bulleted or numbered list to organize your thoughts. This step would be a good place to insert a link or upload an art image. Adding links to your posts gives your readers more information about a subject.

2 Preview your draft. At this point, you may want to spell check or fix any grammatical errors. If you have added a link, check that it is correct and does not load to an inappropriate source.

3 Publish your post.

Language Cam video

Do you want to find out more about protecting the environment? Watch the video.

DOWNLOAD

Citrus10 learned about nature during a class field trip. The travelers in the next selection were challenged by nature as they traveled west nearly 200 years ago.

⏻ **SETTING A PURPOSE**

As you read, pay attention to the details the author gives about the long journey west.

A Long and Difficult Journey

by B. Armitage

A caravan of covered wagons

How long do you think it would take you to walk from the Mississippi to the West Coast?

That probably sounds like an absurd question. But in the mid-1800s, hundreds of thousands of people made that trip. Some people rode in wagons, but others walked alongside them. The journey usually took five to six months.

Imagine yourself making that long and difficult journey. One reason the trip would take so long is that there are many **obstacles** along the way. Just crossing a river could be dangerous, as there are no bridges, of course. Everyone would simply drive their wagon into the river, and out the other side. If the water is too high, or rises too quickly, your wagon might tip over. Then all of your food, supplies, and other belongings would wash away. Sometimes people even drowned.

Many settlers followed a path called the California Trail. It went from Independence, Missouri, to Salt Lake City, Utah, and then southwest into central California. In order to get to Salt Lake City, settlers had to cross the Rocky Mountains. There were only a couple of passes through which it's safe to travel, and the tops of the mountains are covered with snow all year long. It's fun to throw snowballs in the summertime, but if your wagon got stuck in the snow, you'd be in real trouble.

obstacles: things that block the path or get in the way

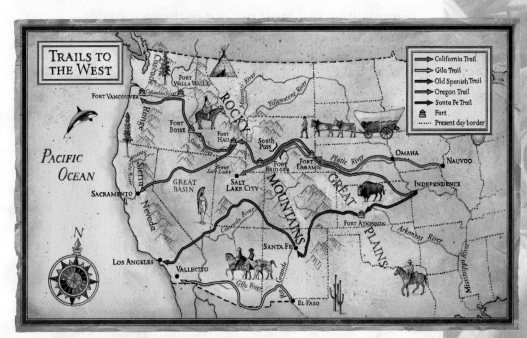

You're exhausted by the time you reach Salt Lake City, but you can't rest. The Great Salt Lake contains salt water, which is not safe to drink. And beyond the lake lies the Great Basin Desert. This desert covers 190,000 square 30 miles, so there's no going around it. The desert covers more square miles than the entire state of California! You have to make your way across the rugged, dry land, and though your cows and horses and oxen have to eat, edible plants are scarce here.

> This is a **long sentence**. Read it again to make sure you understand what it means.

When you finally make it through the desert, things get worse rapidly. You're at the foot of the Sierra Nevada Mountains. They're not as tall as the Rockies, but they're much steeper. Climbing them is 40 hard, and your progress is slow.

But you can't afford a delay. By late autumn it will start to snow. Snow will cover the ground and hide the trail. Deep snow will make travel impossible. You must get out of the mountains before the snow starts.

Today, moving across the country is usually fairly easy. But for the first Americans who did it, this long journey was a tough and dangerous challenge.

An old house in the Sierra Nevada mountains ▼

⏻ COLLABORATIVE DISCUSSION

Discussing the Purpose With a small group, discuss which details support the idea that the journey west was long and difficult.

Speak Out! Imagine you were traveling west in the mid-1800s. What do you think would be the most difficult part of the journey? Share your ideas with a partner.

Analyzing the Text Cite Text Evidence

1. **Main idea** What is the central idea of this text?

2. **Summarize** Explain how each paragraph supports this central idea.

Vocabulary Strategy: Synonyms

trip (line 3)   **journey** (line 4)   **quickly** (line 10)   **rapidly** (line 37)

The words *journey* and *trip* are used several times in this selection. These words are *synonyms*; they both mean "the act of traveling from one place to another." A synonym for the word *rapidly* is *quickly*. Synonyms are words that have about the same meaning. This chart shows synonyms for some other words in the text:

Synonym	Definition
absurd (line 1)	ridiculous, silly
exhausted (line 23)	very tired
scarce (line 35)	small amount, not plentiful

Practice and Apply Think of synonyms for the following words from the text. Use a dictionary to help you.

difficult (line 5)   **rugged** (line 34)

Podcast: Crocodile Meets Godzilla—A Swimming Dino Bigger Than T. Rex

The settlers who traveled from Missouri to California battled nature and the environment along the way. In this podcast, you'll meet an unusual dinosaur that adapted to make the most of its environment.

Background on Dinosaurs

From about 200 million years ago to 66 million years ago, dinosaurs ruled the earth. These animals could be small or large, predators or prey. One of the most well-known dinosaurs is the *Tyrannosaurus rex*. The *T. rex* was a huge meat-eater that stood about 21 feet tall. Eventually, most dinosaurs went extinct, which means that they disappeared from the earth. Dinosaurs are the distant relatives of birds. Birds evolved from dinosaurs over millions of years. In fact, scientists consider birds to be a kind of dinosaur.

⏻ SETTING A PURPOSE

As you listen, think about what the *Spinosaurus* would have been like. Try to picture the dinosaur in your head. Think about how the scientists describe *Spinosaurus*. How did they decide that it was a swimming dinosaur? How would you describe it?

Crocodile Meets Godzilla—
A Swimming Dino Bigger Than T. Rex

Spinosaurus lived in an area with a lot of swamps and many rivers.

Spinosaurus had small legs. It would have been slow and awkward on land.

Spinosaurus' jaws were long, with teeth that were perfect for catching fish.

Spinosaurus was fifty feet long. That is longer than a school bus.

Spinosaurus was a large aquatic predator, like a giant crocodile.

Spinosaurus had nostrils up near its eyes, so that it could keep them above water while swimming.

⏻ COLLABORATIVE DISCUSSION

Discussing the Purpose With a partner, write down a list of details about *Spinosaurus*. Then, put them together to make a description of *Spinosaurus*. Discuss how you picture *Spinosaurus*. Do you agree about what it would have been like?

DOWNLOAD

The Gold Rush: An American Dream

Many people traveled west in search of gold. Read on to find out about the Gold Rush and how gold formed in the California hills.

READING TOOLBOX

Identifying Cause-and-Effect Relationships

Events are referred to as cause-and-effect when one event brings about, or causes, the other. The event that happens first is the **cause**. The one that follows is the **effect**.

- To find the effect of an event, ask yourself, "What happened next?"

- To find out what caused an event, ask yourself, "What happened before this?"

- Look for **signal words**, like *because, since, therefore, as a result,* and *so.* These words help readers figure out cause-and-effect relationships.

⏻ SETTING A PURPOSE

As you read, pay attention to the examples of cause-and-effect in "The Gold Rush: An American Dream."

The GOLD RUSH: An American Dream

by Eloise Sloan

You may have heard of the Gold Rush. In 1848, gold was discovered in Coloma, California. Coloma is about 140 miles northeast of San Francisco. People from all over the world made their way to San Francisco. From there, they headed inland looking for gold.

In 1848, the European population of California was about 10,000. (There was no count of the Native American population). By the end of 1849, because gold was discovered there, 100,000 more people **rushed** to California. Approximately 40,000 were miners seeking to fulfill their dreams of finding fortune. The rest were businesspeople who sold tools, clothes, and food to the miners.

But the story of the Gold Rush doesn't start in
10 1848. It actually starts 400,000,000 years earlier. In a lot of ways it's a story about water, and how it moves. Before we can talk about that, though, there are two things you need to know.

rushed: (v.) hurried

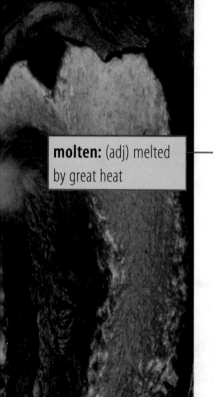

molten: (adj) melted by great heat

First, the earth's surface is solid rock. On parts of the earth's surface, there is water on top of the rock. Below the surface, the deeper you go, the hotter it gets. If you go deep enough, the earth becomes **molten** rock called *magma*.

Second, four hundred million years ago, the land that is now California was buried under the Pacific Ocean.

20   And now the story begins. Along the ocean floor, water seeped through cracks in the rock. The lower the water seeped, the hotter it got. As a result, the hot water dissolved minerals in the rock around it. Eventually, the water got so hot that it shot back up into the sea. As the steam cooled, the minerals that had been dissolved floated down and settled on the sea floor. One of these minerals was gold.

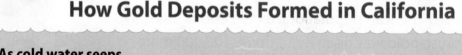

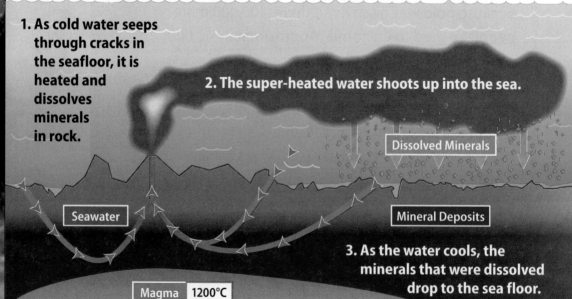

How Gold Deposits Formed in California

1. As cold water seeps through cracks in the seafloor, it is heated and dissolves minerals in rock.

2. The super-heated water shoots up into the sea.

Dissolved Minerals

Seawater

Mineral Deposits

3. As the water cools, the minerals that were dissolved drop to the sea floor.

Magma   1200°C

Then, under the Pacific Ocean, the section of rock that held the seabed moved east. Slowly, very slowly, it hit
30 another section of rock. This movement caused it to bend, crumple, and **heave** upward. When the seawater drained away, this land became the Sierra Nevada Mountains.

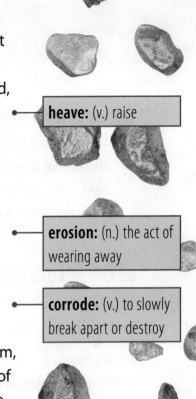

heave: (v.) raise

The mountains took tens of millions of years to form. Over tens of millions of years beyond that, wind and rain washed tiny pieces of rock away. Because of this weathering and **erosion**, some of the gold was washed into rivers and streams in flakes and small grains. Gold is very dense, so it settled onto the bottom of the stream. Because it doesn't **corrode**, it was cleaned to a bright
40 shine by the water.

erosion: (n.) the act of wearing away

corrode: (v.) to slowly break apart or destroy

This kind of gold deposit, as loose sediment in a stream, is called a *placer deposit*. It was the discovery of this kind of gold that sparked the Gold Rush. It was right there on the surface. Miners used wide, shallow pans to sift the gravel from the streams, looking for the flash of gold. For them, the Gold Rush was an American dream.

▼ Panning for gold

⏻ COLLABORATIVE DISCUSSION

Discussing the Purpose With a small group, discuss the cause-and-effect relationships you identified in the text. Why do you think these are examples of causes and effects? What words helped you identify them?

↻ Performance Task

Writing Activity: Cause-and-Effect Work in a small group to identify examples of cause-and-effect in the selection.

A graphic organizer can help you keep track of cause-and-effect relationships in text. The graphic organizer below shows cause-and-effect with an arrow. This can help you remember how one event leads to another. Use a graphic organizer like the one below to show at least one cause-and-effect relationship you read about in this selection.

Cause		Effect
	→	

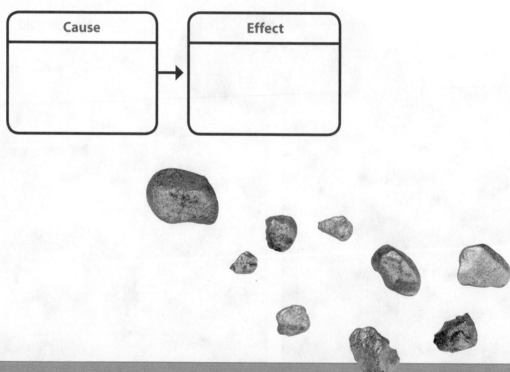

LISTENING TOOLBOX

Active Listening
Always be respectful of others when they are talking.

▶ **Wait for your turn.** As excited as you may be to add to the conversation, don't interrupt.

▶ **Ask questions.** If you don't understand something that has been said, ask about it.

▶ **Let the speaker know that you are listening.** Facing the speaker and making eye contact will help the speaker know you are paying attention. Look at the speaker and be polite, even when you disagree with something he or she is saying.

↻ Performance Task

Speaking Activity: Discussion You read about the Gold Rush and the journey west. With a partner, discuss the dangers of traveling west and the hope of finding gold. Use the following facts and questions to guide your conversation.

● While some miners became rich during the Gold Rush, many miners never found gold. Was the long journey west to find gold worth the many risks?

● If you were living in the mid-1800s, would you have traveled west in search of gold? Why or why not?

● Do you think it would have been easy to find gold because it could be found on the top of streams?

DOWNLOAD

Mama Goose and Jonathan

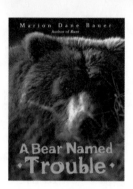

In "The Gold Rush: An American Dream," you read about how gold formed in the California hills. Now read about a boy who tries to understand the natural world of animals.

Know Before You Go

The novel *A Bear Named Trouble* is about a boy named Jonathan who lives in Anchorage, Alaska. Jonathan spends time at the zoo where his father works, imagining what it's like to be different kinds of animals. He pretends he is inside their bodies, seeing and feeling the world as they do. In this chapter, Jonathan imagines what it would be like to be his favorite animal in the zoo—a white, downy goose.

READING TOOLBOX

Reading Fiction

When people read fiction they usually find themselves involved with the story. What are the most important parts of a story?

Plot The plot is what happens in the story. It is what the story is mainly about.

Characters The characters are the people in the story. They are who the story is about.

Setting The setting is where the story takes place.

⏻ SETTING A PURPOSE

As you read, pay attention to the way the author describes the main character and the setting.

Mama Goose and Jonathan

from *A Bear Named Trouble*

by Marion Dane Bauer

Jonathan stood well off the zoo path, deep among the trees, so as to be away from other visitors. Here he could be alone with the pure white goose that was his favorite creature in all the zoo.

"Come, Mama Goose," he called, reaching into his pocket for the corn he always carried when he came to the zoo. "Come. Look what I have for you."

She tipped her head to one side, studying him, then suddenly flapped her great white wings and honked 10 loudly. Jonathan jumped, just a little, and some **kernels** flew from his hand. As tame as she was, Mama Goose could still startle him when she did that.

kernels: (n.) pieces of grain, such as wheat, rice, or corn

When she was very young, she had been a pet. Once she'd grown past the cute, fluffy stage, her owner had decided he didn't want her after all and had donated her to the zoo. Mama Goose had a good life here. All the kids loved her. But no one, not anyone in the world, loved the pure white goose as much as Jonathan did.

"Come, Mama," he called again. And settling onto a 20 patch of ground that wasn't too snowy, he held out a handful of corn.

Mama Goose took a cautious step toward him. She always did that, too, acted as if she had forgotten him, as if she didn't remember he was the one who came to see her every single day.

She bobbed her head up and down, took another step. Jonathan held his breath.

And then there she was . . . not just **pecking** the kernels of corn out of his hand but **clambering** with her wide
30 flat feet right over his legs and settling into his lap. She always gave her tail a final shake when she settled down, murmuring deep in her throat. Kind of a low chuckle.

"Hello," Jonathan whispered, running one hand down her silken neck. He took another handful of corn from his jacket pocket and held it out. Mama Goose gobbled the kernels eagerly, then tilted her head to peer with one bright eye into his face.

pecking: (v.) biting or picking at

clambering: (v.) climbing, often awkwardly, with hands and legs

"Who are you?" she seemed to be saying. And, not incidentally, "Do you have any more corn?"

40   Jonathan laughed. "I'm Jonathan," he said. "I've told you that before. And yes . . . here's more corn."

She watched intently as his hand disappeared into his pocket and emerged again. Then she bent her elegant neck to receive the new offering.

"Just wait until Rhonda sees you," Jonathan said, watching her eat. "She loves birds, and she's going to love you more than all the gulls over Lake Superior. More than the bald eagles, too."

Rhonda was his little sister, but she wasn't here in
50 Alaska with him and their father yet. When Dad moved to Anchorage to take his new job as a keeper at the Alaska Zoo, Rhonda and their mother had stayed behind in Minnesota so Mom could finish out her teaching job in Duluth. Jonathan had wanted Rhonda to come with him and Dad, but Mom had **objected**. "Rhonda needs me," she'd said, as though Jonathan, being all of ten years old, didn't.

In June, once school let out and their house was sold, Jonathan and Dad would fly back to Duluth and
60 bring Mom and Rhonda and their **yellow lab**, Marigold, and Rhonda's beta fish, Boy Blue, to their new home in Anchorage. And then, at last, they would be a family again. But this was only April. June was a long way away.

Jonathan stroked the goose's elegant long neck again, feeling the living warmth beneath the feathers. "You'll like Rhonda, too," he told her.

Slowly, carefully, Jonathan encircled the white goose with his arms and buried his face in the feathery softness of her breast. She tolerated his
70 embrace briefly, then bent down to peck his ear.

objected: (v.) to have disagreed or shown disapproval of something

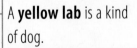

A **yellow lab** is a kind of dog.

The **suffix -ed** is added to make a verb into an adjective.

Do you think the word **waddled** sounds like what it means?

Can you picture a goose with **feathers** when you read this paragraph?

"Ow!" he said, releasing her and grabbing the **offended** ear. "That wasn't very nice."

But nice or not, Mama Goose rose on her stubby legs, shook her feathers back into alignment, then climbed off his lap. As she **waddled** away, her tail feathers twitched with each step.

Jonathan smiled at the picture her rear end made — Mama Goose always made him smile — and scrambled to his feet. Though he had managed to avoid sitting in a patch
80 of snow, his own rear was cold and more than a little damp. He wasn't done with the white goose, though, even if she was done with him. There was the game to be played still.

He closed his eyes and stood perfectly still for a long moment, breathing in the alive smell of the wet earth. When he opened them again, he was ready. It was a game he'd played with his sister since she was little. He'd pretend his way inside a bird or an animal, then he'd tell Rhonda exactly what being that animal was like.

He and Rhonda were still playing the game, even if they
90 had to do it on the telephone now. That meant he had to store up details for the next phone call. He couldn't make the game seem real without the right details.

Jonathan squinted his eyes, studying Mama Goose, who was busy pecking at something hidden in the damp leaves.

Feathers. First there would be the feathers, soft and stiff at the same time. Feathers all over their bodies. And beaks, of course. He brought his hand up in front of his mouth, defining in the air the size and shape of a beak.

"I know," Rhonda would say, impatient for him to get on
100 to the good part, the part where the flying began. "All birds have feathers and beaks."

"But," Jonathan would remind her for the hundredth time, "you have to be *inside* the feathers, *inside* the beak. You have to feel them."

"And inside the wings!" she would say, and without even seeing her, he would know that her cheeks were plumped out with a teasing grin.

What do you **picture in your mind** when you read this sentence?

But Jonathan refused to be hurried. He never let himself be hurried when they were playing the game, no matter
110 how impatient Rhonda got. Waiting a little didn't hurt her. Rhonda hated waiting, but then she *was* rather spoiled. Everyone in the family admitted that Rhonda was spoiled, even Dad, who was the one who spoiled her the worst.

Next, Jonathan would remind her about Mama Goose's eyes, how she has one eye on each side of her head. "That's so she can see in every direction at once," he'd explain, "so she won't get caught by **predators**." But, of course, Mama Goose didn't have to worry about predators. Life in the zoo was safe.

predators: (n.) animals that hunt other animals

120 "Our feet," Jonathan spoke out loud now, as though Rhonda were by his side and could hear, "are big and flat. You'd think a goose's feet would be cold, standing bare like that on the snow, but they aren't. It's got something to do with the veins being close together. I don't remember exactly what."

Finally, he got to the part he knew Rhonda was waiting for. He reached his arms out wide and said, "And our wings are strong. When we stretch them out, they catch the air. I can feel the way the air lifts me off the ground. I can feel
130 the flying in my wings. Can you feel it, too?"

And without even having to close his eyes to concentrate, he heard Rhonda's answer. She looked up at him with those **sky blue eyes** that always captured every fragment of the light and said, "Yes, Jonnie, yes. I can feel it. Just like you. We can fly!"

Do you like this **description** of Rhonda's eyes?

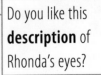

121

UPLOAD

COLLABORATIVE DISCUSSION

Discussing the Purpose Talk with a partner about the selection "Mama Goose and Jonathan." How did the author use words to help you paint a picture of the story?

Analyzing Literature Would you recommend this selection to a friend? Why or why not? Discuss with a partner what your favorite part was. Explain why you enjoyed that part the most.

↻ Performance Task

Speaking Activity: Talk about Fiction In a small group, talk about the plot, characters, and setting of "Mama Goose and Jonathan." Answer the following questions.

- **Plot** Were you interested in the plot? Did the plot make you want to keep reading to find out what happens next?

- **Characters** Who are the characters in "Mama Goose and Jonathan"? Was the main character described in a way that you almost feel like you know him? What did you think about Jonathan?

- **Setting** Did the author make the setting real? Could you picture the zoo in your mind? What words did she use to create a mood or a feeling?

↻ **Performance Task**

Writing Activity: Write about Fiction Choose one part of "Mama Goose and Jonathan" that you discussed with your classmates, and think once more about the plot, the character, or the setting. Write your thoughts or opinions in your own words.

- Ask yourself: Why did I choose this part? How did it make me feel?

- Ask yourself: Did the author use words that made the selection come to life? Would I have used different words if I were writing this story?

- Ask yourself: What did the author do very well in this selection? What did the author not do so well?

Speak Out! In a small group, take turns retelling what happened in "Mama Goose and Jonathan."

LISTENING TOOLBOX

Group Discussion
When you are discussing something in a group, it is important to listen to what your classmates are saying. Be sure to take turns when you are sharing your opinions and ideas.

Useful Phrases

▷ Would you please repeat that? I'm not sure what you mean.

▷ I agree with some of what you say, but _____.

▷ I heard Maria say, and Julio just pointed out, but I would like to add _____.

DOWNLOAD

"Mama Goose and Jonathan" is about a boy who spends a lot of time with animals. Now you will discover different ways to describe groups of animals.

⏻ **SETTING A PURPOSE**

As you read, think about the words that are used to describe the animals in different and unusual ways.

A Rascal of Students

by Arturo Aranjo

A *collective noun* is a singular word for a collection of things. For example, a collection of cows is a *herd*, and a group of fish is a *school*. In fact, *group* and *collection* are collective nouns, too!

What does **school** mean here?

©Comstock/Getty Images

There are also much more interesting collective nouns, such as a *pride* of lions, or a *murder* of crows. Many of these unusual words for groups of animals,

10 or species, were invented by English noblemen in the mid-fifteenth century though some are more recent. Collective nouns were hunting terms at first. Over time, they changed to become part of an educated gentleman's vocabulary. These terms were first written down by a woman named Dame Juliana Berners in 1482.

> This is a **long sentence**. Read it again to be sure you understand its meaning.

You'll notice that many of these terms

20 describe the animals involved. Lions were considered proud, so they collect in *prides*. People associate crows with death, and so a number of them is a morbid *murder*. You can probably guess why a bunch of porcupines is a *prickle*, or a group of squirrels is a *scurry*. Those words tell you how the animals act. A *clutter* of cats and a *cloud* of bats also make sense, since those words describe how a

30 group of those animals might look.

a pride of lions

a prickle of porcupines

a scurry of squirrels

a cloud of bats

a clutter of cats

125

A **parliament** of owls makes sense because a parliament is a group of people who discuss the business of some governments. And owls do look very wise. Some of these collective nouns, however, are just silly. A *zeal* of zebras sounds good, even if it doesn't tell you anything about zebras!

40 The English gentlemen even had a word to describe a group of boys. It was *rascal*!

Here are some other collective nouns. Can you guess why these names were chosen?

a smack of jellyfish

a gaggle of geese

a troop of monkeys

a zeal of zebras

an army of toads

an exaltation of larks

an ostentation of peacocks

an unkindness of ravens

a parliament of owls

a swarm of bees

an army of frogs

a pod of whales

a paddling of ducks

a business of ferrets

a crash of rhinos

a congress of baboons

⏻ **COLLABORATIVE DISCUSSION**

Discussing the Purpose Talk with a partner about the selection "A Rascal of Students." Why do you think the author chose the examples that you saw and read about?

Vocabulary Strategy: Using a Dictionary

When you come across an unfamiliar word, you can try to use context clues to help you figure out the meaning of the word. In the selection, you might have been able to figure out the meaning of the word *species* (line 10) using context clues. If that did not help you figure it out, use the dictionary. If you use a digital dictionary, you can even hear how the word is pronounced.

Here is an example of a dictionary entry:

> **species** (spē'shēz, -sēz) *n. pl.*
> Definition A group of plants or animals having a similar appearance: *So far, the wildlife photographers have seen at least one of every species—even a polar bear.*

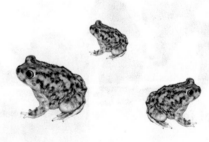

©Jack Goldfarb/Design Pics/Corbis

○ Performance Task

Speaking: Make up your own collective nouns Authors use many kinds of figurative language to help the reader picture what they are trying to describe. **Onomatopoeia** is the use of a word that sounds like what it means.

Here are some examples of onomatopoeia from the selection:

a prickle of porcupines
a scurry of squirrels
a smack of jellyfish
a crash of rhinos
a paddling of ducks

In a small group, talk about these examples. Then work together to invent your own collective nouns using onomatopoeia. You do not have to use only animals. For example:

a jangle of telephones
a twang of guitars
a honk of horns

Speak Out! Share with your classmates which collective noun from the selection is your favorite, and why.

Black Beauty

You just read a selection about groups of animals that have interesting names. Now read a story about a horse that is told from the horse's point of view.

Know Before You Go

POINT OF VIEW When an author tells a story, sometimes he or she chooses to tell it from the first-person **point of view**. This means that the **narrator**, or the voice that tells the story, is a character in the story, telling it using first-person pronouns such as *I, me, we,* and *us.* Use of the first-person point of view allows the reader to imagine what it would be like to be the narrator. "Black Beauty" is a first-person narrative. In the story, Anna Sewell imagines what Black Beauty must be feeling, and allows him to express those feelings as the narrator of the story.

BACKGROUND By showing us what Beauty is thinking and feeling, Sewell helps us relate to his suffering and pain. Because of the book *Black Beauty*, many people became aware of the cruel ways that work horses were treated, and many cruel practices were stopped.

⏻ SETTING A PURPOSE

As you read, pay attention to the point of view. Do you think that using the first person makes the story better?

ANNA SEWELL'S
BLACK BEAUTY

retold by Meredith Mann

I WAS BORN ON A FARM IN THE ENGLISH COUNTRYSIDE. MY MOTHER AND I LIVED IN THE FIELDS OF SQUIRE GORDON AND HIS WIFE.

You're a real beauty, aren't you? That shall be your name, Black Beauty.

I hope you will grow up to be gentle and good, and never learn bad ways. Do your work with a good will, and never bite or kick, even in play.

WHEN I WAS OLD ENOUGH TO UNDERSTAND, MY MOTHER GAVE ME SOME VERY GOOD ADVICE.

I TOOK HER ADVICE TO HEART, AND ALWAYS TRIED TO BE GOOD. WHEN MY MASTER NEEDED ME TO RUN, I RAN AS FAST AS I COULD.

I HAD MANY FRIENDS, THE BEST ONES BEING MERRYLEGS AND GINGER.

ONE NIGHT WHILE RIDING HOME IN A STORM, MY GROOM, JOHN MANLY, AND I CAME TO A RIVER BRIDGE. I REFUSED TO MOVE, BECAUSE I COULD TELL THAT THE BRIDGE WAS FLOODED.

Good boy, Beauty.

WHEN LADY GORDON GOT SICK, I WAS RIDDEN A LONG WAY IN THE RAIN . . .

. . . AND THEN CARRIED THE DOCTOR ALL THE WAY BACK.

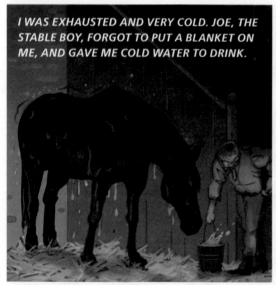

I WAS EXHAUSTED AND VERY COLD. JOE, THE STABLE BOY, FORGOT TO PUT A BLANKET ON ME, AND GAVE ME COLD WATER TO DRINK.

I BECAME VERY ILL.

I'm sorry Beauty, I'll always be careful in the future.

©Escletxa

WHEN THE LADY'S HEALTH GOT WORSE, THE GORDONS DECIDED TO MOVE. GINGER AND I WERE SOLD TO LORD AND LADY W.

LADY W. INSISTED THAT HER HORSES KEEP THEIR HEADS HELD HIGH, SO GINGER AND I WERE FORCED TO WEAR A BREAKING REIN.

IT WAS EXTREMELY PAINFUL, AND STRAINED OUR BACKS AND NECKS. GINGER GOT VERY ANGRY.

ONE NIGHT, REUBEN SMITH, OUR CARETAKER, RODE ME OUT AND STOPPED AT AN INN.

HE RODE ME HARD OVER SHARP STONES ON THE WAY HOME.

I FELL AND SCARRED MY KNEES.

WITH UGLY SCARS FROM THE FALL, I WAS NO LONGER FIT TO BE A CARRIAGE
HORSE AND WAS SOLD TO A LONDON TAXICAB DRIVER NAMED JERRY.

HE WAS A GOOD
MAN WHO
TREATED ME WELL.

MANY OTHER HORSES WERE
WORKED TO DEATH.

BUT JERRY ALWAYS TOOK
A REST ON SUNDAY . . .

. . . SO I WAS ABLE TO
REST, TOO.

ONE COLD NIGHT, WAITING
OUTSIDE AFTER A PARTY, JERRY
CAUGHT A TERRIBLE CHILL.

©Esclerxa

HE DID NOT LEAVE HIS BED FOR MANY DAYS, AND I FEARED I WOULD LOSE HIM.

He must leave the city. The country would be a better place for him.

I WAS HAPPY THAT MY KIND MASTER WOULD RECOVER, BUT FATE WAS NOT SO KIND TO ME.

FOR TWO YEARS, I WAS PUT TO HARD WORK, PULLING HEAVY CARTS DAY AND NIGHT.

I WAS SO TIRED FROM THE WORK THAT MY MASTER SOLD ME.

FOR SALE

BUT WHEN ALL HOPE WAS LOST, I WAS FOUND BY AN OLD FRIEND.

Hey there Beauty, do you remember me? It's your young Joe . . .

AND AFTER MANY YEARS OF TOIL AND MISERY, I RETURNED HOME TO THE COUNTRY, AND TO PEACE AND FRIENDSHIP.

⏻ COLLABORATIVE DISCUSSION

Discussing the Purpose In a small group, talk about "Black Beauty." Did you like how the story was told from Black Beauty's point of view? Did the narration in the first person make the story better? If you were the author, would you have written the story this way?

Speak Out! Give a brief review of "Black Beauty." Did you like this story? Why, or why not? Be sure to give specific reasons in your review.

SPEAKING TOOLBOX

Giving a Presentation

When you give a presentation, keep the following tips in mind:

▶ **Don't forget to practice.** If you can, it's best to rehearse your presentation. Check your body language in a mirror.

▶ **Use physical clues.** Your posture, hand gestures, and facial expressions can help listeners understand your points.

▶ **Use the right tone.** Your tone sets the mood—upbeat or serious, thoughtful or direct. When you set the tone, keep your audience in mind. What is the best way to address your listeners?

©Fsclerxa

READING TOOLBOX

Summarize a Story

When you summarize a story, you tell it in your own words.

- Make sure you include the most important events in the story.

- Be certain to include the main characters in the story.

- Use your own words, but don't change the author's meaning.

↻ **Performance Task**

Writing Activity: Summarize the Story   First, re-read the graphic novel, "Black Beauty." In a group, talk about the most important parts of the story. Then summarize the story in your own words. When you are done writing, read over what you have written.

You know that you have summarized the story successfully if someone who has not read the story can understand exactly what the story was about, and what happened.

Performance Task

Writing Activity: Response to Literature

In this unit, you have read selections that describe nature in different ways. You have read selections in different genres. Now it's your turn to write a response to literature that includes your opinion of a selection that you read.

Planning and Prewriting

Connect to the Theme

Nature often plays a big role in fiction. Authors and poets describe nature and animals using colorful adjectives, interesting word choices, and figurative language.

When you write a response to literature, you are letting readers know what you thought about something you read. Think about what you liked best about each selection. Think about what you disliked. Would you recommend it to a friend? What would you change?

Choose Your Topic

You have thought about the theme of nature. Read the questions below, and choose one that seems interesting. This question will be your topic.

- If you were the author of "Black Beauty" would you have written from the point of view of the horse? Why, or why not?

- Did the author's use of figurative language add to your enjoyment of "Mama Goose and Jonathan"? Why, or why not?

- Did Jonathan in "Mama Goose and Jonathan" seem like a real person? What did you think of this character?

You may also choose your own topic.

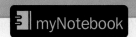

Decide the Basics

You should now have your topic. This topic will become your main idea. You will support your idea with examples and details from the selection. Use the notes below to help guide your decision making.

Characters

- Are the characters believable?
- How are the characters described?
- What are the characters' relationships to one another?

Plot

- What are the important story events?
- What is the problem in the story?
- Is the problem solved at the end of the story?

Style Elements

- How does the author express the theme?
- How is the setting important to the plot?
- What details suggest the mood and the tone of the story?
- How does the author use word choice and point of view to emphasize important ideas?

Point of View

Who tells the story? The **point of view** is how a writer chooses to tell a story. The **first-person** point of view means the narrator is a character in the story. The third-person point of view means the narrator is not a character in the story.

Dialogue

- What do the characters think or say?
- Does the dialogue sound like real people thinking or speaking?

Performance Task

Finalize Your Plan

You know what you want to say in your response to literature. Now it's time to plan the structure of your response.

Use the diagram in the Writing Toolbox to help you.

WRITING TOOLBOX

Elements of a Response to Literature

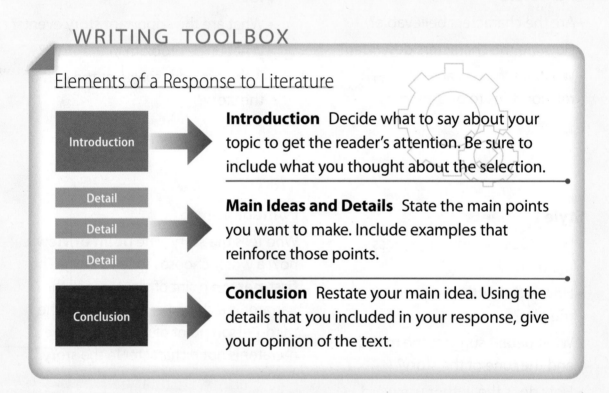

Introduction Decide what to say about your topic to get the reader's attention. Be sure to include what you thought about the selection.

Main Ideas and Details State the main points you want to make. Include examples that reinforce those points.

Conclusion Restate your main idea. Using the details that you included in your response, give your opinion of the text.

Draft Your Response to Literature

You've got it all planned out. You've decided on your main idea and you have all the supporting evidence you need. You have a way to organize your ideas. Now it's time to start writing! As you write, think about:

- **Purpose and Audience** What do you want your readers to know?

- **Clarity** Make sure your ideas are clearly stated. Arrange your sentences in a logical order.

- **Support** Include examples that support your ideas.

- **Connecting Words** Use connecting words to show how one idea links to another.

Revise

Self Evaluation

Use the checklist and rubric to guide your analysis.

Peer Review

Exchange your response to literature with a classmate. Use the checklist to comment on your classmate's work.

Edit

Edit your response to literature to correct spelling, grammar, and punctuation errors.

Publish

Finalize your response to literature and choose a way to share it with your audience.

Unbreakable Spirit

There is no journey upon this earth that a man may not make if he sets his heart to it.

— H. Rider Haggard, author

Essential Question

How can we show our spirit in little ways and in big ways?

The Language of Spirit

Having spirit is often about solving problems and overcoming challenges. Most people, at some point in their lives, face difficulties. Managing difficulties and moving forward, especially when it is really hard, is what spirit is all about.

We all have special talents that help us show our spirit. Each of us has something we are especially good at. Some people are very patient. Some people are great at helping others. Some people are great listeners. Some people are great at telling stories. These are talents that help make us who we are.

Leadership and determination are talents, too. These talents allow us to help others when they need it and to keep our spirit no matter what stands in our way.

In this unit, you will learn about the many ways in which people show spirit. In "Cello Girl" you will read about a young girl's determination to play the cello even though she is hearing-impaired. You will explore strength and perseverance in the selections "Catch That Wave" and "Nelson Mandela." You will also find out about the amazing spirit of the Navajo Code Talkers.

> **Why is it important to have spirit?**
> **How does spirit help us grow?**

You Can Say That Again:
Synonyms and Antonyms

Words that mean about the same thing are **synonyms**. *Small* and *little* are synonyms. So are *big* and *large*. **Antonyms** are words that have opposite meanings. *Small* and *big* are antonyms. So are *little* and *large*. Finding out about a word's synonyms and antonyms can help you learn about the word and its meaning. Synonyms and antonyms can help you add a bit of spirit to your writing, too! Here are some words about spirit, along with their synonyms and antonyms.

Word	Synonyms	Antonyms
courage	bravery, fearlessness, valor	cowardice, fearfulness
determination	perseverance, dedication, persistence	wavering, indifference, doubt
strength	vigor, toughness	weakness
enthusiasm	energy, eagerness, zeal	laziness, lifelessness, indifference

↻ Performance Task

Think of someone who has shown spirit. It might be someone you know. It could be someone you've heard or read about, or even someone you've seen in a movie or on TV. What makes you think this person has spirit? Use the information on these pages or in **Browse** magazine to help you organize your thoughts. Write a short speech about why you think this person has spirit. Don't forget to use your **Activity Book**, too.

➜ *Browse magazine*

DOWNLOAD

In this blog, you'll get to know Cello Girl, who was determined to be in the orchestra even though her hearing is impaired. Having determination is a big part of having spirit.

⏻ SETTING A PURPOSE

While you read, think about Cello Girl's character. What does this blog entry tell you about who she is as a person?

Breaking into Orchestra
CELLO GIRL

Enter your email address:

Subscribe me!

SEARCH

💬 Comments 3

Hello! I'm one of those "deaf" kids from school. Actually, Imy hearing is impaired. I can hear a little—more when I'm using my hearing aids. If you're from my school you know there's a bunch of us in a special program. We have our own classes (for sign language and stuff like that), and some of us go to regular classes with sign language interpreters to help us out. The interpreters go with us on field trips, or when we join a school club. We do all kinds of things at school. You see us everywhere!

Well, almost everywhere. The school policy is that kids in our program can't be in orchestra. But I wanted to change that. I come from a musical family—both of my parents are music teachers. My dad teaches violin, and my mom teaches cello. I knew from when I was little that I wanted to play an instrument.

When I was six, my dad brought home a tiny violin and a tiny cello for me to try. The violin was so cute! But it was almost impossible for me to hear. The cello was easier—the notes are lower and I hear those better. Also, because I hold the cello with my whole body, I can feel the vibrations. My mom started to teach me on the tiny cello. At first I just played open strings to feel and hear the difference between, say, an open G and an open C. Then I started learning scales and songs. My mom would sing, and I would accompany her on the cello. It was fun, and I got pretty good!

I knew playing in a group would be hard, but I figured with the help of the interpreter I could follow the conductor and keep up. I wouldn't have guessed that getting into the orchestra would be even harder!

At the beginning of fourth grade, I went to sign up. My mom went with me. At first Mrs. Brooks, the orchestra teacher, said no. She explained that it was a school policy. I said I thought the policy was unfair, especially because most of the other kids were beginners and I already knew how to play.

There was an awkward silence.

My mom asked if I wanted to do something else instead. "Ceramics?"

I said, "No!"

Mrs. Brooks said, "Well, maybe I can just hear you play a little bit."

I played "The Happy Farmer" by Robert Schumann. As she listened, Mrs. Brooks's eyebrows rose higher and higher behind her glasses. A smile spread across her face.

"Oh my!" she said. "Well now. We'll have to see about that policy, won't we? Welcome to orchestra!"

And that was that. Not so hard after all!

Posted by Cello Girl, 4:31 p.m.

ARCHIVES

September

August

July

June

May

April

March

February

January

©Getty Images

⏻ COLLABORATIVE DISCUSSION

Discussing the Purpose Talk with a small group about Cello Girl's character. How does this blog entry give you an idea about who she is? Which words or parts of the story help you paint a picture of her?

Exploring the Theme Cello Girl shows determination. What other qualities or traits show that someone has spirit?

Write On! Like many bloggers, Cello Girl gives readers the opportunity to post comments about the blog. Write a short comment to Cello Girl. You may wish to state your opinion about what she wrote. You can also share a similar story. 💬 **Comments**

↺ Performance Task

Writing Activity: Schedule Posts on Your Calendar
Many bloggers like to write posts ahead of when they want to publish them. For instance, if you will be away on a school trip or a family vacation, you can set up several blog posts on a calendar to be published while you're away. This way, your blog automatically sends posts and continues to update your readers.

1 Write three posts that will be published at a later date. Your blog software should have a scheduling feature that allows you to set up your calendar so that you can publish your posts in the future.

2 Write an entry about a favorite book or a favorite movie that you wish to publish at a later date.

3 Send a reminder about an upcoming event, such as a science fair at a local museum. Make sure that your blog post gives an accurate date and time. You don't want to invite readers to an event at a wrong location or day.

4 Write a blog post to celebrate an upcoming holiday, like Earth Day or Memorial Day. Set it up so that the future blog date matches the specific date in mind. Add a special design for fun!

Language Cam video

Watch the video to find out more about what it means to have spirit.

CATCH A WAVE

In "Breaking into Orchestra" you read about how a young girl's determination helped her to perform in the school orchestra. Read on to find out why surfers need determination, too.

READING TOOLBOX

Learning to Write an Outline

Writers often create an outline to organize their thoughts and research before they begin to write. An outline shows the important ideas the writer wants to include and lists them in order. An outline helps writers:

▶ stay focused.

▶ be sure they make the points they are trying to make.

▶ include only the best examples to support their ideas.

▶ tell a clear story or give a clear message.

The **subheadings** in this selection are like an outline. They show the important ideas of the text and how the author organized her thoughts and research. Subheadings often help readers, too. Subheadings help readers quickly scan and find information in text.

⏻ SETTING A PURPOSE

As you read, look for subheadings in the text and think about how they help you know the author's important ideas.

Catch a Wave

by Jennifer Taylor

When people think of a sandy beach on a sunny day, the image of surfers hanging ten might pop into their minds. Along the coasts of the United States, surfing is a part of the culture. Strong, constant winds and the shape of the land under the water cause breaking waves that are just right for riding.

What information in this sentence helps you understand what causes good waves for surfing?

Spirit of Surfing

Surfing can be a thrilling pastime. Gliding along a wave looks like smooth sailing, but it's not easy! It takes strength, skill, and practice, not to mention **endurance** and a love for
10 the water. You need good balance to keep from falling over. You need strong muscles to steer the board. You won't surf well the first time you try, so you need dedication, too. Learning to surf means being thrown into the water and struggling with the board. In a way, surfing means fighting the waves and overcoming all the energy and motion that make them up.

endurance: (n.) the ability to do something difficult for a long time

Action of Waves

Surfing, of course, also takes waves. But how do waves form? And why do they break along the shore? What **conditions** create that perfect wave? Surprisingly, the answers don't start with the water. They mostly start with the wind!

Ocean waves form when wind blows across the surface of the water. First, ripples form. Then, as the wind pushes against the ripples, the ripples turn into waves. Waves vary. They can be tall or short. They can come one right after another. They can also be spread far apart. All of this is determined by the wind.

conditions: (n.) the things that affect the way something is

▲ The tallest waves, which are perhaps the most exciting to surf, form when fast-moving winds blow for a long time over a large area.

©Digital Vision/Getty Images

Here's an odd fact: A wave can travel thousands of miles across the ocean, but the water in a wave hardly moves at all. As the wind blows across the surface of the water, it transfers some of its energy to the water. The water is set in motion, but it doesn't move forward as you might expect. Instead, it moves in circles. The energy is pushed forward through the ocean, but the water itself doesn't travel. So what we call a wave is really just the energy that moves through the water.

Near the coast, things change. Here the water becomes **shallow** as the seafloor slopes up toward the shore. The bottom of the wave scrapes along the ground and slows down, but the top of the wave keeps moving quickly. Soon the wave starts to tip over and the wave "breaks." If conditions are right, the top curls over, forming a crest that surfers can ride.

shallow: (adj.) the opposite of *deep*

The Length of Waves

Wave movement

The shallower the water, the shorter the wave's length.

Surfing Culture

Surfing became a part of popular culture around 60 years ago in the 1950s and 1960s. The sport became associated, or connected, with its own unique 'surfer' clothing style, 'surfer' slang, and 'surfer' music. At that time, surfing became as much a community of people as a sport. Today, surfing has
50 become part of a major lifestyle, taking on a spirit that goes beyond the water.

⏻ COLLABORATIVE DISCUSSION

Discussing the Purpose With a small group, talk about the important ideas in the text and how they are organized. How do the subheadings help you remember and understand the important ideas?

Exploring the Theme Why does surfing take spirit? Talk with a partner about the sport. Use examples from the text in your discussion.

↻ Performance Task

Writing Activity: Write an Outline Suppose you wanted to write a report about a sport or activity you enjoy. What would you want readers to know about the sport? Make an outline for a report.

- Ask yourself, "What are the most important things I want readers to know?" For example, is it important for readers to know the history of the sport? Do I want to explain the rules or how the game is played? Should readers know why I love the sport and why it's fun to do?

- Ask yourself, "What is the best order for telling the information? What will paint a clear picture for readers?"

Speak Out! Choose a sport you think takes spirit to play. Write a short speech to tell about it. Remember to include facts and examples to support your ideas.

DOWNLOAD

You just read about the spirit of surfing. Now read on to find out about the fascinating code talkers.

⏻ **SETTING A PURPOSE**

As you read, pay attention to the order in which the events occured.

Code Talkers

by Joe Cummings

When he was in boarding school, Chester Nez was punished if he spoke Navajo, his native language. But more than 60 years later, he was awarded the Congressional Gold Medal for doing just that—speaking Navajo.

◀ Chester Nez

The military wars against American Indians were
10 over by the late 1800s. The government of the United
States, however, wanted to change their culture.
In 1883, laws were passed that **prohibited** certain
American Indian religious practices. Children were
also encouraged to attend **boarding schools,** where
they were taught "American" culture. Chester Nez was
a student at one of those boarding schools.

American Indians were not granted full citizenship
until 1924. One reason that this law was finally passed
was in appreciation of the thousands of American
20 Indians who volunteered to fight for the United States
in World War I. Not only were they brave and gifted
fighters, but some of the men became "code talkers."

The enemy was very good at breaking the codes
used by the Allied Forces, but they didn't know any
of the many American Indian languages. Members of
the Choctaw Nation, among others, simply spoke in
their own language, and their messages were safe.

prohibited: (v.) not allowed

boarding school: (n.) a school where students live

▼ A field radio from World War II

Chester Nez was still in boarding school when he was asked to be a code talker with the United States Marine Corps during World War II. The military had learned from their success in the first war, and **recruited** hundreds of American Indians—mostly Navajos. It is thought that there were only about 30 people in the world who were not Navajo but understood the language. All the same, the code talkers developed codes in their languages. Even members of their tribes back home wouldn't be able to understand what they were saying. For example, a fighter plane was called a "**hummingbird**," a battleship was called a "whale," a platoon was a "mud," and February was "squeaky voice." (The code words were all spoken in Navajo.)

Code talkers were often in the middle of the fighting, carrying and operating their radio equipment. They were given messages in English, and immediately translated them in their heads and transmitted them. Any time there was need for extra **security**, they would use the codes, in their language, that they had developed.

30

40

recruited: (v.) asked to join

hummingbird

security: (n.) the act of protecting from harm

50 Governments are very secretive about military ideas used during wartime, and for years laws prevented the public from knowing anything about the code talkers. However, in 1968, twenty-three years after the end of World War II, the secrets were **released**.

For his efforts during the war, Chester Nez was awarded the Congressional Gold Medal by President George W. Bush in 2001. He later wrote a popular book, *Code Talker*, about his experiences in 60 the Pacific in World War II. Nez died in 2014, the last of the Navajo code talkers. But Chester Nez wasn't really his name—it was the English name he was given in kindergarten.

> What in this paragraph helps you understand the meaning of **released**?

▼ Two Navajo code talkers sending messages during a battle in 1943

 **COLLABORATIVE DISCUSSION**

Discussing the Purpose Informational text is often written in time order. With a small group, talk about the major events in "Code Talkers." What happened first? Then what happened? Use time-order words such as *first, next,* and *later* in your discussion.

Vocabulary Strategy: Identify Suffixes

government (line 10)   **equipment** (line 45)

Look at the words above. Both of them end with the suffix *-ment*. When you add *-ment* to the end of a verb, it changes the verb to a noun. To *equip* means "to provide necessary supplies." *Equipment* means "the necessary supplies that are provided." Here are some other words with the suffix *-ment*.

move	movement
agree	agreement
achieve	achievement
measure	measurement
manage	management

Practice and Apply Use the suffix *-ment* to help you define words and change verbs into nouns.

1. Use what you know about each verb listed above to define the word with the suffix.

2. Add the suffix *-ment* to the following words to make new words. How many of these words do you recognize?

argue	accomplish	punish	settle	embarrass

↻ Performance Task

Writing Activity: Take Notes Note-taking is an important skill when doing research. When you take notes, you record the main ideas in a text. You can go back later to help remember what you've read. Reread the selection taking notes as you read. Here are some tips for taking good notes:

- If you are reading a book or article, write down the title and the author's name. If you are reading from the Internet, copy the complete URL and name of the website.

- Write the main ideas of the text and the important points the author makes. Include the page numbers where you found key information.

- Try not to copy whole sections of the text. Instead, try to summarize the main ideas. Remember, when you summarize, you retell the main ideas in your own words.

Speaking Activity: Report Use the notes you took about "Code Talkers" to prepare a short report.

Make sure your report begins with an introduction. Your introduction will explain what you are going to discuss in your report.

Also be sure that your report ends with a conclusion.

A conclusion often summarizes the main ideas of your report. When you are finished, read your report aloud to a partner.

DOWNLOAD

Podcast: The Big Race

In the selection you just read, the code talkers worked hard to help the war effort. In the story you'll listen to next, a girl realizes that she does not want to give up no matter what.

Background on Radio Plays

The selection you're about to hear is a radio play. This type of entertainment was very popular in the United States during the early twentieth century. Radio plays often have a narrator and different characters. There are no images, so the narrator or characters describe what is happening in the story. Sometimes music and sound effects also help listeners imagine the setting and the action.

Radio plays became less popular after the television was invented in the 1950s. However, they didn't disappear completely. One radio play in the United Kingdom has been on the air for over 50 years. Also, some people today are making new radio plays using the Internet.

 SETTING A PURPOSE

While you listen, think about Shonda's problem and possible solutions to her problem. Remember, a *problem* is a situation that needs to be overcome. A *solution* is a way of dealing with a difficult situation or problem.

The Big Race

Tim's Solution

Shonda should run really fast at the start of the race so Rachel can't catch up.

Shonda is worried about losing a race to Rachel.

Rachel's Solution

Shonda won't win the race as long as she gives up when she gets tired.

Shonda's Solution

I should train harder so I can keep going during the race.

⏻ COLLABORATIVE DISCUSSION

Discussing the Purpose In a small group, discuss the solutions Tim, Rachel, and Shonda come up with for Shonda's problem. Which solutions do you agree or disagree with? Do you think Shonda's solution is enough to solve her problem?

DOWNLOAD

Disorientation

You heard about a girl who would not give up even though she lost a race. Now read about two children who are determined to make it through a terrible storm.

In *The Magic Trap*, the novel this selection is taken from, brother and sister Jessie and Evan face a number of challenges. They're trying to set up a magic show for the neighborhood. Their parents are separated, and while their mother normally takes care of them, she's out of town on business. Their father, who promised to take care of them, is not at home. And now they have to deal with a hurricane!

READING TOOLBOX

Author's Choice of Words

Authors choose the words that they use to create a feeling or atmosphere for the reader. What the characters say and think, and the author's use of description add to the mood that he or she is trying to convey. Mood can be described by adjectives such as *angry, serious,* or *funny.*

Mood is part of the author's **style**, which involves choices about *how* something is said rather than *what* is said.

⏻ SETTING A PURPOSE

As you read, think about how the author's use of words help you to understand how Jessie and Evan feel.

Disorientation

from *The Magic Trap*

by Jacqueline Davies

It was a sound like an explosion that yanked Evan back awake. At first he thought he hadn't slept at all, but then he saw that there was daylight outside—a dark murkiness, but daylight nonetheless. The sound was so loud, it even woke Jessie, who could sleep through an army invasion.

"What was that?" she shouted, looking at Evan with wild eyes. The sound of the outside storm seemed even louder than before, as if it was rushing

10 into the house through a **gaping** hole.

Evan and Jessie hurried out of their mother's room and followed the noise of the storm. When they looked in Jessie's bedroom, they couldn't believe their eyes. A large tree **limb** was sticking right through the wall and lay across Jessie's bed. There was a hole about the size of a car door, and rain was pouring through it, soaking the bed and the floor. Chunks of plaster from the ceiling had fallen on top of the mess.

gaping: wide open; very large

This is a **multiple-meaning** word. Here, *limb* means "a branch of a tree."

The *term flip* out is an **idiom**. It means "to get very excited or upset."

Can you figure out what **to shake the thought loose** means?

Evan looked at Jessie, expecting her to **flip out**,
20 but the expression on her face was very still. Jessie
didn't like *anything* to mess up her room, not even
one tiny bit. What was she thinking now?

Jessie pointed at her bed. "If I'd slept there, I'd be
dead," she announced, like a reporter stating a fact.

"Nah," said Evan, who didn't even want to think
about that. But what if Jessie *had* been in her bed?
What would he have done then? **To shake the
thought loose**, he asked, "What tree is it?"

They carefully crossed the room to the hole in the
30 house and peered out.

"Oh, Evan! It's the Climbing Tree!"

It was true. The Climbing Tree had snapped in
half, and the top of it had crashed into their house.
Evan felt a stab of pain—it was almost as if someone
had died. The Climbing Tree was more than just a
place to hang out. There were times when it had felt
like Evan's only friend in the world. Times when he'd
needed to get away—from the house, from Jessie,
from the fighting between his mom and his dad,
40 from his own impatience or frustration or confusion.

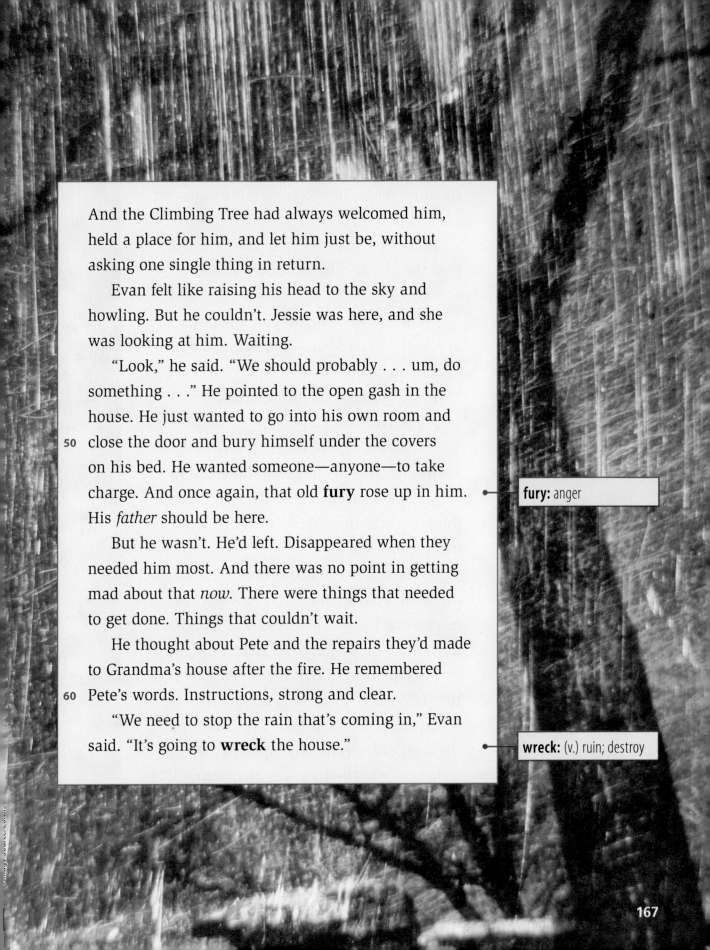

And the Climbing Tree had always welcomed him, held a place for him, and let him just be, without asking one single thing in return.

Evan felt like raising his head to the sky and howling. But he couldn't. Jessie was here, and she was looking at him. Waiting.

"Look," he said. "We should probably . . . um, do something . . ." He pointed to the open gash in the house. He just wanted to go into his own room and
50 close the door and bury himself under the covers on his bed. He wanted someone—anyone—to take charge. And once again, that old **fury** rose up in him. His *father* should be here.

fury: anger

But he wasn't. He'd left. Disappeared when they needed him most. And there was no point in getting mad about that *now*. There were things that needed to get done. Things that couldn't wait.

He thought about Pete and the repairs they'd made to Grandma's house after the fire. He remembered
60 Pete's words. Instructions, strong and clear.

"We need to stop the rain that's coming in," Evan said. "It's going to **wreck** the house."

wreck: (v.) ruin; destroy

"Wreck the house?" shouted Jessie, waving at the tree in her bed.

"Well, even *more*," said Evan. "Water is a house's worst enemy." It was as if Pete were standing there. *You gotta keep the water out. That's job number one.*

70 Evan sent Jessie down to the garage to grab the plastic tarps that their mother kept there.

"How are we going to hold the tarps in place?" asked Jessie when she came back upstairs.

Evan looked at the hole. "Nails," he said decisively.

Jessie's eyes grew wide. "Nails? In the wall? Mom is going to kill you if you do that!"

"Jess, look at this! It's a disaster. I don't 80 think a few nails in the wall are going to make it any worse!"

So they pounded about twenty nails into the wall, securing the tarp at the top of the hole. Jessie had the bright idea of hanging the bottom of the tarp over the tree branch and out the hole so that the water would run off outside. Even so, a fair amount of water was still pushing its way in around the sides of the tarp, which flapped in the 90 vicious wind. **The tree was also acting like a straw**, drawing the water in from outside and

> Can you picture what the author means when she says that **the tree was also acting like a straw**?

dumping it on the bed. Jessie, who was good at figuring out how things work, had an idea. She and Evan wedged the two smaller tarps between the tree and the mattress, and then they shaped the tarps so that there were two gullies in the plastic. The water that poured on top of the tarp gathered in the gullies and ran off into two buckets that Jessie positioned

100 on the floor. It was sort of like the marble tracks that she and Evan sometimes built.

"That's the best we can do," said Evan.

"We just have to remember to change the buckets, because they're filling up pretty quick," said Jessie. It was true. There was already almost an inch of rainwater in each bucket. How could the sky hold that much water?

They carried the heavy, **sodden** towels

110 they'd used to wipe up the puddles down to the laundry room and piled them on the dryer. No electricity, so there was no way to dry the towels. In the kitchen, they each poured a bowl of cereal, but decided not to open the refrigerator door, in the hopes that the food inside would stay cold enough until the power came back on. They sat in the dim room, away from the sliding glass doors in case any more tree limbs fell, and ate their

120 bowls of dry cereal.

sodden: very wet

⏻ COLLABORATIVE DISCUSSION

Discussing the Purpose Talk with a partner about the selection, "Disorientation." How did the author use words to help you understand what Jessie and Evan were experiencing?

Vocabulary Strategy: Shades of Meaning

When an author wants to describe something, he or she will often search for the perfect word. There are many words that mean about the same thing, but some words work better in certain sentences. For example: Which of the following sentences gives you a clearer picture?

> The **cold** water was a **good** drink on a **hot** summer day.
>
> The **icy** water was a **perfect** drink on a **steamy** summer day.

The following words have slight differences in meaning:

Big	Large	Huge
Wreck	Crash	Smash
Wet	Soaked	Sodden
Smart	Clever	Brilliant
Peer	Look	Stare

Practice and Apply

1. Look at the chart. Write a sentence using one of these words. Then write the same sentence using a word that means almost the same thing. Which sentence do you think works better?

2. What are some other words that mean almost the same thing? Write sentences using both words.

↻ Performance Task

Speaking Activity: Share Ideas In a small group, talk about the author's choice of words in "Disorientation."

How do the following sentences from the selection help you to understand how Evan is feeling?

> *The Climbing Tree was more than just a place to hang out. There were times when it had felt like Evan's only friend in the world.*

Now, how does the last sentence of the selection make you feel?

> *They sat in the dim room, away from the sliding glass doors in case any more tree limbs fell, and ate their bowls of dry cereal.*

Which sentence do you think is the most dramatic or interesting?

Share your ideas with your classmates.

LISTENING TOOLBOX

Active Listening

Always be respectful of others when they are speaking.

- Wait for your turn. As excited as you may be to add to the conversation, don't interrupt.

- Ask if you don't understand what's been said.

Are You Having Pun Yet?

The characters in the story that you just read showed spirit and determination in the face of danger. In this selection, lift your spirit with some fun and laughter.

READING TOOLBOX

Reading for Entertainment

People love to read for entertainment. Sometimes they can get lost in a story. Sometimes they are fascinated by facts. You can learn a lot by reading articles that are filled with information.

You can also learn a lot when you read stories, poems, or plays. You can find out how other people live. You can discover how other people think. You can explore other cultures or even travel through time. Reading for fun is full of possibilities. Believe it or not, you can also learn simply by reading some jokes!

⏻ SETTING A PURPOSE

As you read, think about how understanding the multiple meanings of the words helps you understand the puns.

Are You Having **Pun** Yet?

by Matilda Sokolov

I'm reading a book about anti-gravity. I just can't put it down.
When a clock is hungry it goes back four seconds.
To whoever invented zero: Thanks for nothing!

What do those jokes have in common? They're all puns! A pun is a joke that plays on the words in it.

Sometimes a pun uses the fact that some words sound alike, like this one: "I'm really good friends with 25 letters of the alphabet . . . I don't know why." If that doesn't make sense, try thinking of what sounds just like the word "why" and you'll see how that pun works. A pun might also put more than one word together to sound like another word.

13 "If I had a pet newt I would call him "Tiny," because he'd be my newt." That's a pun based on the word "minute," which can mean "very small."

Sometimes a pun uses a word that has more than one meaning: "To write with a broken pencil is pointless." It could also work by using a phrase that could mean multiple things. For example: "I couldn't quite remember how to throw a boomerang, but eventually it came back to me." If you know that a boomerang

23 returns to the person who threw it, "**eventually** it came back to me" could be about the person's memory or about a boomerang. (Of course, after it's been explained, that joke probably isn't that funny anymore.)

Have you ever heard a joke that was like a little story? That kind of joke usually has one line at the end that makes the whole thing funny—the punch line. Sometimes the punch line of a joke is a pun.

33 See if you can guess what the pun might be at the end of this joke.

eventually: at some time later

"A guy goes to a restaurant after a long day at work and orders a sandwich. After his first bite, he hears a high-pitched voice. 'Hey mister! Nice pants,' it says. He looks around, doesn't see anything, and quickly shrugs it off. After a little bit, he takes another bite and hears the voice again. 'Hey mister! Sweet shoes.' Again, he looks around, and sees nothing but a waiter who is busy attending to other customers. Shaking his head, he takes another

43 bite. 'Hey mister! Cool shirt.' He puts down his sandwich, frustrated at this **phantom** voice, and calls to the waiter, who comes over. 'Excuse me,' he begins, 'what is that high-pitched voice I keep hearing?' 'Oh, those are the peanuts,' the waiter replies. 'They're complimentary.'"

Puns are actually a very old form of humor. Shakespeare uses puns all the time in his plays! So if you like making

50 puns and someone else thinks it's annoying, just tell them you want to be like William Shakespeare and they'll understand. After all, where there's a Will there's a way!

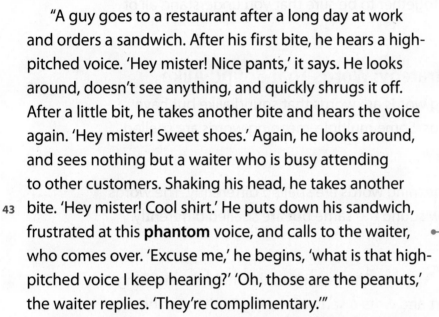
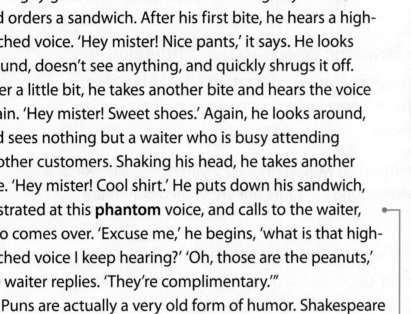

phantom: (adj.) of something sensed, but with no physical reality

175

⏻ **COLLABORATIVE DISCUSSION**

Discussing the Purpose In a small group, talk about the puns you read. Talk about the different meanings of the words. Work together to be sure that you understand all of the puns.

Vocabulary Strategy: Words That Sound Alike

Multiple-meaning words are words that sound alike but have different meanings. Some multiple-meaning words are spelled the same.

Some multiple-meaning words are spelled differently. The words in the chart below sound the same but are spelled differently.

Practice and Apply Choose one of the multiple-meaning words in the chart and write a sentence using both meanings in one sentence. You might even write a pun!

not/knot	aunt/ant
rays/raise	in/inn
allowed/aloud	knight/night
for/four	pear/pair
peak/peek	flower/flour

⟳ Performance Task

Writing Activity: Learn About Search Terms You heard a little bit about William Shakespeare in "Are You Having Pun Yet?" Are you curious to learn more? You can use the Internet to help you find out more. Search terms are the words and phrases you use to find out more about a topic.

When you research a topic, you may use the Internet to help you find information. You use **search terms**.

- With a partner, talk about what search terms you would use to find out more about William Shakespeare.

- Write down at least three terms, and then discuss the terms with your partner.

SPEAKING TOOLBOX

Working Together

▶ When you work with a partner, make sure you take turns speaking so that you can share your ideas.

▶ Remember that when it is your turn to speak, you want your partner to give you his/her full attention.

Nelson Mandela

Now you will read about a man who truly had an unbreakable spirit.

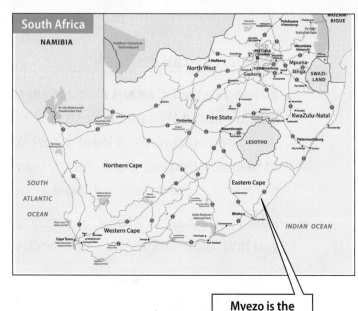

Know Before You Go

BACKGROUND South Africa is called the Rainbow Nation. It has 11 official languages. Many families moved there from other parts of Africa. Then, people from Europe arrived. Finally, in 1910, South Africa became an independent nation.

Mvezo is the birthplace of Nelson Mandela.

Some people think that the South African flag is a mix of older flags. Some think that the colors of the flag have meanings.

difficulties South Africa has faced

the African skies

the beautiful land

riches from minerals

the different people of South Africa

⏻ SETTING A PURPOSE

As you read, think about how the author of this graphic novel used facts and research to describe the incredible spirit of Nelson Mandela.

Nelson Mandela

by Jessica Cohn

IT IS JULY 1918. IN THE VILLAGE OF MVEZO, IN SOUTH AFRICA. A BABY IS BORN.

The name suits him, I think.

Wah!

HE IS GIVEN THE NAME ROLIHLAHLA. IT MEANS "TROUBLEMAKER."

THE BABY IS PART OF THE THEMBU PEOPLE. HIS FATHER WORKS FOR THE KING.

Come see your brother!

THE BABY CRIES AND THEN GROWS QUIET. IN TIME, THE WHOLE WORLD WILL HEAR FROM HIM. HE WILL BECOME KNOWN AS NELSON MANDELA, THE FREEDOM FIGHTER.

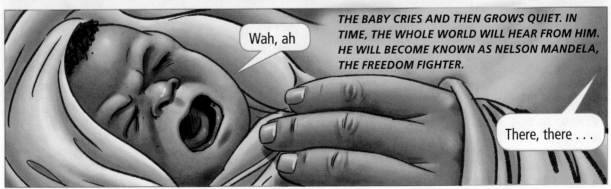

Wah, ah

There, there . . .

179

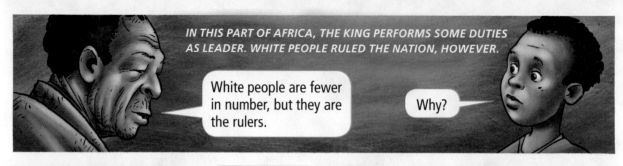

IN THIS PART OF AFRICA, THE KING PERFORMS SOME DUTIES AS LEADER. WHITE PEOPLE RULED THE NATION, HOWEVER.

White people are fewer in number, but they are the rulers.

Why?

You will be called *Nelson*. You will learn to write it.

WHEN HE IS OLD ENOUGH TO GO TO SCHOOL, THE BOY'S TEACHER GIVES HIM AN ENGLISH NAME. THIS IS THE TRADITION.

AT HOME, YOUNG NELSON LISTENS CAREFULLY TO STORIES ABOUT HIS PEOPLE.

. . . And that is why being kind is important. Very, very important.

HE LEARNS TALES ABOUT HIS PEOPLE'S BRAVERY. HE WONDERS WHY THEY NO LONGER RULE THEMSELVES.

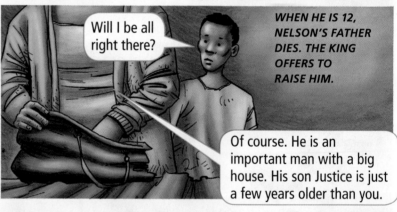

Will I be all right there?

WHEN HE IS 12, NELSON'S FATHER DIES. THE KING OFFERS TO RAISE HIM.

Of course. He is an important man with a big house. His son Justice is just a few years older than you.

NELSON LEARNS TO LIKE LIFE IN THE ROYAL HOUSE. HIS MOTHER VISITS HIM. HE CONTINUES HIS SCHOOLING. IN SCHOOL, NELSON LEARNS TO BE A LEADER.

IN COLLEGE, NELSON IS ELECTED TO THE STUDENT COUNCIL. MOST OF HIS FELLOW STUDENTS BELIEVE THE COUNCIL HAS NO REAL POWER. HE REFUSES TO TAKE THE POSITION.

Only 25 people voted. That is not a real election. I refuse to take part until you hear our demands.

ALREADY, NELSON HAS NOBLE IDEAS ABOUT HOW LIFE SHOULD BE. HE ACCOMPANIES SOME FRIENDS TO THE CITY OF JOHANNESBURG.

Good-bye to the old life.

Just look at how big the city is!

Hey!

NELSON WORKS AS A SECURITY OFFICER AT A MINE. IN THE CITY, WHITE PEOPLE RUN THE BUSINESSES. MOST AFRICANS ARE POOR. THEY LIVE OUTSIDE THE CITY.

HE BEGINS TO STUDY LAW. THREE MAIN PURPOSES HAVE ALREADY BEGUN TO GUIDE HIM.

Just a hundred more pages to go . . .

HE BELIEVES THAT ALL PEOPLE DESERVE DEMOCRACY, QUALITY, AND THE POWER OF EDUCATION.

NELSON MANDELA JOINS THE AFRICAN NATIONAL CONGRESS (ANC). IN 1944, HE HELPS FORM THE ANC YOUTH LEAGUE.

Freedom is not just a word . . .

I like the name Thembekile.

FOR A SHORT TIME, HE IS MARRIED TO A NURSE NAMED EVELYN. THEY HAVE TWO SONS AND TWO DAUGHTERS.

THE ANC FIGHTS TO ALLOW AFRICANS TO RULE THEMSELVES. THE GOVERNMENT OF SOUTH AFRICA RESPONDS BY INTRODUCING APARTHEID.

We will not be ignored!

Open your books.

APARTHEID DIVIDES PEOPLE BY THE COLOR OF THEIR SKIN. THEY MUST LIVE IN DIFFERENT PLACES. THEY MUST GO TO SEPARATE SCHOOLS.

THERE ARE EVEN SEPARATE DOORWAYS TO THE SHOPS.

What are you doing here, anyway?

IF YOU ARE OVER 16 AND NOT WHITE, YOU MUST CARRY A PASSBOOK THAT SHOWS WHERE YOU LIVE. IF YOU GO OUT WITHOUT ONE, YOU CAN BE SENT TO JAIL.

IN THE EARLY 1950S, NELSON IS A MEMBER OF THE DEFIANCE CAMPAIGN.

We have more members than ever before . . .

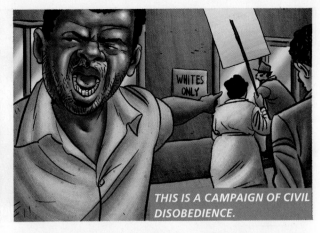

THIS IS A CAMPAIGN OF CIVIL DISOBEDIENCE.

No more apartheid.

CIVIL DISOBEDIENCE IS A FORM OF PROTEST. PEOPLE WANTED TO OVERCOME APARTHEID THROUGH PEACEFUL MEANS.

THE PEOPLE OF THE DEFIANCE CAMPAIGN PROTEST AGAINST LAWS THEY FIND UNJUST.

NO MORE PASSES

No more apartheid.

MANY WHITE PEOPLE JOIN THE FIGHT. A NUMBER OF GROUPS FORM. IN 1954, THE GROUPS JOIN TOGETHER TO FROM THE CONGRESS ALLIANCE.

THE CONGRESS ALLIANCE SIGNS THE FREEDOM CHARTER.

It begins like this. "We, the people of South Africa, declare for all our country and the world to know: that South Africa belongs to all who live in it, black and white . . ."

183

THE PEOPLE IN GOVERNMENT ARE AFRAID. THEY ARREST NELSON AND OTHERS.

Did you or did you not plan to overthrow the government?

EVENTUALLY, THEY SET HIM FREE.

IN 1958, NELSON MARRIES AGAIN. HIS WIFE IS A SOCIAL WORKER NAMED WINNIE. THEY HAVE TWO DAUGHTERS.

RAT-A-TAT RAT-A-TAT

THE PROTESTS CONTINUE. IN 1960, THOUSANDS MARCH IN THE TOWN OF SHARPEVILLE. THE POLICE SHOOT AND KILL 69 PROTESTERS. THEY INJURE HUNDREDS MORE.

Run!

IT LEADS TO A STATE OF EMERGENCY. THE ANC IS BANNED.

Hut, hut . . .

IN SECRET, THE ANC FORMS AN ARMY. THEY CALL THEMSELVES UMKHONTO WE SIZWE, WHICH MEANS "SPEAR OF THE NATION."

NELSON TRAINS AS A SOLDIER. HE TRAVELS AROUND AFRICA TO GAIN SUPPORT FOR THE GROUP. WHEN HE RETURNS TO SOUTH AFRICA, HE IS ARRESTED.

I knew you looked familiar . . .

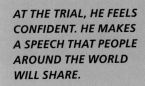

AT THE TRIAL, HE FEELS CONFIDENT. HE MAKES A SPEECH THAT PEOPLE AROUND THE WORLD WILL SHARE.

I have cherished the ideal of a democratic and free society in which all persons will live together in harmony. . . . It is an ideal for which I am prepared to die.

How can I live without news from the papers or the radio?

NELSON MANDELA GOES TO JAIL IN 1964. HIS CELL IS VERY SMALL.

THE ANC HAS BEEN RUNNING THE RELEASE MANDELA CAMPAIGN. PEOPLE ALL AROUND THE WORLD HAVE BEEN PROTESTING.

MANDELA

End apartheid!

Release Mandela!

HE IS NOT SET FREE UNTIL 1990. WHILE IN PRISON, HE HAS BECOME A GRANDFATHER.

"I HAVE WALKED THAT LONG ROAD TO FREEDOM."
—Nelson Mandela

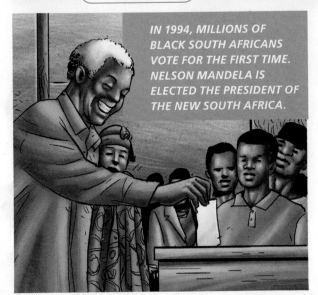

IN 1994, MILLIONS OF BLACK SOUTH AFRICANS VOTE FOR THE FIRST TIME. NELSON MANDELA IS ELECTED THE PRESIDENT OF THE NEW SOUTH AFRICA.

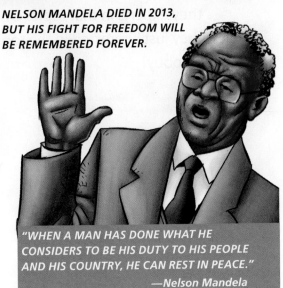

NELSON MANDELA DIED IN 2013, BUT HIS FIGHT FOR FREEDOM WILL BE REMEMBERED FOREVER.

"WHEN A MAN HAS DONE WHAT HE CONSIDERS TO BE HIS DUTY TO HIS PEOPLE AND HIS COUNTRY, HE CAN REST IN PEACE."
—Nelson Mandela

UPLOAD

⏻ **COLLABORATIVE DISCUSSION**

Discussing the Purpose In a small group, talk about the information presented in this graphic novel.

RESEARCH TOOLBOX

Gathering Information

When you want to find information about a topic, you have to do research. You probably go to the library or use a search engine online to learn about what you are going to talk or write about. But be careful where you get your information from!

▶ **Check your sources.**

Whether you are getting information from a book or from the Internet, it is important to be sure that the authors of the information are reliable. Are they experts in that topic? Or are they just interested in the topic as a hobby?

▶ **Check your facts.**

Confirm your research against more than one source. For instance, if you are writing about an event in history, check two or more sources to make sure that the date of the event is the same in each of them.

▶ **Double check your work.**

Once you have information you can trust, organize it in a clear way. Then, go over it again to make sure you have included the information correctly.

©Ferlotya

↻ Performance Task

Writing Activity: In Your Own Words In a small group, review the graphic novel that describes the life of Nelson Mandela.

Work together to determine what the most important parts of the selection are. Ask yourself, "What information is necessary in order to understand who Nelson Mandela was?" Then write a paragraph that includes the most important facts that were in this selection.

Speak Out! What do you admire the most about Nelson Mandela? Use information from the graphic novel when you give your opinion.

Performance Task

Writing Activity: Research Report

In this unit you have read about people who have shown spirit in the face of difficulty. Which of these people interested you the most? Did you read something that made you want to find out more? Your task is to write a research report on the theme of "showing spirit."

Planning and Prewriting

Connect to the Theme

Nelson Mandela had it. So did the Code Talkers. But people don't have to be famous to have spirit. An athlete with a disability who trains for a marathon has it. A girl with a stutter who runs for student council has it. A boy with a vision impairment who enjoys painting has it. Dealing with challenges and moving forward is what having spirit is all about. By rising above their circumstances, people with spirit encourage others to be the best they can be. In this activity you will be writing a research report about a person with "spirit." Who will it be?

Choose a Topic

After you've picked a person to write about—let's say it's Nelson Mandela—it's time to choose a topic. "Nelson Mandela" wouldn't work—it is too big a topic. You'll need to narrow it down. Is there a part of his life you want to focus on? Is there one event you want to research? As a topic, "Nelson Mandela's Early Life" or "Nelson Mandela's Years in Prison" might be better.

Decide the Basics

Now that you have a topic, it's time to gather your sources, take notes, and make an outline.

Gather Your Sources

You'll probably want to go to the library for information or research your topic online. But no matter what sources you use, make sure they're reliable. This is especially true for Internet sources. There's a difference between someone's opinion posted on a website and an online article written by an expert.

Check Your Facts

Since you'll be writing a research report about an actual person, you'll be dealing with facts. Facts have to be correct. Using more than one source will help you double-check your facts. An encyclopedia entry, a news article, and a biography give you different kinds of information. If you're having trouble finding a certain fact in one place, you might find it in another.

Take Notes

Here are some tips for taking good notes:

- For print sources, write down the title of the book or article and the author's name. For online sources, copy the complete URL and name of the website.

- Write down the important points the author makes. Include the page numbers where you found information.

- Avoid copying whole sentences. Instead, summarize a section of text, or tell it in your own words.

Make an Outline

An outline lists all your ideas and puts them in order. It shows which facts are most important and which facts are details. An outline helps you stay on topic, keeps you focused on the points you're trying to make, and establishes a clear story or message. And when you start to write, an outline will help you organize and structure the information you want to present.

Performance Task

Finalize Your Plan

You've got your outline. Now you need to decide how to present the information. Follow the structure shown in the Writing Toolbox.

WRITING TOOLBOX

Elements of a Research Report

Opening Paragraph	Present your topic. Introduce the subject and why you've chosen him or her to write about. "Hook" your readers with an interesting detail or a quotation from the person you are writing about.
Main Idea and Supporting Details	Make sure that your main idea is stated clearly. Each paragraph should include details that support the main idea.
Conclusion	The conclusion should follow and sum up how the details support your main idea. You may want to include an insight about the person as a result of the research you did.

Draft Your Research Report

Now start writing! As you write, here are some things to think about:

- **Audience** What effect do you want your report to have on readers? Will it give them a better understanding of the person you wrote about?

- **Purpose** Tell why you chose this person early on in your report so readers can follow the points you're making. Is it clear why you think this person has "spirit?"

- **Title** The title of your report should identify the subject of the report or refer to him or her in a way that makes the reader want to learn more.

- **Structure** Use the Writing Toolbox diagram to help organize your information. Be sure to link your paragraphs together in a way that makes sense.

- **Transitions** Make sure your sentences flow smoothly. Use connecting words like *later, finally,* and *then* to show the timing of events.

- **Conclusion** Use a concluding paragraph to tie your ideas together. Restate and expand on the reason you think this person has spirit. You may want to include comments of your own based on the research you did.

Revise

Self Evaluation Use the checklist and rubric to guide your analysis.

Peer Review Exchange your report with a classmate. Use the checklist to comment on your classmate's report.

Edit

Edit your report to correct spelling, grammar, and punctuation errors.

Publish

Finalize your report and choose a way to share it with your audience.

©Gianluca battista/Demotix/Corbis

Change It Up

We must all obey the great law of change. It is the most powerful law of nature.

— **Edmund Burke, statesman**

Essential Question

What are some things that we can do to make sure we continue to grow and change?

The Language of Change

Everyone experiences change throughout life. Change occurs from our very first moments of life. Infants grow and develop each day. They learn to crawl, then toddle, and then walk. They learn to speak and communicate with others. In time, they go to school, and then they turn into grownups. People move, make new friends, and have new experiences throughout their lives.

Technology changes our lives over time. People discover and invent new things almost every day. Most inventions are built on the discoveries and inventions that others made before them. Cell phones were built in part from the telephone, which was in turn built in part from the telegraph.

Progress comes from change. When people or technologies change for the better, we call it *progress*. Progress is the process of improving or developing something over time.

In this unit, you will read selections about progress and change. You will find out how we are trying to produce electricity in a cleaner way. You will discover how movie-making in Hollywood has changed over time to bring you the spectacular films you see today. You will also learn about texting and its beginnings more than 150 years ago.

> **What effect does progress have on our lives?**

©Ollyy/Shutterstock

Agents of **Change**: Prefixes and Suffixes

When you add a prefix or a suffix to a word, its meaning changes. You know that a **prefix** is a word part added to the beginning of a root word. A **suffix** is a word part added to the end of a base word. Prefixes and suffixes change the meaning of words in ways that you can figure out with a little practice. These parts of words can be used as clues to the meaning of a word. Here are some common prefixes and suffixes.

Prefix	How it Changes a Word	Examples
in- *dis-* *un-*	changes a word to mean "not"	inactive, incorrect dislike, dishonest unusual, untie
pre-	changes a word to mean "before"	precaution, preschool

Suffix	How it Changes a Word	Examples
-ful	changes a word to mean "full of"	careful, helpful
-less	changes a word to mean "without"	fearless, useless

↻ Performance Task

Choose an invention that you think has changed our lives.
Use these pages and **Browse** magazine as you think about your choice. Then present your chosen invention to a small group of students. Tell them about the invention and why you chose it. Explain how it has changed our lives. Don't forget to use your **Activity Book**, too.

→ *Browse magazine*

In this blog, you'll find out about Ivan the Science Kid and other students who want to change the world by inventing fascinating inventions that are actually useful.

⏻ SETTING A PURPOSE

While you read, think about Ivan's blog and the comments he receives. What do these comments tell you about these blog visitors?

Ivan the Science Kid

Enter your email address:

Subscribe me!

SEARCH

🔍

💬 **Comments** 4

What Should I Invent?

My school has an Inventor's Fair coming up, and I really want to enter something. But first I have to think of what to invent. My problem is, I want to invent something **useful**—you know, like a skateboard, night-vision binoculars, or pre-packaged peanut butter and jelly sandwiches. It seems like so many inventions are pretty much **useless**—you know what I mean, like, dolls that talk or… vacuum cleaners. I don't want to waste my time with stuff like that.

Anyone have ideas for useful things I could try to invent? I promise to give you credit. Or maybe we could work together. *I'm listening!*

Posted by Ivan the Inventor, 3:45 p.m.

 Like 3   Dislike 0 REPLY

©Virinaflora /Shutterstock

COMMENTS

Pre-packaged PB&Js are ridiculous! They taste awful, and making a fresh PB&J only takes a minute. But that's not the point. I don't think an invention is useful or not useful based on if you like it. A useful invention is something like a bike, warm clothing, or cup-holders for the car—things people need and use every day.

<u>Posted by I Make My Own, 4:11 p.m.</u>

👍 Like 8   👎 Dislike 0   REPLY

Well, people will have different opinions about pre-packaged PB&Js, but I agree with *I Make My Own.* An invention can be useful even if you yourself don't like it or use it much. I think there are lots of people who would be sad if the vacuum cleaner had never been invented. Useful inventions can be time savers. They help solve a problem. They can help keep us alive. Or maybe they are just fun.

I think you should invent a way to feed your dog when you're not home. Or how about a way to keep your younger brothers and sisters busy so they won't bug you all the time?

<u>Posted by Annoyed Big Sister, 5:21 p.m.</u>

👍 Like 8   👎 Dislike 0   REPLY

A lot of inventions are apps for cell phones. Maybe you could figure out an app that will come up with ideas for inventions! It sounds like a joke, but I'm sort of serious.

<u>Posted by App Master, 5:33 p.m.</u>

👍 Like 6   👎 Dislike 0   REPLY

Hey everyone, thanks for pitching in! Do you think I could invent a way (an app?) for my dog to let himself out into the yard when we're not home? That would be really useful!

<u>Posted by Ivan the Inventor, 6:45 p.m.</u>

👍 Like 5   👎 Dislike 0   REPLY

ARCHIVES

September

August

July

June

May

April

March

February

January

⏻ COLLABORATIVE DISCUSSION

Discussing the Purpose Talk with a small group about Ivan the Inventor and the blog visitors who had ideas for inventions. Which comments told you the most about these visitors?

Exploring the Theme Ivan the Inventor wants to invent something that people can use every day. Do you think any of these inventions could actually work?

Write On! Like many blogs, Ivan the Science Kid gives readers the opportunity to post comments about the blog. Write a short comment to Ivan. You may wish to state your opinion or suggest your own invention.

↻ Performance Task

Writing Activity: Helpful Tips When Writing Blog Posts
When you write blog posts, think about the tone of your blog and your audience. In other words, what kind of mood or attitude are you trying to bring to your blog?

1 Do you want your blog to be informative, educational, or entertaining? Think about your topic. If you are writing tips about technology , the tone of your blog should be informative. If you are blogging about your move to a new city, your tone can be more conversational. It can be written as if you are just talking with a friend.

2 Think about your audience. Some bloggers consider their readers to be a community. They might just start their posts with "Hi, readers!" Other bloggers use a more formal style. Even if your tone is conversational, be sure to proofread your blog posts. Pay attention to your spelling and grammar. Make sure to use language that is respectful. Use appropriate language and always be polite.

3 If your blog is time-sensitive, or needs to be read right away, some blog software allows your readers to subscribe to, or sign up for, your blog. Your readers will be informed when you publish a new entry.

Language Cam video

Do you want to hear more about interesting inventions? Watch the video.

Where Do We Get Our Energy?

Ivan the Inventor was trying to think of amazing inventions. Now think about the invention of electricity, which is something we all use every day. Then read on to find out how we generate electricity from fuel.

READING TOOLBOX

Reading Hard Words

This selection contains scientific terms that describe sources of energy. You can break some of them down into root words, prefixes, and suffixes. You'll need to use different strategies to figure out the meaning of words that cannot be broken down into these familiar parts.

▶ **Give the text a first read** to see what it's mainly about. Try to read all the way through to the end without stopping to figure out the meaning of each new word. Even without knowing the meaning of every word, you can probably figure out the main ideas of the text.

▶ **Study the pictures.** The photographs and illustrations often show places or things mentioned in the text. These can help you understand what the author is writing about.

▶ **Use context clues.** Read the sentences right before and after an unfamiliar word. These can often help you define the new word.

⏻ SETTING A PURPOSE

As you read, write down the words that are new to you.

Where Do We Get Our Energy?

by Tarek Ali

You use electricity every day. Electricity powers refrigerators, toasters, televisions, computers, and all mobile devices. You know you can plug these items into a socket to turn them on or charge them. But did you ever think about where the electricity that flows through a socket comes from?

Generating Electricity

Most of the electricity we use is **produced** in electric power plants. Almost all electric plants use steam to turn **turbines**. When the turbines spin, mechanical energy is changed into electrical energy in the generator.

10 This creates electricity. In many power plants, steam is made by burning coal, oil, or natural gas. These fuels are *nonrenewable* sources, meaning that only a certain amount exists. When we use them up, they're gone. These energy sources also create pollution when they are burned.

produced: made; created

turbines: engines that have blades that spin by pressure from steam

Electric Power Plant

Coal supply

Water

Steam line

Turbine

Generator

Transmission lines

Transformer

Boiler

Condenser

◀ A power plant turns fuel into electricity.

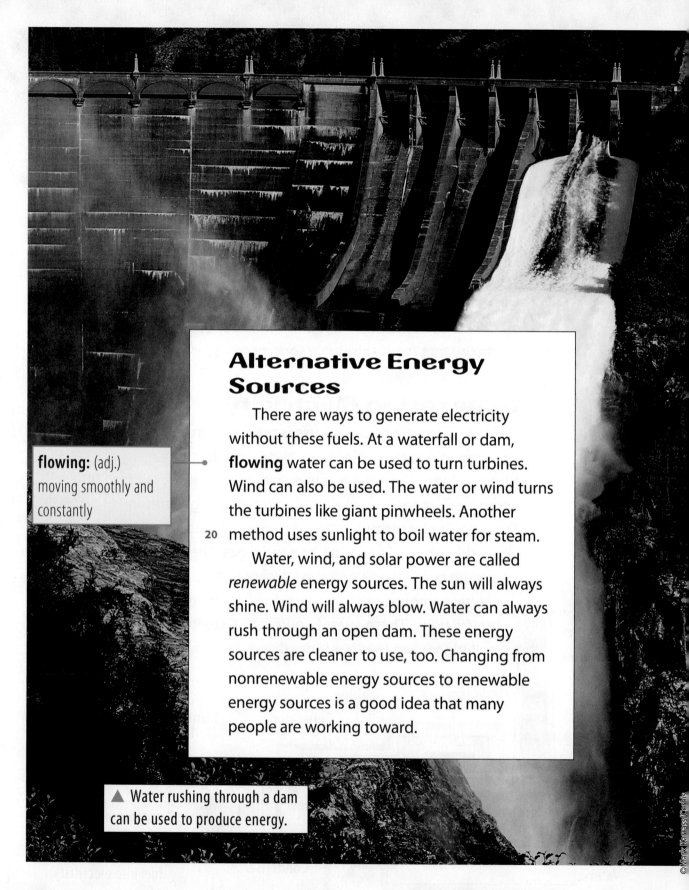

Alternative Energy Sources

There are ways to generate electricity without these fuels. At a waterfall or dam, **flowing** water can be used to turn turbines. Wind can also be used. The water or wind turns the turbines like giant pinwheels. Another
20 method uses sunlight to boil water for steam.

Water, wind, and solar power are called *renewable* energy sources. The sun will always shine. Wind will always blow. Water can always rush through an open dam. These energy sources are cleaner to use, too. Changing from nonrenewable energy sources to renewable energy sources is a good idea that many people are working toward.

flowing: (adj.) moving smoothly and constantly

▲ Water rushing through a dam can be used to produce energy.

©Mark Karrass/Corbis

Alternative Energy in the United States

Many United States companies are developing
renewable energy systems from wind and solar
sources. Researchers, engineers, and other
partners have been working together to find ways
to produce more energy using these sources. Over
one-tenth of the electricity in the United States is
produced with renewable sources, and attempts to
increase that include some impressive projects.

In the Mojave Desert, the Ivanpah Solar Power
Facility was brought online in 2013. Acres of curved
mirrors focus the harsh desert sunshine onto a
central tower that contains water. The water in the
tower boils. Then the turbines turn with the steam.
It was the largest solar power plant in the world
when it was built.

Solar panels capture energy from the
sun and change it into electricity. ▼

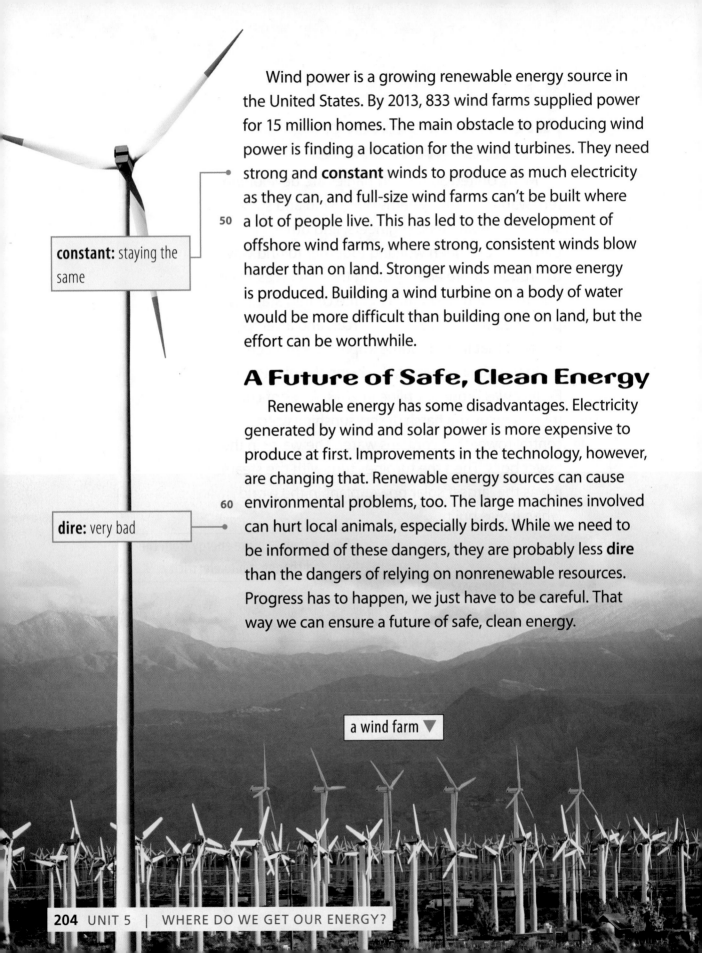

Wind power is a growing renewable energy source in the United States. By 2013, 833 wind farms supplied power for 15 million homes. The main obstacle to producing wind power is finding a location for the wind turbines. They need strong and **constant** winds to produce as much electricity as they can, and full-size wind farms can't be built where

50 a lot of people live. This has led to the development of offshore wind farms, where strong, consistent winds blow harder than on land. Stronger winds mean more energy is produced. Building a wind turbine on a body of water would be more difficult than building one on land, but the effort can be worthwhile.

constant: staying the same

A Future of Safe, Clean Energy

Renewable energy has some disadvantages. Electricity generated by wind and solar power is more expensive to produce at first. Improvements in the technology, however, are changing that. Renewable energy sources can cause

60 environmental problems, too. The large machines involved can hurt local animals, especially birds. While we need to be informed of these dangers, they are probably less **dire** than the dangers of relying on nonrenewable resources. Progress has to happen, we just have to be careful. That way we can ensure a future of safe, clean energy.

dire: very bad

a wind farm ▼

⏻ COLLABORATIVE DISCUSSION

Discussing the Purpose With a small group, review your list of unfamiliar words. Together, use context and picture clues to guess the meaning of these words. Then use the dictionary to look up their meaning.

Exploring Language Work with a partner to break down the terms *renewable* and *nonrenewable* into root words, prefixes, and suffixes. Then define these terms in your own words.

READING TOOLBOX

Reading Hard Words

Many science words were used in this selection. Was it important to know the exact definition of each word? What was important to know about these words?

Speak Out! Should people try to use less electricity in their day-to-day lives? Why or why not? Write a short speech explaining your opinion. Be sure to support your opinion with facts and details.

Let's Go to the Movies

Alternative forms of energy are changing the ways we produce electricity. Read on to find out how movies, which depend on electricity, have also changed over time.

READING TOOLBOX

Identifying Sequence of Events

Both narrative and informational texts often tell stories or events in the order in which they happened. The order in which events take place is called a sequence. Identifying sequences can help you better understand and remember what you read. To identify sequence:

- Look for time-order words and phrases such as *in the beginning, later on, next, then, after,* and *finally.*

- Look for dates and times, such as the names of months and years. These tell you when things happened.

- Ask yourself: What happened first? What happened next?

⏻ SETTING A PURPOSE

As you read, pay attention to the sequence in which movies changed over time.

Let's Go to the Movies

by Mark Bailey

Think about some of the things that you like to do. You might enjoy watching movies and television, playing video games, or seeing videos online. All these things were made possible by people who came to California a little over a hundred years ago.

In 1900, Hollywood was a village two miles north of Los Angeles with a post office, a hotel, two stores, and five hundred people. It was filled with large houses and orange groves. Soon, all of this would change.

When movies were first produced, in the late 1800s,
10 the first American movie companies were located near New York City. In the 1910s, however, most of them moved west. The sunny weather in Southern California meant companies could shoot outside without spending money on lights.

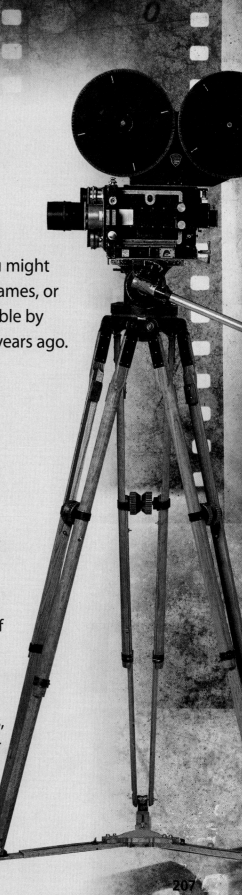

By the 1920s, film studios were producing a constant stream of silent movies. The name Hollywood came to represent American movies. Hollywood had already changed a lot!

In 1927, the first movie with sound was released. This
20 was just the first of many ways technology would change movies over time. But in 1929, the country **plunged** into the Great Depression. Many Americans had little money during the 1930s, but movies were cheap. For fifteen cents, people could forget their troubles in a world of fantasy. Hollywood made cheerful musicals, gangster dramas, and comedies about rich people in beautiful apartments. The first color movies were also made at this time.

In 1941, the United States entered World War II. Patriotic movies played across the country. Wacky comedies kept
30 families' spirits up while their sons and brothers were fighting. Newsreels were shown before the films, keeping people informed.

Television entered American homes in the 1950s. People became less interested in going out to the movies. So Hollywood introduced **spectacle**, hoping that people would be excited by gigantic sets and thousands of extras. It also showed off technological progress with wide screens and the first version of 3-D.

plunged: fell or dropped suddenly

Use context clues to help you understand the meaning of the word **spectacle**.

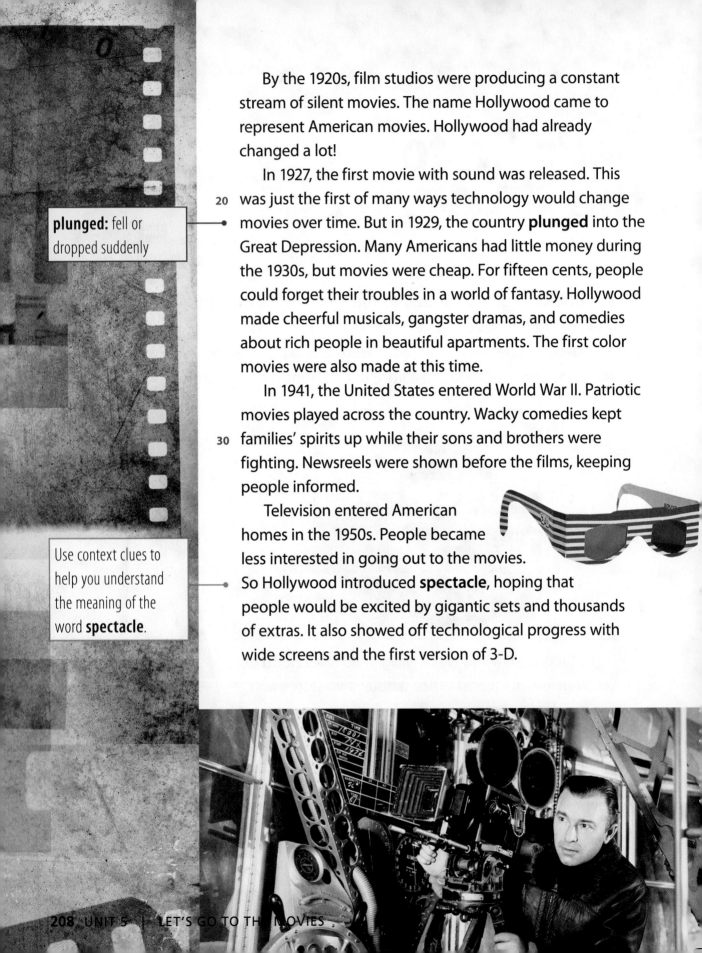

40   The late 1960s were a time of experiment and change. Young filmmakers made small, personal films independent of movie studios. Then, in the 1970s, movies became popular again when directors like George Lucas and Steven Spielberg entered the field. In the summer of 1975, *Jaws*, and then in the summer of 1977, *Star Wars* each made more than a hundred million dollars. Now movie companies plan exciting blockbusters with lots of special effects to release each summer.

50   In the 1990s, new animation companies appeared. Until then, few animation films were released each year. These companies and others make many animated movies that kids and adults can enjoy.

   All of this happened before you were born. But summer blockbusters, independent films, animated movies, and of course, color and sound are still part of the movie scene. The movies you see today are the result of all the ways movies

60 have changed in a hundred years.

⏻ COLLABORATIVE DISCUSSION

Discussing the Purpose With a small group, talk about how movies changed over time. First, movies were produced in New York. Then what happened? When were sound and color introduced? What about special effects?

Exploring the Theme Over time, new technologies, like color film and animation, changed the way movies were made and how they looked. How do these changes show progress? Talk with a partner about change and whether change is good, bad, or both. Does change always lead to progress?

READING TOOLBOX

Identifying Sequence of Events

This selection gives a brief history of movies. You can organize and summarize this information using a graphic organizer like the one shown below.

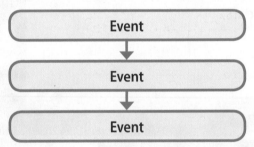

Create a sequence graphic organizer in your notebook. Then reread the text and note each big event or change in movie history. You can also list dates as you come across them in the text. Use your graphic organizer later on to help you understand and remember what you've read.

↻ Performance Task

Speaking Activity: Discussion Think about a movie you've seen recently. Then think about the ways in which movies have changed over the past one hundred years. Answer these questions as you discuss movies with a partner.

- What was the name of the movie and what was it mainly about? Who were the main characters? How would you describe them?

- Were there special costumes or special effects used as part of the setting or plot?

- How might the movie have been different if it were made 20 years ago? How might it have been different if it were made a hundred years ago?

SPEAKING TOOLBOX

Formal and Informal Language

When you need to speak to an adult or someone you do not know, it is important to speak respectfully.

▶ **Formal language** is a polite way to speak to someone. You use formal language when you are speaking to someone such as your teacher, or to another adult of authority such as a school principal. When you are in a group setting with your friends, it is natural to speak informally.

▶ **Informal language** is casual, everyday speech that you use with your friends. Examples of informal language include idioms and slang. Idioms are expressions whose meanings are different from the literal meanings. Slang is informal language used by a specific group.

Podcast: Two Poems by William Wordsworth

The last selection talked about the history of movies. In the podcast you'll listen to next, you'll meet an English poet who created beautiful pictures with words.

Background on William Wordsworth and Romantic Poetry

William Wordsworth (1770–1850) was born in an area of England called the Lake District. This area is famous for its beautiful lakes and forests. The beauty around Wordsworth influenced his poetry, which expresses a deep love of nature.

The Romantic Movement in English poetry lasted from the late 1700s to the mid-1800s. This movement had little to do with what we would now call romance. Instead, Romantic poets used a new style of poetry to write about emotion, imagination, and nature. They often used images to express themselves. Other famous Romantic poets of the time included Lord Byron, Samuel Coleridge, and John Keats.

⏻ SETTING A PURPOSE

As you listen to the poems, think about how the images make you feel. Pay attention to the way that Wordsworth creates images of colors, actions, and natural landscapes in your mind.

Two Poems by William Wordsworth

Images in the Podcast

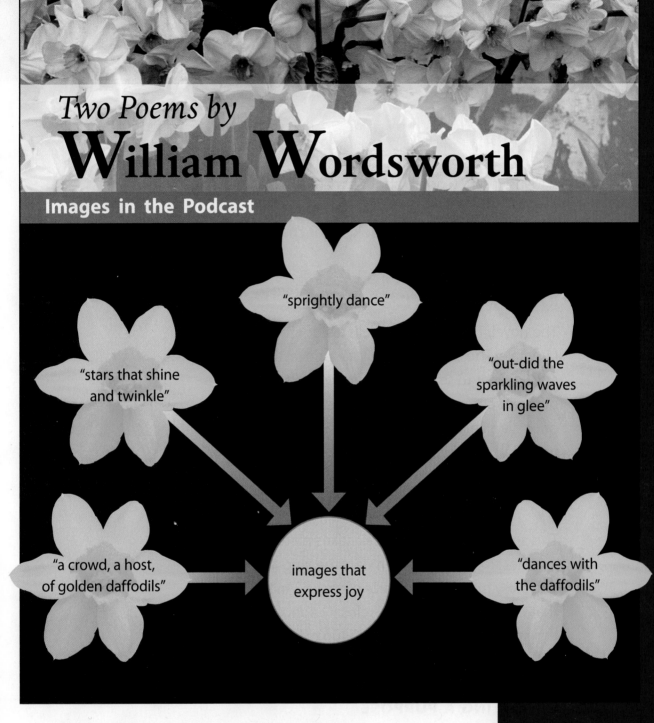

"sprightly dance"

"stars that shine and twinkle"

"out-did the sparkling waves in glee"

"a crowd, a host, of golden daffodils"

images that express joy

"dances with the daffodils"

⏻ COLLABORATIVE DISCUSSION

Discussing the Purpose With a partner, write down the descriptive words or phrases you hear in the poems. Then arrange them by the emotions they make you feel. What words would you use to describe the same things?

The King

You just heard a poem about a man who was inspired by a beautiful field of daffodils. Now read a story about a little prince looking for change all over the universe.

Know Before We Go

The novel, *The Little Prince*, tells a story that is like a fairy tale. The character, the little prince, travels from small planet to small planet meeting all kinds of different people. Finally, he comes to Earth. The little prince is a child, and spends much of the story trying to understand adults, whom he thinks do things for no good reason and only seem to want to tell other people what to do.

This section of *The Little Prince* takes place as he visits another small planet and meets the king living there. The story makes fun of parts of society, in the hope that readers will think more closely about things. In this story, the author is making fun of adults who always want to be in charge of things.

⏻ SETTING A PURPOSE

As you read, think about how the author uses dialogue to help the reader see how funny and silly the king really is.

The KING

from
*The Little
Prince*

by Antoine de Saint-Exupéry

The first one was inhabited by a king. Wearing purple and ermine, he was sitting on a simple yet majestic throne.

"Ah! Here's a subject!" the king exclaimed when he **caught sight** of the little prince.

And the little prince wondered, *How can he know who I am if he's never seen me before?* He didn't realize that for kings, the world is extremely simplified: All men are subjects.

10   "Approach the throne so I can get a better look at you," said the king, very proud of being a king for someone at last.

The phrase **caught sight** is an idiom and means that a person noticed something or someone suddenly.

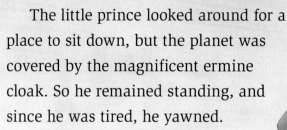

The little prince looked around for a place to sit down, but the planet was covered by the magnificent ermine cloak. So he remained standing, and since he was tired, he yawned.

"It is a **violation** of etiquette to yawn in a king's presence," the monarch told him. "I forbid you to do so."

"I can't help it," answered the little prince, quite embarrassed. "I've made a long journey, and I haven't had any sleep . . ."

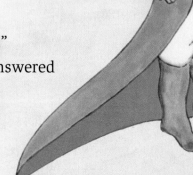

"Then I command you to yawn," said the king. "I haven't seen anyone yawn for years. For me, yawns are a curiosity. Come on, yawn again! It is an order."

"That **intimidates** me . . . I can't do it now," said the little prince, blushing deeply.

"Well, well!" the king replied. "Then I . . . I command you to yawn sometimes and sometimes to . . ."

He was sputtering a little, and seemed annoyed.

For the king insisted that his authority be universally respected. He would tolerate no disobedience, being an absolute monarch. But since he was a kindly man, all his commands were reasonable. "If I were to command," he would often say, "if I were to command a general to turn into a seagull, and if the general did not obey, that would not be the general's fault. It would be mine."

"May I sit down?" the little prince timidly inquired.

20

30

40

"I command you to sit down," the king replied, majestically gathering up a fold of his ermine robe.

But the little prince was wondering. The planet was tiny. Over what could the king really reign? "Sire . . . ," he ventured, "excuse me for asking . . ."

"I command you to ask," the king hastened to say.

50   "Sire . . . over what do you reign?"

"Over everything," the king answered, with great simplicity.

"Over everything?"

With a discreet gesture the king pointed to his planet, to the other planets, and to the stars.

How does this sentence help you to picture the **setting**?

"Over all that?" asked the little prince.

"Over all that . . . ," the king answered.

For not only was he an absolute monarch, but a universal monarch as well.

60   "And do the stars obey you?"

"Of course," the king replied. "They obey immediately. I tolerate no **insubordination**."

insubordination: the act of not following orders

Such power amazed the little prince. If he had wielded it himself, he could have watched not forty-four but seventy-two, or even a hundred, even two hundred sunsets on the same day without ever having to move his chair! And since he was feeling rather sad on account of remembering his own little planet, which he had **forsaken**, he ventured to ask a favor of the king: "I'd

Use **context clues** to help you understand the meaning of forsaken.

70   like to see a sunset . . . Do me a favor, your majesty . . . Command the sun to set . . ."

"If I commanded a general to fly from one flower to the next like a butterfly, or to write a tragedy, or to turn into a seagull, and if the general did not carry out my command, which of us would be in the wrong, the general or me?"

How does the king's **dialogue** add to your understanding of the king's personality?

80

"You would be," said the little prince, quite firmly.

"Exactly. One must command from each what each can perform," the king went on. "Authority is based first of all upon reason. If you command your subjects to jump in the ocean, there will be a revolution. I am entitled to command obedience because my orders are reasonable."

"Then my sunset?" insisted the little prince, who never let go of a question once he had asked it.

"You shall have your sunset. I shall command it. But I shall wait, according to my science of government, until conditions are favorable."

"And when will that be?" inquired the little prince.

"Well, well!" replied the king, first consulting a large
90 calendar. "Well, well! That will be around . . . around
. . . that will be tonight around seven-forty! And you'll see how well I am obeyed."

The little prince yawned. He was regretting his lost sunset. And besides, he was already growing a little bored. "I have nothing further to do here," he told the king. "I'm going to be on my way!"

"Do not leave!" answered the king, who was so proud of having a subject. "Do not leave; I shall make you my minister!"

100 "A minister of what?"

"Of . . . of justice!"

"But there's no one here to judge!"

"You never know," the king told him. "I have not yet explored the whole of my realm. I am very old, I have no room for a carriage, and it **wearies** me to walk."

"Oh, but I've already seen for myself," said the little prince, leaning forward to glance one more time at the

wearies: makes tired

other side of the planet. "There's no one over there, either . . . "

110   "Then you shall pass judgment on yourself," the king answered. "That is the hardest thing of all. It is much harder to judge yourself than to judge others. If you succeed in judging yourself, it's because you are truly a wise man."

    "But I can judge myself anywhere," said the little prince. "I don't need to live here."

    "Well, well!" the king said. "I have good reason to believe that there is an old rat living somewhere on my planet. I hear him at night. You could judge that old rat.

120 From time to time you will condemn him to death. That way his life will depend on your justice. But you'll pardon him each time for economy's sake. There's only one rat."

    "I don't like condemning anyone to death," the little prince said, "and now I think I'll be on my way."

    "No," said the king.

    The little prince, having completed his preparations, had no desire to aggrieve the old monarch. "If Your Majesty desires to be promptly obeyed, he should give me a reasonable command. He might command me, for

130 instance, to leave before this minute is up. It seems to me that conditions are favorable . . . "

    The king having made no answer, the little prince hesitated at first, and then, with a sigh, took his leave.

    "I make you my ambassador," the king hastily shouted after him. He had a great air of authority.

    "Grown-ups are so strange," the little prince said to himself as he went on his way.

> How does the little prince's **dialogue** add to your understanding of his personality?

> How does this one thought help you figure out the **theme** of the story?

⏻ COLLABORATIVE DISCUSSION

Discussing the Purpose In a small group, talk about the dialogue and how it helps you understand the characters.

READING TOOLBOX

Parts of Narrative Fiction

▶ **Dialogue** Dialogue iswhat the characters say. You can learn a lot about a character through his or her dialogue.

▶ **Thoughts** Sometimes an author will let you "hear" what the character is thinking.

▶ **Theme** Many stories have themes, or big ideas. Most authors do not state the theme directly. It is up to the reader to come to his or her own conclusion using the author's clues.

↻ Performance Task

Speaking Activity: Talk About Narrative Fiction In a small group, talk about the "The King."

Dialogue Did the dialogue between the king and the little prince interest you? Do you think that is the way these characters would speak if they were real people?

Thoughts The author shares some of the little prince's thoughts in this piece. Did you think this was interesting? What did they help you know about the little prince's character?

Theme What did the author really think about the king and the little prince? Which lines in the story help you answer?

Speak Out! In a small group, take turns retelling what happened in "The King."

LISTENING TOOLBOX

Listening to Others

▶ When someone else is telling a story, make sure you pay attention even though you may be eager for your turn to speak.

▶ Remember that when your turn comes, you want your audience to give you their full attention.

↻ Performance Task

Writing Activity: Dialogue Make up a conversation that you think the king and the little prince might have. You may use part of the story or make up a whole new part of your own. You may also include what the king and the little prince are really thinking in your writing.

Ask yourself:

● What kind of language does the king use? Is it formal or informal? Is it just a little bit silly? What does he say that gives you more information about his character?

● What kind of language does the little prince use? Is it formal? Is it informal? What does he say that tells you more about what he is really like?

Do U Like 2 Txt?

In the "The King," you read about a boy who explores distant planets. In the next selection, you'll explore how communication has changed over many years.

READING TOOLBOX

Compare and Contrast Information

"Do U Like 2 Txt?" tells a short history of electronic communication over the last two centuries, and how it has changed with the invention of new technology. When you read about how things develop over time, it is sometimes useful to make comparisons. That way you can quickly understand how things are the same as in the past and how they are different.

- When you compare, you think of ways things are alike. Look for signal words and phrases such as *like, similar to, also,* and *as in.*

- When you contrast, you think of ways things are different. Look for signal words and phrases such as *unlike, but, in contrast,* and *while.*

⏻ SETTING A PURPOSE

As you read, pay attention to ways in which electronic messages have stayed the same over time and ways in which they have changed.

Do U Like 2 Txt?

by Yvette Marcelin

Think quickly! You've got just a few seconds to say hi to a friend across the country before getting to school. You come up with a phrase and send it: "Hw r u ts mng?" Meaning, "How are you this morning?" That message seems like a modern text message, but it was sent over a century ago, in the late 1800s.

Shortening words and phrases to make communication faster has been done
10 throughout history. The practice of cutting words down to just a few letters is called abbreviation, which itself can be shortened to "abbr."

The Telegraph

About two hundred years ago, in the mid-1830s, the invention of a device called the telegraph created a new way for people to communicate. It allowed them to quickly send messages over long distances for the first time. The telegraph sent messages
20 through electrical wires. An operator had to spell out each word in a message using a special code for each letter. Then an operator on the other end had to listen to the code and write out the message.

Letter Writing Abbreviations

Etc.	Etcetera, which means "and so on"
Encl.	Enclosed, referring to something else sealed in the envelope with the letter
PS	Post Script, or "after the text"
No.	Number
St.	Street
RSVP	repondez s'il vous plait, a French abbreviation which means "please respond"

early telegraph machine ▶

223

When they didn't have other messages to send, operators chatted with each other across the country. To save time, they abbreviated words. To express emotion, they sent messages like "ha ha ha" to tell the other operator
30 that they found something funny. The longer they paused between each "ha," the stronger the expression. Here are some more abbreviations that telegraph operators used.

Telegraph Operator Abbreviations	
Hw r u ts mng	(How are you this morning?)
Pty wl	(pretty well)
G a	(Go ahead)
Min pen	(Wait a minute as I adjust my pen)

Text Messaging

Instead of the telegraph machine of long ago, today people use cell phones and mobile devices to quickly send messages and chat with friends. While it takes much less time to type letters on a keyboard than it did to tap out the code for a letter on the telegraph, people nowadays still want to save time and space. Text

40 messages can usually fit only a certain number of letters per message. People like to finish writing and hit "send" as quickly as they can. If you want to let someone know you have to put down your phone, it's faster and easier to just type "brb" than "I'll be right back."

We also use some abbreviations to get across emotions when texting or emailing. Much like the telegraph operators sending "ha ha ha," people today use "lol" or "rofl" to

50 stand for "laughing out loud" and "rolling on the floor laughing." Which textspeak abbreviations do you like to use?

This is a **long sentence**. Read it again to be sure you understand what it means.

Textspeak Abbreviations

gr8	great
cu	see you
btw	by the way
afaik	as far as I know
asap	as soon as possible
luv	love
thx	thanks
atm	at the moment

1:30 PM

Message   Edit

hi cu soon?

can't atm brb

ok gr8

cu asap

thx

Send

⏻ COLLABORATIVE DISCUSSION

Discussing the Purpose Work with a partner to compare and contrast modern text messages and telegraph messages sent long ago. In what ways are the messages similar? In what ways are they different?

Exploring the Theme With a small group, discuss how technology has changed the way we communicate with one another. Has communication changed for the better? Why or why not?

Vocabulary Strategy: Prefixes and Root Words

The word *telegraph* is made up of the prefix *tele-* and the root word *graph*. *Tele-* means "at a distance," while *graph* refers to something written, drawn, or recorded. When put together, *telegraph* means "something written at a distance." Knowing the meaning of this prefix and root word can help you figure out the meaning of other related words.

Here are some other words that contain the prefix *tele-*.

telephone, **tele**vision, **tele**scope

Here are some words that contain the root word *graph*.

auto**graph**, photo**graph**, bio**graph**y

Practice and Apply Use what you know about the meaning of the prefix *tele-* and the root word *graph* to try to define the words above.

Speak Out! Today's computers are possible, in part, because of the telegraph and its use of scientific discoveries. With a small group, talk about what your life might be like without such inventions. How would your day-to-day activities change? How would school be different?

LISTENING TOOLBOX

Active Listening
Act the way you would like listeners to act when you speak.

▶ **Give your full attention to the speaker.** You may think you know what the person is going to say next, but you may be wrong!

▶ **Ask questions.** If you are not sure you understand what the speaker has said, just ask.

↻ Performance Task

Writing Activity: Plan Ahead—Narrative Fiction Plan a story about a telegraph operator. Decide who your narrator will be. Then use the following questions to help you.

• Where and when does the telegraph operator live?

• What kind of mood do you want to create? Is the story funny, with an operator who is goofing up messages all the time? Is it exciting, with an operator sending secret messages?

• What are the main events of the story? What colorful details can you add? How will it begin? How will it end? How can you build the story to reach an interesting conclusion?

The Prince and the Pauper

You just read about big changes in the way people communicate. Now read about two boys who make a very big change!

Know Before You Go

ABOUT THE AUTHOR Mark Twain (1835–1910) was a famous American author. His real name was Samuel Langhorne Clemens. Mark Twain is most famous for his novels, *The Adventures of Tom Sawyer* and *The Adventures of Huckleberry Finn*.

ABOUT THE NOVEL *The Prince and the Pauper* is an adventure story about two boys who look alike, but whose lives are very different. One is a prince, the other is a pauper. They meet by accident and exchange the clothes they're wearing. As a result, the two boys change their roles in life, at least for a little while.

THE CHARACTERS

| **Tom Canty** | **Prince Edward** | **John Canty** | **Father Andrew** | **The King of England** |
| the pauper | the prince | Tom's father | a kind priest | Edward's father |

⏻ SETTING A PURPOSE

As you read the graphic novel, think about the events in the story and how they lead up to the conclusion.

Mark Twain's
The Prince and the Pauper

retold by Mercedes Roffe

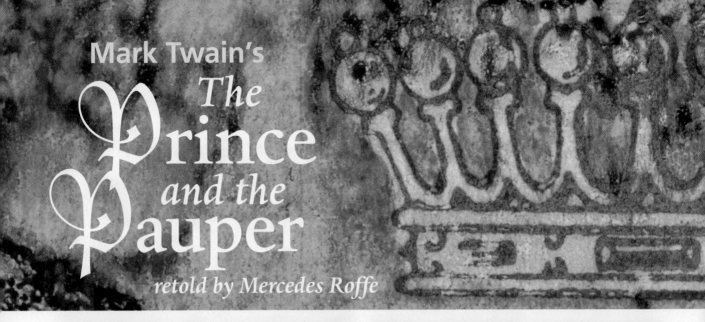

IN THE CITY OF LONDON, ONE DAY IN THE SIXTEENTH CENTURY, A BOY WAS BORN TO A VERY POOR FAMILY. THEY NAMED HIM TOM. TOM CANTY.

One more mouth to feed!

I'll make sure he'll earn his bread soon enough.

THE SAME AUTUMN DAY, IN THE SAME CITY OF LONDON, A BOY WAS BORN TO THE ROYAL FAMILY. HIS FATHER WAS THE KING OF ENGLAND. THEY NAMED HIM EDWARD, PRINCE OF WALES.

A baby boy!

Welcome to our future king!

TOM GREW UP AND, AS HIS FATHER HAD PROMISED, HE WAS SOON SENT TO WORK.

WHEN TOM HAD FREE TIME, HE LOVED TO LISTEN TO FATHER ANDREW'S TALES OF CASTLES AND PRINCES. HE ALSO LEARNED TO READ AND WRITE.

Thank you, Father Andrew!

Enough stories for today, Little Tom. Go home and take this bread for your dinner.

229

TOM GREW FOND OF THE PRIEST'S WORLD OF BEAUTY AND ABUNDANCE. IT WAS LIKE A LULLABY AS HE LAY ON HIS THIN STRAW, TIRED AND HUNGRY.

In the name of the king, my father…

HE EVEN IMAGINED HIMSELF AS A ROYAL. AND NOT JUST ANY ROYAL, BUT THE PRINCE HIMSELF.

ONE DAY, TOM WANDERED RIGHT UP TO THE DOORS OF THE PALACE. SUDDENLY, A HAND PUSHED HIM.

Hey, young beggar, be off!

How dare you treat the boy that way? Open the gates, and let him in!

IT WAS PRINCE EDWARD HIMSELF! THE PRINCE TOOK TOM TO HIS CHAMBERS. HE SAW THAT TOM WAS HUNGRY AND ORDERED A MEAL FOR HIM.

Tell me about your life, my friend.

I live near the city. My dad is rough, but sometimes I swim and run with my friends.

I'd give my father's kingdom to enjoy that one time!

THE BOYS DECIDED IT WOULD BE FUN TO SWITCH PLACES, SO THEY EXCHANGED THEIR CLOTHES.

Don't we look just like twins?

I'd never dare to say that, sir. But you're right!

BUT THEN THE PRINCE NOTICED A WOUND ON TOM'S HAND, AND WENT TO REPRIMAND THE GUARD.

Ha ha ha! His Highness!

You again, young beggar. Be off!

How dare you speak that way to the Prince of Wales? My father, the king, will hang you if you dare lay your hands upon me!

THE CROWD AT THE PALACE DOORS DID NOT RECOGNIZE THE PRINCE AND CHASED HIM AWAY.

SO THE PRINCE STARTED TO WANDER. HE DIDN'T KNOW WHERE HE WAS. BUT SOMEHOW HE FOUND HIMSELF IN TOM'S NEIGHBORHOOD. EVERYTHING LOOKED SO GRIM . . .

But surely Tom's family will help me get back to the palace.

MEANWHILE, IN THE PRINCE'S CHAMBERS . . .

Why is it taking so long for the Prince to come back?

JUST THEN, A PAGE CAME TO ANNOUNCE THE PRINCE'S COUSIN, LADY JANE GREY.

My Lady, I am not the Prince. I'm Tom.

What are you saying, Sir? Are you sick?

LADY JANE RAN TO TELL THE KING THAT THE PRINCE WAS UNWELL.

MEANWHILE, PRINCE EDWARD WAS HAVING A DIFFICULT TIME WITH TOM'S FATHER.

Your father is right here. Watch out or I will break your bones.

Please take me to my father, the king. He will make you rich.

231

SOON ENOUGH, JOHN CANTY SENDS THE PRINCE TO WORK WITH A BAND OF THIEVES.

AND POOR TOM HAS TO FACE THE KING, WHO WANTS TO MAKE SURE HIS SON, THE PRINCE, IS QUITE WELL.

TOM HAS TO ATTEND ONE OFFICIAL CEREMONY AFTER ANOTHER.

BUT THERE WAS ONE VERY BIG PROBLEM.

Please try to remember where the Seal of England is.

I don't remember.

THE KING USED THE SEAL TO SIGN HIS DECREES. HE HAD GIVEN IT TO EDWARD. TOM DID NOT KNOW WHAT IT WAS.

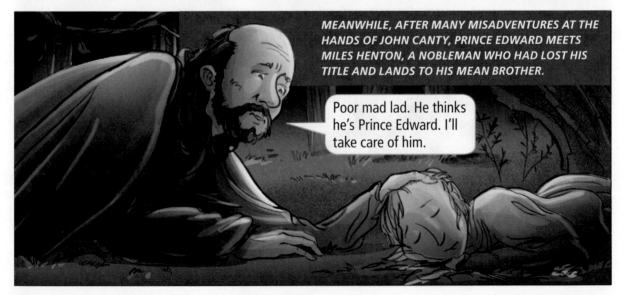

MEANWHILE, AFTER MANY MISADVENTURES AT THE HANDS OF JOHN CANTY, PRINCE EDWARD MEETS MILES HENTON, A NOBLEMAN WHO HAD LOST HIS TITLE AND LANDS TO HIS MEAN BROTHER.

Poor mad lad. He thinks he's Prince Edward. I'll take care of him.

THEN SUDDENLY THE KING DIED. NEWS OF THE KING'S DEATH IS SPREAD THROUGHOUT THE KINGDOM.

THE FOLLOWING MORNING, IN THE PALACE, TOM CANTY IS DRESSED AND FED, AND PREPARED FOR HIS CORONATION. HE RIDES IN A GRAND PROCESSION THROUGH LONDON.

JUST WHEN THE ARCHBISHOP IS ABOUT TO PLACE THE CROWN ON TOM'S HEAD, PRINCE EDWARD INTERRUPTS.

I am Prince Edward Tudor, the heir to King Henry's throne.

He's Prince Edward, the new King of England. Your Majesty, where have you been?

NOBODY KNEW WHO WAS THE PRINCE AND WHO WAS THE PAUPER. FINALLY, AN IMPORTANT QUESTION WAS ASKED.

If you are the real prince, where is the Seal of England?

Inside the armor, next to my chambers, Sir. I put it there myself.

SO THE YOUNG EDWARD TUDOR, THE NEW KING OF ENGLAND, WAS CROWNED BEFORE A CHEERFUL CROWD.

THE PRINCE WAS GRATEFUL TO HIS FRIENDS.

Tom, you will now be the king's ward. I will take care of your mother and sisters, too.

And to you, my loyal Miles, I restore the title of the Earl of Kent.

EDWARD WAS A CARING KING WHO RIGHTED MANY OF THE WRONGS HE HAD SEEN IN HIS DAYS AS A PAUPER.

⏻ COLLABORATIVE DISCUSSION

Discussing the Purpose With a small group, discuss the events in "The Prince and the Pauper." How did the events lead up to the conclusion? Did the ending make sense? What did you think was going to happen?

↺ Performance Task

Speaking Activity: Discuss Events and Details Talk about the events and details in the graphic novel. In a small group talk about the following questions:

1 What was the problem at the beginning of the story? Do you think the author introduced the situation well?

2 Did the setting help you to understand and enjoy the story?

3 Did you think the characters were interesting?

4 Did the sequence of events make sense and help you understand the story?

5 How did the characters change during the story?

Speak Out! How were the prince and the pauper alike? How were they different? Use evidence from the story to support your opinion.

↻ Performance Task

Writing Activity: Write a Conclusion In a small group, talk about the ending of the graphic novel. What do members of the group think about the ending? Would you have ended the story differently? How else could the story have ended?

Write your own ending for the graphic novel. Continue the story so that we find out what happens to Tom and Edward next. How did Tom's life change? What about Edward's life? Be sure to use the details from the graphic novel when you write your conclusion.

Here are some useful words to help you in your writing. You can look them up in a dictionary if you do not know their meaning.

Useful Words

▷ kingdom
▷ grateful
▷ loyal
▷ coronation
▷ ceremony
▷ title

Performance Task

Writing Activity: Narrative

You have been reading stories and informational texts about change. Now, it's your turn to write a narrative about change!

Planning and Prewriting

Connect to the Theme

Your narrative can be fictional or it can be based on a personal experience that changed you in some way. If you choose fiction, your narrative can be real or it can be imaginary. Your narrative can be about a person or an event. What things on this list are you interested in writing about?

Realistic
- Moving to a new neighborhood
- Exploring a cave

Imaginary
- Moving to a new kingdom
- Exploring a different time in history

If you are writing about a person or event, you could write about:

Realistic
- A family member or celebrity you admire
- A historical event

Imaginary
- A fictional character that influenced you
- An imaginary event

Write Down Three Ideas

Write three possible ideas based on one of the situations on the list that you think can be the start of a narrative. You may also choose one of your own.

Read your ideas. How excited are you about each one? Rate them, from 0 (not excited) to 5 (really excited). Which one has the highest rating? That's your story line!

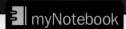

Decide the Basics

Now that you have your idea, it's time to plan your narrative, and decide your main conflict or problem, your characters, your setting, and your point of view. Use the notes below to help guide your decision making.

Conflict or Problem

A **conflict** is a struggle that is the focus of the narrative.

Think about:

- What is the conflict or problem in your narrative?
- Who faces this conflict or problem?
- Is your conflict exciting enough?

Characters

Characters are the people, animals, or imaginary creatures that take part in the action.

Think about:

- Who is the main character of your narrative?
- Are there other characters?
- How would you describe your characters?
- Do you feel strongly about your characters? Do you love them or dislike them?

Setting

The **setting** is the **time** and **place** of the action.

Think about:

- **Time**: When is your narrative set?
- **Place**: Where is your narrative set?
- Is the setting going to play an important role in your narrative?

Point of View

The **point of view** refers to how a writer chooses to narrate (or tell) a story. When a narrative is told from the **first-person** point of view, the narrator is a character in the story. In a narrative told from **the third-person** point of view, the narrator is not a character in the story. A writer's choice of narrator affects the information the readers receive.

Performance Task

Finalize Your Plan

You know the basics of your narrative: the conflict, the characters, the setting, and the point of view. Now it's time to plan your plot structure. Follow the structure of the diagram in the Writing Toolbox.

WRITING TOOLBOX

Elements of a Narrative

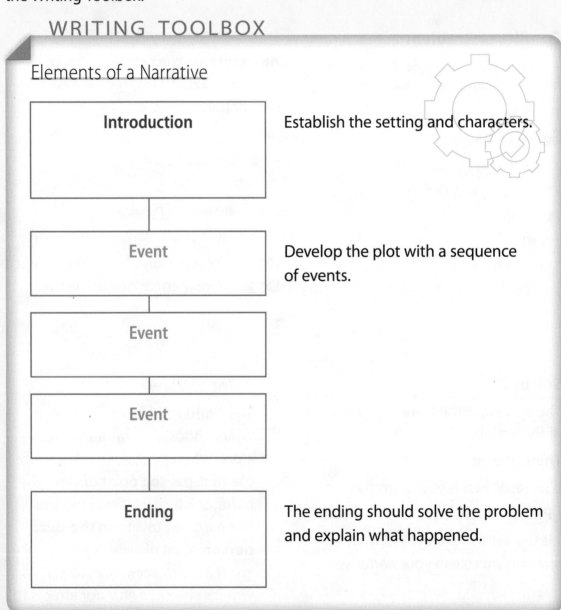

Introduction	Establish the setting and characters.
Event	Develop the plot with a sequence of events.
Event	
Event	
Ending	The ending should solve the problem and explain what happened.

Draft Your Narrative

You have the basics of your narrative. Start writing! As you write, think about:

- **Purpose and Audience** What effect do you want the narrative to have on readers? Who will read or listen to your story?

- **Main Character, Setting, and Conflict** Introduce the main character, setting, and conflict.

- **Point of View** Establish your point of view.

- **Elements of a Story Diagram** Refer to the Writing Toolbox to create the sequence of events.

- **Transitions** Use transitional words and phrases to help your reader follow the sequence of events.

- **Descriptive Language** Use descriptive words and sensory language to create a detailed picture.

- **Climax** Make sure the narrative has an exciting ending.

- **Conflict Resolution** Tell how the conflict is resolved.

Revise

Self Evaluation

Use the checklist and rubric to guide your analysis.

Peer Review

Exchange your narrative with a classmate. Use the checklist to comment on your classmate's story.

Edit

Edit your narrative to correct spelling, grammar, and punctuation errors.

Publish

Finalize your narrative and choose a way to share it with your audience.

Paths to Discovery

He who never made a mistake

never made a discovery.

— Samuel Smiles, author

Essential Question

How can discovery inspire
us to keep searching?

The Language of Discovery

Discovery is finding out about new things. We discover new things about ourselves throughout life as we experience new situations. We also make discoveries about our world as we explore what is happening around us.

Exploring our natural world can inspire us. Often when we observe or investigate nature, we are filled with wonder and awe. People, including scientists, artists, engineers, and musicians, use inspiration from nature to create and invent new things.

Inspiration leads us to make the world and ourselves better. People are capable of great accomplishments when they are inspired to act. Inspiration gives us strength and courage to try new things and grow as people.

In this unit, you will find out about discoveries that have lead to change or a new understanding of our world. You will find out how John Muir helped to preserve Yosemite and the California valley. You will read about the fascinating formation of the Black Hills. You will also find out how time keeping has changed over time and you will take a journey 20,000 leagues under the sea.

How do discoveries lead to growth and progress?

John Muir ▶

A *Rolling* Stone **Gathers** No Moss: **Adages**

An **adage** is an old, short saying that has come to be accepted as truth. Adages remind us to do, or not to do, certain things in a few words. Try and explain the following adages in your own words. Then imagine situations that illustrate the meaning of the adages.

> Practice makes perfect.
>
> Live and learn.
>
> Two heads are better than one.
>
> Look before you leap.
>
> Nothing ventured, nothing gained.
>
> Strike while the iron is hot.

↻ Performance Task

Think about a discovery you recently made or heard about. It may be something you found out about yourself. It could be a new fact or bit of information you learned that inspired or surprised you. Talk with a partner about the discovery. Use page 242 and **Browse** magazine as you brainstorm topics. Don't forget to use the **Activity Book**, too.

DOWNLOAD

There are many ways to make discoveries. Read ahead to find out about the memorable trip this blogger took to visit some national parks.

⏻ **SETTING A PURPOSE**

While you read, think about how the blogger includes interesting details about the trip he took.

Explorer 11

On the Road with G.G. and Gamps

Friday, 3:53 p.m.

Hey there. It's Memorial Day weekend, and I'm heading out for *three days on the road* with G.G. and Gamps. No, that's not the name of a band. It's my grandparents. G.G. is Grandma Grace. Gamps is what my little brother calls my grandpa.

A few years ago G.G. and Gamps sold their home and bought a "lightly used" RV. They're planning to travel for a while before settling down. This weekend they swung by to pick me up, and we're headed north. I'm writing this blog to keep track of our progress. It's Friday afternoon, just after school, and we are ready to *hit the road*!

Friday, 8:57 p.m.

We stopped at MacKerricher State Park for the night. We arrived in time to explore the tide pools and see the seals sunning themselves on the beach. Gamps

Enter your email address:

Subscribe me!

SEARCH

💬 Comments 0

©createvil/Shutterstock

made a fire and cooked dinner. (He has skills!) The RV looks small on the outside, but I have my own "bedroom area." That's where I'm writing from *right now*.

Saturday, 11:16 a.m.
We are on the road again, heading north to highway 101 and the Redwood National and State Parks. G.G. and Gamps have been there before and say it's the best. I can't wait!

Saturday, 8:12 p.m.
Well, they were right, this place is *awesome*! It's all about the trees—the enormous, incredible, mind-blowing trees! The park is filled with coast redwoods, the tallest trees in the world. My neck aches from staring up at them. And they are huge around the bottom, too. In the forest, you feel like you're in a movie about dinosaurs or the beginning of time. We had a picnic dinner on the beach and watched the sun set. Now I'm exhausted and ready for bed.

Monday 8:23 p.m.
Oops, I forgot to write in my blog yesterday! On Sunday we took our bikes and went on a long ride, through the forest, then out onto a road along the beach. We went on some scenic drives, too—we even saw one of those "drive thru trees." In the evening we went to a campfire program led by a ranger. That sounds dorky, but it was pretty fun. How cool it would it be to work as a park ranger! I wonder how you get that job? I'll have to ask a ranger next time I'm at a park.

Today we drove home. Tomorrow?
Yup, you guessed it: *back to school!*

ARCHIVES

September

August

July

June

May

April

March

February

January

UPLOAD

⏻ COLLABORATIVE DISCUSSION

Discussing the Purpose The blogger shared a memorable experience in his blog entry, On the Road with G.G. and Gamps. The blogger described his experience in a way so that the reader can picture what he saw and felt.

Exploring the Theme What would you like to explore and discover?

Write On! Like many blogs, *Explorer 11* gives readers the opportunity to post comments about each blog post. Write a short comment about this blog post. You may want to comment on the blogger's experience or share a memorable moment of your own.

⟳ Performance Task

Writing Activity: Share With Other Blogs Now that you have successfully started a blog, brainstormed ideas, chosen a design, scheduled posts, and are aware of respectful blogging rules, you are ready to share your blog with others. Sharing with other bloggers is one of the most exciting parts of blogging.

1 Participate with bloggers you may know by leaving comments or asking questions about their blog posts. If a blogger replies to your comment, you can then continue the conversation. Also, by leaving a comment, you have the chance to tell about your own blog. Many blog forms allow you to include your blog website.

2 Find new blogs that are similar to yours. Leave comments on these blogs and join the conversation. You might learn something new, or you might be asked to explain something further. Either way, participating in an online community is an interesting experience.

3 Ask your readers if they have questions or comments about each of your blog posts. For example, if you write about a cultural tradition that's important to your family, invite your readers to share their own cultural traditions or stories.

4 Ask your readers to suggest future topics.

Language Cam video

Watch the video to find out more about kids making discoveries.

DOWNLOAD

John Muir's Path to Nature

You just read about Explorer 11's trip to national parks. Now read about the man who is responsible for the creation of our beautiful national parks.

READING TOOLBOX

Chronological Order

When authors use **chronological order**, they describe events in the order they happened. One way they do this is by including the dates they occurred. Many informational texts, biographies, and autobiographies are arranged in chronological order. The dates make it easier for the reader to understand and follow the events that the author is describing.

⏻ SETTING A PURPOSE

As you read, pay attention to the dates that are included in this selection.

©Todd Bannor/Alamy

John Muir's Path to Nature

by Eleanor Yee

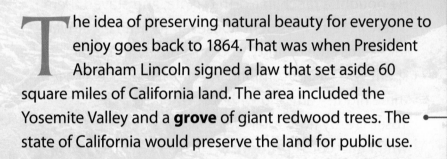

The idea of preserving natural beauty for everyone to enjoy goes back to 1864. That was when President Abraham Lincoln signed a law that set aside 60 square miles of California land. The area included the Yosemite Valley and a **grove** of giant redwood trees. The state of California would preserve the land for public use.

> **grove:** a small group of trees

Unfortunately, many people ignored the law. One man, named James Mason Hutchings, owned a hotel in the Yosemite Valley. In 1869, he decided to start logging in the protected area. He hired a man named John Muir to build and run the sawmill.

10

Muir was an **unusual** man. Two years earlier, he had walked from Indiana to Florida. In Yosemite, he spent his free time hiking through the awesome natural beauty, and came to feel a special connection with nature. In 1873 he moved to Oakland, California, and began writing magazine articles that captured the natural beauty of the wilderness, promoting the protection of wilderness areas.

> Use the **prefix *un-*** to help you understand the meaning of the word *unusual*.

249

Meanwhile, in 1871, a group of explorers traveled to
what is now Wyoming to investigate some wild rumors.
Prospectors told tales of boiling mud and steam shooting
out of the ground. The fantastic stories turned out to
be true. In 1872, President Ulysses S. Grant signed a law
protecting the area, thus creating Yellowstone Park. It was
the first national park in the world.

In 1890, two national parks were created in California's
Sierra Nevada mountains. The first was Yosemite, fulfilling
John Muir's hopes. The second was Sequoia, protecting
the giant redwood trees there.

Theodore Roosevelt, an **outdoorsman** and hunter,
became president in 1901. About twenty years earlier, he
had fallen in love with the vast open spaces of the West.
He bought a ranch in North Dakota, and stayed there
often. In 1903, President Roosevelt took an eight-week
tour across the country, and on a break from that tour he
spent two weeks camping in Yellowstone. He also spent
three nights camping with John Muir in
Yosemite. By now, Muir was a famous
writer and **conservationist**. He persuaded
Roosevelt to expand Yosemite
National Park to include the
Yosemite Valley.

Break down this long
compound word into
smaller words to help you
understand its meaning.

conservationist:
someone who works to
protect animals, plants,
and natural resources

Yosemite National Park, California

©Digital Vision/Getty Images

President Roosevelt went on to create five more national parks. He also created 18 national monuments, including Devil's Tower in Wyoming and the Grand Canyon. He established bird sanctuaries, **game** refuges, and millions of acres of national
50 forests. In 1908, a forest in Marin County, California, became Muir Woods National Monument. Roosevelt named it after his friend John Muir.

Unfortunately, while Congress passed laws to establish parks, it did nothing to protect them. Soldiers patrolled some areas, but there was a lot of land and not a lot of soldiers. Ranchers brought in cattle, which ate the plants. Loggers cut down trees. Hunters killed wildlife. Tourists carved
60 their names in rocks and trees. In 1916, President Woodrow Wilson established the National Park Service to patrol, preserve, and protect the nation's national parks.

▲ Theodore Roosevelt

The word **game** is a multiple-meaning word. Here it means animals that people hunt.

Horse-drawn wagon going through tunnel in giant redwood tree. ▼

251

UPLOAD

⏻ COLLABORATIVE DISCUSSION

Discussing the Purpose The author describes the sequence of events that led to the creation of our national parks. Do the dates help you understand this selection?

If there were no dates, do you think it would be difficult to follow what happened?

↻ Performance Task

Speaking: Use Dates In a small group, talk about the use of dates in the selection. How does the author use dates to help the reader follow the sequence of events?

Then think about a series of events that you know about or that happened to you or someone you know.

Tell the members of your group what happened and when. Make certain that the sequence is clear to your audience. Include dates in your presentation, and add interesting details and descriptions.

Did the use of dates help the members of the group understand you better?

LISTENING TOOLBOX

How Well Did I Understand?

Ask yourself the following questions:

▶ Did I listen carefully when someone else was speaking?

▶ Did I use the dates included in the presentation to help me understand the sequence of events?

▶ Did I understand the topic or event that was presented?

▶ Did I know most of the words the speaker used?

▶ Were the words and sentences mostly clear or confusing?

▶ When I didn't understand, did I ask a question?

↻ Performance Task

Writing: Create a List with Dates and Events In a small group, read the selection again and pay special attention to the dates included.

Then write down each date in the selection.

As a group, work together to fill in each event that is described next to the date when it happened.

Be sure to check your work when you are done.

Did you remember to include every date? Did you include every event?

The Black Hills

You just read about John Muir and his discoveries in nature. Now read on to find out about some of the oldest mountains in nature, the Black Hills.

READING TOOLBOX

Reading Diagrams

A **diagram** is a picture used to help explain something. Diagrams are often used in science to show information so that it is easier to understand. Diagrams help you picture what the text is describing. Here are some things to look for when reading diagrams.

▶ **Captions and labels** are used to help you understand different parts of the diagram.

▶ **Arrows** are used to show direction or how things in the diagram move.

▶ **Colors** in a diagram may have meaning. They can give you clues to help you understand the different parts of the diagram.

⏻ SETTING A PURPOSE

As you read, pay attention to the photos and diagram. Think about how they help you understand the text.

THE Black Hills

by Ben Klug

Some of the oldest mountains in the United States are in South Dakota. They are called the Black Hills. Huge stone peaks rise above the **dark forests** below that give the hills their name. But the Black Hills did not always exist!

More than two billion years ago the Black Hills of South Dakota wouldn't have been hills. They wouldn't have been in South Dakota, either, because this was before there was a South Dakota, or any other state.
10 This was long before humans walked the earth.

These geological formations first started deep underground as huge granite deposits. Granite is a hard rock formed from **molten** magma that rises from the depths of the earth, like in a volcano. But unlike the lava from a volcano, this molten rock didn't reach the surface before it cooled down and hardened. It stayed underground for over a billion years, slowly rising as more rock formed under it, and eventually the molten rock was pressed toward
20 the surface.

> Why do you think the **dark forests** give the hills their name?

> **molten:** (adj.) made into liquid by heat

255

Meanwhile, on the surface over the granite, many changes took place. The most important of these changes was when the entire area was under water. A long, long time ago, a sea stretched from what is now Canada to what is now Texas. It covered the middle of North America. This sea eventually drained away, but before it did it left layers of sand, mud, and seashells. These things hardened into rock. This type of rock is called *sedimentary* rock, because it consists of

30 those kinds of materials, which are called *sediments*. This sedimentary rock is softer than granite.

With the sea gone, weather slowly wore down the sedimentary rock in a process called **erosion**. **Eventually**, this exposed the parts of the granite that would become the Black Hills. Because the granite was so much harder than the sedimentary rock, it did not erode away as quickly. Parts of the granite began to stick up out of the sedimentary rock, forming hills. The forests in the Black Hills still grow on that sedimentary

40 rock, while the bare granite peaks rise up through it.

erosion: (n.) the process of wearing away

eventually: (adv.) at some later time

◀ Devils Tower, a granite hill, sticks up out of the surrounding landscape of sedimentary rock and forest.

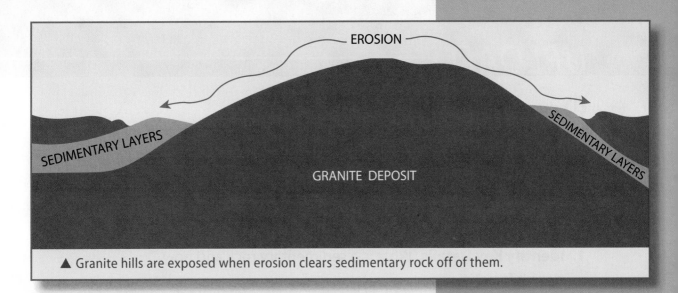

▲ Granite hills are exposed when erosion clears sedimentary rock off of them.

Eventually, people came to live in the Black Hills. Since the Black Hills are millions of years old, they existed long before humans appeared. They were waiting when Native Americans settled in the region. The people of the Sioux Nation consider the Black Hills to be sacred, and have many myths about them. In modern times, the Black Hills attract millions of tourists each year.

50 There are six national parks in the Black Hills, including Mount Rushmore. An unfinished monument to Native American leader Crazy Horse is also in the Black Hills. The Black Hills are filled with the possibilities of discovery.

Mount Rushmore is a famous American monument. The faces of four American Presidents are carved directly into the granite of a mountainside. Each face is sixty feet tall—about as tall as three adult giraffes. The presidents represented are George Washington, Thomas Jefferson, Theodore Roosevelt, and Abraham Lincoln. ▼

⏻ COLLABORATIVE DISCUSSION

Discussing the Purpose Talk with a partner about the photos and the diagram in this selection. How did these features help you to understand the text?

Analyzing the Text Cite Text Evidence

1. **Identify Key Details** What is a sedimentary rock and how does it form?

2. **Identify Key Details** Why didn't the granite in the Black Hills erode away?

Vocabulary Strategy: Specialized Vocabulary

This selection includes some words about geology that may not be familiar to you. Specialized vocabulary is the words and terms that are particular to a job, activity, or area of study. For example, you may not know the meaning of *sedimentary* (line 28), but context will help you determine the meaning of the word as it is used in the selection. Use context from the selection to help you determine the meaning of these other specialized words.

Term	Guessed Meaning	Dictionary Meaning
peaks (line 3)	tops	
formation (line 11)		
granite (line 12)		
deposits (line 12)		
magma (line 13)		
volcano (line 14)		
exposed (line 34)		

Practice and Apply Use context in the selection to help you figure out the words on the Vocabulary Strategy chart. Then use a dictionary to find the meaning of the word.

↻ Performance Task

Writing Activity: Write About a Discovery Think about a discovery you have made that surprised you in some way. It could be something you discovered about yourself. It could be something you discovered in nature, at school, or in some other place you visited. Make an outline for a presentation about the discovery. Answer these questions as you create your outline.

- **Who** was I with?
- **What** did I discover and what caused me to discover it?
- **Where** was I?
- **When** did I discover this?
- **Why** was the discovery surprising or important?
- **How** did I make the discovery?

Trade outlines with a partner. Take turns talking about your discoveries, outlines, and ideas. Give your partner feedback and share your own thoughts and ideas about his/her discovery.

Review the questions above when you talk about your outline with your partner.

Speak Out! Is a discovery only something that is found or can a discovery be something that you realize about yourself?

What do you think?

Podcast: My First Summer in the Sierra

The last selection you read described how a part of South Dakota's terrain was formed. The podcast you'll listen to next describes a man's experiences and feelings as he travels through the mountains.

Background on John Muir

John Muir was one of the first conservationists in the United States. A conservationist is a person who wants to protect nature so it is not changed or damaged by people. Muir was born in Scotland in 1838, but he moved to Wisconsin in 1849. Muir spent his life exploring and writing about nature in the United States. Much of his work encouraged conservation. In 1868, he first visited the Sierra Nevada in California as a sheepherder. The Sierra Nevada is a mountain range in the western United States. He wrote about his experiences in his journal. These writings describe the natural environment of the region.

 SETTING A PURPOSE

As you listen, think about the details Muir describes in these journal entries. What does he focus on? Does his focus change depending on where he is?

(tl) ©Irina Nartova/Shutterstock; (tr) ©rangizzz/Shutterstock; (inset) ©Houghton Mifflin Harcourt

Excerpt from

My First Summer in the Sierra

Details in the Podcast

John Muir's Trip to the Sierra Nevada

At the camp	◆ the food everyone ate
Exploring the Sierra Nevada	◆ the weather and temperature ◆ descriptions of the plants that he saw ◆ the animals he observed in the mountains ◆ the bones of animals that used to live in the mountains
Leaving the Sierra Nevada	◆ his memories of the natural beauty of the mountains ◆ how the Sierra Nevada made him feel

⏻ COLLABORATIVE DISCUSSION

Discussing the Purpose With a partner, discuss some of the details John Muir included in his journal. Then talk about the details of your day in class. Which details would you include in a journal?

Out of the Antartic

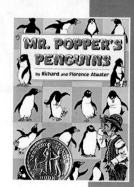

You just heard the journals of John Muir who was fascinated by the beauty of nature. Now read about an ordinary man who discovers that he can communicate with the South Pole.

Know Before You Go

Mr. Popper and his wife, the main (human) characters of *Mr. Popper's Penguins*, live in America in the 1930s. Mr. Popper is a house painter who dreams of exploring the world, especially Antarctica. People did not know very much about Antarctica in the early 20th century.

Scientists and explorers made expeditions to this continent and the South Pole. In the 1930s, communication with such an expedition would only be possible by radio. In this story, Admiral Drake is one such explorer on an expedition. Read on to discover the special surprise Mr. Popper receives one day—all the way from the South Pole!

⏻ SETTING A PURPOSE

As you read, think about how the authors describe Mr. Popper's exciting and memorable experience.

Out of the Antarctic

from *Mr. Popper's Penguins*

by Richard and Florence Atwater

"September thirtieth!" said Mr. Popper in an excited tone. "You don't mean that tonight is Wednesday, September twenty-ninth?"

"Why, yes, I suppose it is. But what of it?"

Mr. Popper put down his book of *Antarctic Adventures* and moved **hastily** to the radio.

hastily: quickly

"What of it!" he repeated, pushing the switch. "Why, this is the night the Drake Antarctic **Expedition** is going to start broadcasting."

expedition: a trip taken by a group of people for a purpose

10 "That's nothing," said Mrs. Popper. "Just a lot of men at the bottom of the world saying 'Hello, Mamma. Hello, Papa.'"

"*Sh!*" commanded Mr. Popper, laying his ear close to the radio.

There was a buzz, and then suddenly, from the South Pole, a **faint** voice floated out into the Popper living room.

faint: (adj) not heard clearly

"This is Admiral Drake speaking. Hello, Mamma. Hello, Papa. Hello, Mr. Popper."

20 "Gracious goodness," exclaimed Mrs. Popper. "Did he say 'Papa' or 'Popper'?"

"Hello, Mr. Popper, up there in Stillwater. Thanks for your nice letter about the pictures of our last expedition. Watch for an answer. But not by letter, Mr. Popper. Watch for a surprise. Signing off. Signing off."

"*You* wrote to Admiral Drake?"

"Yes, I did," Mr. Popper admitted. "I wrote and told him how funny I thought the penguins were."

"Well, I never," said Mrs. Popper, very much

30 **impressed**.

> **impressed:** felt admiration or interest

Mr. Popper picked up his little globe and found the Antarctic. "And to think he spoke to me all the way from there. And he even mentioned my name. Mamma, what do you suppose he means by a surprise?"

"I haven't any idea," answered Mrs. Popper, "but I'm going to bed. I don't want to

40 be late for the Ladies' Aid and Missionary Society meeting tomorrow."

What with the excitement of having the great Admiral Drake speak to him over the radio, and his curiosity about the Admiral's message to him, Mr. Popper did not sleep

50 very well that night. He did not see how he could possibly wait to find out what the Admiral meant.

Captain Drake ▶

264 UNIT 6 | OUT OF THE ANTARCTIC

When morning came, he was almost sorry that he had nowhere to go, no houses to paint, no rooms to paper. It would have helped to pass the time.

"Would you like the living room papered over?" he asked Mrs. Popper. "I have quite a lot of Paper Number 88, left over from the Mayor's house."

60 "I would not," said Mrs. Popper firmly. "The paper on now is plenty good enough. I am going to the first meeting of the Ladies' Aid and Missionary Society today and I don't want any mess around to clean up when I get home."

"Very well, my love," said Mr. Popper meekly, and he settled down with his pipe, his globe, and his book of *Antarctic Adventures*. But somehow, as he read today, he could not keep his mind on the printed words. His thoughts kept **straying away** to Admiral

70 Drake. What could he have meant by a surprise for Mr. Popper?

Fortunately for his peace of mind, he did not have so very long to wait. That afternoon, while Mrs. Popper was still away at her meeting, and Janie and Bill had not yet come home from school, there was a loud ring at the front door.

"I suppose it is just the postman. I won't bother to answer it," he said to himself.

The bell rang again, a little louder this time.
80 Grumbling to himself, Mr. Popper went to the door.

It was not the postman who stood there. It was an **expressman** with the largest box Mr. Popper had ever seen.

"Party by the name of Popper live here?"

"That's me."

> Read the sentence that comes before to help you figure out what **straying away** means.

> **expressman:** someone who is making a delivery

265

"Well, here's a package that's come Air Express all the way from Antarctica. Some journey, I'll say."

Mr. Popper signed the receipt and examined the box. It was covered all over with markings. "UNPACK

90 AT ONCE," said one. "KEEP COOL," said another. He noticed that the box was punched here and there with air holes.

You can imagine that once he had the box inside the house, Mr. Popper lost no time in getting the screw driver, for by this time, of course, he had guessed that it was the surprise from Admiral Drake.

He had succeeded in removing the outer boards and part of the packing, which was a layer of dry ice, when from the depths of the packing case he suddenly

100 heard a faint *"Ork."* His heart stood still. Surely he had heard that sound before at the Drake Expedition movies. His hands were trembling so that he could scarcely lift off the last of the wrappings.

There was not the slightest doubt about it. It was a penguin.

Do you think **ork** is a good word to describe the way a penguin would sound?

(bg) ©Ralf Somers/Fotolia; (l) ©Digital Zoo/Digital Vision/Getty Images

⏻ COLLABORATIVE DISCUSSION

Discussing the Purpose How did the authors use interesting details, description, and dialogue to tell about a very unusual experience.

Do you think the authors set up their story well?

Do you think that Mr. Popper had a memorable experience?

↻ Performance Task

Speaking Activity: Tell a Story Retell the story in your own words. Pretend that you are Mr. Popper and that you are telling someone about what happened to you.

Prepare your presentation in the first person (use the word "I") so that you and your audience are involved in the story.

Be sure to include details, descriptions and, especially, how you would feel if somebody sent you a penguin in the mail.

SPEAKING TOOLBOX

Presentation
Let your listeners know that you are speaking to them, not yourself.

▶ Speak loudly enough so that everyone can hear you clearly.

▶ Don't be afraid to be dramatic! You want your listeners to be interested and involved in your presentation.

DOWNLOAD

You just read about how Mr. Popper used a radio to receive information about the Antarctic. Now read about a discovery that was invented to help people know the time.

⏻ **SETTING A PURPOSE**

As you read, think about how sundials were used to solve a problem.

How to Make a Sundial

by William Franklin

The History of Sundials

You're sitting in class and you wonder how much longer until lunch. What can you do? Look at a clock or watch, of course. Long ago people didn't have a way to quickly check the time. Instead, they used the Sun.

Each day the Sun appears to rise in the eastern sky, makes a huge **arc** across the sky and then appears to set in the west. By tracking the Sun's changing position, people can estimate the time. What if people wanted to know the exact time? How could this problem be solved?

arc: a line or shape that is curved so that it looks like part of a circle

10   Sundials, one of the earliest clocks invented by people, show time more **precisely** by using the Sun and the shadows it casts. A sundial is a tool with markings that tell you what time it is when a long, skinny object, called the gnomon, casts a shadow on one of the markings. In the morning when the Sun is in the east, the shadow points toward the west. In the middle of the day when the Sun is high overhead, the shadow

20 points slightly north. Near sunset when the Sun is in the west, the shadow points east.

    Over the centuries, many new technologies were developed to help us tell time more easily. While we usually don't use them to tell time today, sundials were an important invention.

precisely: accurately or exactly

You read a sundial by comparing the gnomon's shadow to the marked lines. When the shadow lines up with the marking for 10:00 a.m., you know that is the time. ▼

Make Your Own Sundial

You'll need:

- a paper plate
- a long skinny object for the gnomon
- tape
- a pen or pencil
- rocks or tape
- a sunny day

What you need to do:

1 Put a paper plate in a spot that gets sun all day long. You can hang it from a wall or lay it flat on the ground. Keep the paper plate in place with rocks or tape.

2 Use tape to attach the gnomon to the paper plate so it sticks straight up and casts a shadow on the paper plate.

Architect Santiago Calatrava was inspired by the ancient tool when he designed California's Sundial Bridge early in this century.

3 At the beginning of an hour, mark the gnomon's shadow and write the hour next to it. For example, at 8 a.m. you can make a mark on the shadow. Then write down the time.

4 Keep making marks at the new places that the shadow falls every hour or every half-hour, until the Sun goes down.

5 **Now you can use your sundial to tell the time.**

⏻ COLLABORATIVE DISCUSSION

Discussing the Purpose Talk with a partner about sundials. How did they solve the problem of telling time in a simple way?

If the Sun's pattern in the sky were not regular, would sundials still work as a way of telling time?

READING TOOLBOX

Problem and Solution

In this selection, you read about an ancient technology that was developed to solve the problem of telling time. Presenting a problem and offering a solution is one way to organize your thoughts or your writing.

▶ A **problem** is something that needs to be solved. It may be something that causes trouble or difficulty.

▶ A **solution** is a way of dealing with a difficult situation. It is a way of solving a problem.

What was the problem in the selection? What was the solution? Using a graphic organizer such as the one below can help you keep track of problems and solutions described in texts.

Problem

Solution

> **What was the problem in the selection?**
>
> **What was the solution?**

Speak Out! Many people today use a mobile device to keep track of time throughout the day. Do you think watches and clocks will become things that people do not use anymore? Will people continue to use them to tell time? Will they just enjoy them for their beauty and history as we do with sundials? Share your thoughts with a small group. Remember to support your opinions with evidence.

SPEAKING TOOLBOX

Stating your Opinion

When you state your opinion, you should be clear about why you feel the way you do.

Make sure you can support your opinion with facts.

Be sure to listen to other people's opinions and wait your turn to express yourself.

↻ Performance Task

Writing: Write Directions This selection included directions for making a sundial. In a small group, decide what you would like to create. It can be as simple as a paper airplane or a house built from little wooden sticks.

First make a list of the things that you will need.

Then make a list of the steps needed to build the thing that you are creating.

Use the selection as a guide when you write up your directions.

DOWNLOAD

20,000 Leagues Under the Sea

You've just read about how the invention of sundials was a big step forward in science. Now read about an imaginary trip under the sea and what the characters discovered on their voyage.

Know Before You Go

GENRES The selection is based on a book with the same name. The book is an adventure novel by Jules Verne. It was first published in 1870. It is science fiction. In science fiction, the events are not real, but they are still based on science. In fact, there actually were boats that could travel under the water at the time this novel was written.

About the Author

Jules Verne (1828–1905) was a French author. He is often called the father of science fiction. He lived at a time when new inventions like the steam locomotive and electricity were changing the world. Verne wrote adventure stories. He imagined what new inventions could do in the present and in the future. Many of the fantastic things in his books—submarines, rockets that travel into space, and news broadcasts—all are real today. Some of his other famous books are *Around the World in 80 Days* and *A Journey to the Center of the Earth*.

⏻ SETTING A PURPOSE

As you read, pay attention to the exciting details that Jules Verne included in this adventure story.

Jules Verne's
20,000 Leagues Under The Sea

retold by Meredith Mann

FOR SIX WEEKS WE SEARCHED. THE MEN STAYED ALERT, EAGER TO BE THE FIRST TO SEE THE MYSTERIOUS CREATURE.

UNTIL IT FOUND US . . .

AND ATTACKED US . . .

NED, CONSEIL AND I WERE THROWN CLEAR OF THE SHIP AND WERE LEFT ADRIFT . . .

UNTIL WE WERE RESCUED . . .

I am Captain Nemo. Welcome to the Nautilus.

WE HAD BEEN CAPTURED AND FOUND OURSELVES ABOARD AN INCREDIBLE SUBMARINE, A MARVEL OF SCIENCE THAT COULD TRAVEL UNDER THE OCEAN'S SURFACE.

I AM THE MASTER OF THIS SHIP, GENTLEMEN. I AM ITS CAPTAIN AND ENGINEER.

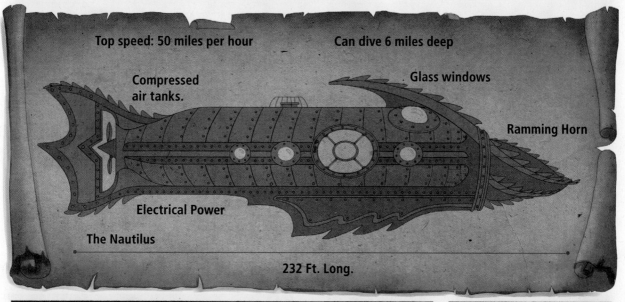

Top speed: 50 miles per hour

Can dive 6 miles deep

Compressed air tanks.

Glass windows

Ramming Horn

Electrical Power

The Nautilus

232 Ft. Long.

The sea provides me with everything I need.

And its vast life is on display.

AS THE WEEKS PASSED, WE WITNESSED MANY WONDERS.

WE VISITED THE GREAT CORAL REEFS OF AUSTRALIA.

WE EXPERIENCED THE UNDERWATER CITY OF ATLANTIS.

WE EVEN PLANTED NEMO'S FLAG AT THE SOUTH POLE.

WHEN WE SURFACED TO EXPLORE A TROPICAL ISLAND, NED HOPED TO ESCAPE.

BUT WE WERE CHASED BACK TO THE NAUTILUS.

WE WERE ATTACKED BY A GIANT SQUID, AND NED LAND SAVED CAPTAIN NEMO'S LIFE.

WHEN WE RETURNED TO THE OPEN SEAS, A WARSHIP ATTACKED US, AND NEMO WAS FORCED TO SINK THE SHIP.

NEMO HATED WHAT HE HAD BECOME, AND WAS AFRAID THAT MANKIND WOULD USE HIS TECHNOLOGY FOR WAR. SO HE SAILED THE NAUTILUS INTO A GIANT WHIRLPOOL.

BUT NED, CONSEIL AND I WERE ABLE TO ESCAPE, AND LIVE TO TELL NEMO'S STORY.

DID THE NAUTILUS SURVIVE? I HOPE SO. WE HAD SAILED UNDER THE SEA FOR TEN MONTHS AND HAD SEEN SO MUCH, AND STILL, I LONGED TO EXPERIENCE MORE WONDERS.

UPLOAD

⏻ COLLABORATIVE DISCUSSION

Discussing the Purpose As a group, discuss the details that Jules Verne included in his story.

Which details do you think are the most interesting?

Which details do you think could have really happened?

Which was your favorite part of the graphic novel and why?

LISTENING TOOLBOX

Discussions

Discussions let you share your thoughts and describe your ideas. When you listen to someone else's thoughts or opinion you might think about things in new and different ways.

▶ Follow class rules for participating.

▶ Wait for your turn and don't interrupt.

▶ Ask if you don't understand what's been said.

▶ Ask questions about the ideas others have shared.

▶ Build on the ideas shared before yours when you make comments.

↻ Performance Task

Writing: Journal Entry With a partner, talk about events in the graphic novel.

Then write a journal entry. Pretend that you were a crew member on the Nautilus and you are writing about your adventure under the sea. Include interesting details and descriptions. Be sure to tell how it felt to be a member of Captain Nemo's crew.

Share your journal entry with your partner.

SPEAKING TOOLBOX

Speaking with Expression and Drama

When you are telling about something exciting and memorable, you should present your story in an interesting way. Here are some tips:

▶ Look directly at the audience members.

▶ Speak clearly.

▶ Speak loudly enough so that everyone can hear you.

▶ Change your tone of voice depending on what you are describing. Don't be afraid to convey emotion when you are speaking.

⟳ Performance Task

Speaking: Take Turns Telling a Story In a small group, talk about the events in the graphic novel. Then take turns retelling what happened. Each student will describe one event. Then it will be the next student's turn.

- The first speaker should give background for the adventure.

- Each speaker should include interesting details that will keep the attention of the listeners.

- The last speaker should make sure the story has a clear ending.

Performance Task

Speaking Activity: Narrative Presentation

You have been reading about different kinds of discoveries. Your task is to plan, write, and give a narrative presentation about a personal discovery.

Planning Your Presentation

Connect to the Theme

A discovery can be something that a scientist figures out after years of research. A discovery can be something that is found under the ground or under the sea. A discovery can be a mysterious package that arrives at your door. A discovery can also be something that you realize about yourself. It could be something you discovered in nature, at school, or in some other place that you visited.

Write Down Some Possible Topics

Since the theme of your presentation is "Discovery," your topic should involve a discovery you made. You will talk about an event or experience that is memorable to you.

Choose your own topic or use one of these examples to help you:

- I was not looking forward to doing something but it turned out great.

- My visit to the zoo (or park, beach, or anywhere else) was incredible.

- My favorite book made me realize something important about myself.

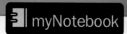

Decide the Basics

Now that you have a topic for your narrative presentation, you'll need to organize your thoughts and decide how you want to express yourself. Use the notes below to help guide your decision making.

Topic

- Write your topic in the form of a sentence.
- Choose a topic that is meaningful to you.
- Think about the most important point you're making.
- Start off with something that will surprise readers or make them curious.

Supporting Details

- Include details and descriptions that make your presentation interesting.
- Include only examples that are important to the topic—don't stray off course!
- Include your feelings and ideas so that your audience understands why your topic is memorable to

Vocabulary

- Remember this is an oral presentation—listeners get one chance to hear it. Use time-order words (*First; Then; Finally*) to help them out.
- Use language that sounds natural.
- Include connecting words and phrases such as *because, since, although*, and *as a result to* make

Tips for Speaking Out Loud

- Speak loudly enough to be heard, at a normal speed. Speak clearly.
- Pay attention to tone and word choice.
- Use language that sounds natural.
- Use physical cues. Hand gestures, facial expressions, and eye contact can help listeners understand your points.

Performance Task

Finalize Your Plan

You now have a topic based on the theme of "Discovery." You know which examples and details you'll use. You may even have a title for your presentation.

Now you need to decide how to present it. Follow the notes in the Speaking Toolbox to help you organize an outline for your presentation.

SPEAKING TOOLBOX

Elements of an Oral Presentation

Introduction	Present your topic. "Hook" your audience with an interesting detail or observation that relates to your topic.
Details	The body of your presentation should include examples, observations, and details that add to your topic. It's a good idea to present them in time order, to make it easier for listeners to follow what you're saying.
Conclusion	The conclusion should sum up the ideas in your presentation. Make certain that it is clear to your audience why the experience you described was memorable to you.

Speaking Before an Audience

As you prepare your presentation, think about:

- **Practice** Rehearse your presentation as much as possible— in front of a mirror, a family member, or even a pet, if you have one.

- **Audience** Know your audience. You will be speaking to your teacher and classmates.

- **Purpose** Think about the effect you want your presentation to have.

- **Style** Present your narrative in a clear and straightforward way.

- **Structure** Use the diagram in the Speaking Toolbox to help you organize your thoughts.

- **Conclusion** Tie your ideas together at the end. Make sure your audience understands why the experience you described was memorable to you.

- **Listening** Remember to treat your listeners the way you would like to be treated.

Revise

Self Evaluation

Use the checklist and rubric to guide your presentation.

Peer Review

Use the checklist to comment on your classmate's presentation.

Student Resources

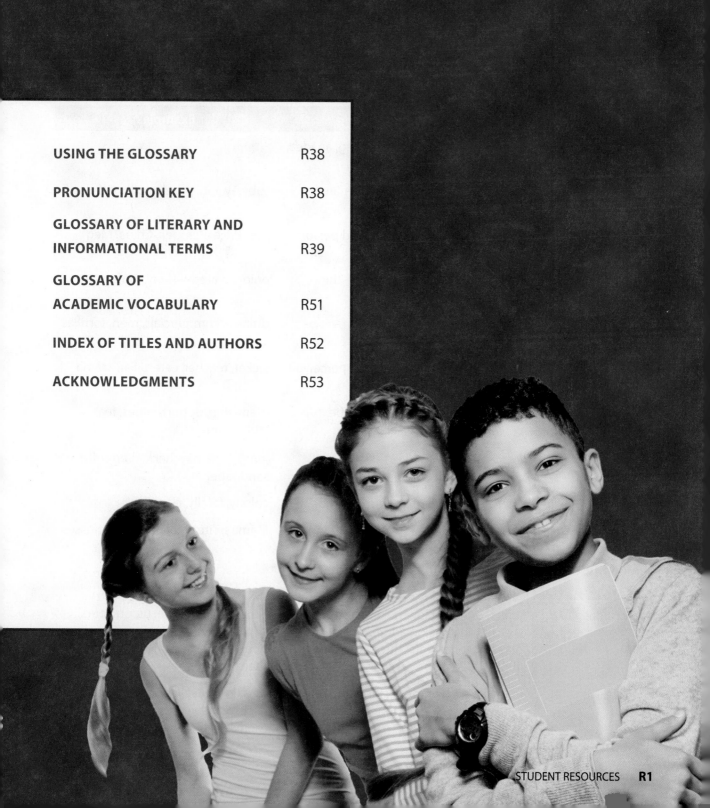

Grammar

Writing that has a lot of mistakes can confuse or even annoy a reader. Punctuation errors in a letter might lead to a miscommunication or delay a reply. A sentence fragment might lower your grade on an essay. Paying attention to grammar, punctuation, and capitalization rules can make your writing clearer and easier to read.

Quick Reference: Parts of Speech

Part of Speech	Function	Examples
Noun	names a person, a place, a thing, an idea, a quality, or an action	
Common	serves as a general name, or a name common to an entire group	subway, fog, puzzle, tollbooth
Proper	names a specific, one-of-a-kind person, place, or thing	Mrs. Price, Pompeii, China, Meg
Singular	refers to a single person, place, thing, or idea	onion, waterfall, lamb, sofa
Plural	refers to more than one person, place, thing, or idea	dreams, commercials, men, tortillas
Concrete	names something that can be perceived by the senses	jacket, teacher, caterpillar, aroma
Abstract	names something that cannot be perceived by the senses	friendship, opportunities, fear, stubbornness
Compound	expresses a single idea through a combination of two or more words	jump rope, paycheck, dragonfly, sandpaper
Collective	refers to a group of people or things	colony, family, clan, flock
Possessive	shows who or what owns something	Mama's, Tito's, children's, waitresses'
Pronoun	takes the place of a noun or another pronoun	
Personal	refers to the person making a statement, the person(s) being addressed, or the person(s) or thing(s) the statement is about	I, me, my, mine, we, us, our, ours, you, your, yours, she, he, it, her, him, hers, his, its, they, them, their, theirs
Reflexive	follows a verb or preposition and refers to a preceding noun or pronoun	myself, yourself, herself, himself, itself, ourselves, yourselves, themselves

continued

Part of Speech	Function	Examples
Intensive	emphasizes a noun or another pronoun	(same as reflexives)
Demonstrative	points to one or more specific persons or things	this, that, these, those
Interrogative	signals a question	who, whom, whose, which, what
Indefinite	refers to one or more persons or things not specifically mentioned	both, all, most, many, anyone, everybody, several, none, some
Relative	introduces an adjective clause by relating it to a word in the clause	who, whom, whose, which, that
Verb	expresses an action, a condition, or a state of being	
Action	tells what the subject does or did, physically or mentally	run, reaches, listened, consider, decides, dreamed
Linking	connects the subject to something that identifies or describes it	am, is, are, was, were, sound, taste, appear, feel, become, remain, seem
Auxiliary	precedes the main verb in a verb phrase	be, have, do, can, could, will, would, may, might
Transitive	directs the action toward someone or something; always has an object	The storm **sank** the ship.
Intransitive	does not direct the action toward someone or something; does not have an object	The ship **sank.**
Adjective	modifies a noun or pronoun	**strong** women, **two** epics, **enough** time
Adverb	modifies a verb, an adjective, or another adverb	walked **out, really** funny, **far** away
Preposition	relates one word to another word	at, by, for, from, in, of, on, to, with
Conjunction	joins words or word groups	
Coordinating	joins words or word groups used the same way	and, but, or, for, so, yet, nor
Correlative	used as a pair to join words or word groups used the same way	both . . . and, either . . . or, neither . . . nor
Subordinating	introduces a clause that cannot stand by itself as a complete sentence	although, after, as, before, because, when, if, unless
Interjection	expresses emotion	wow, ouch, hurrah

Quick Reference: The Sentence and Its Parts

The diagrams that follow will give you a brief review of the essentials of a sentence and some of its parts.

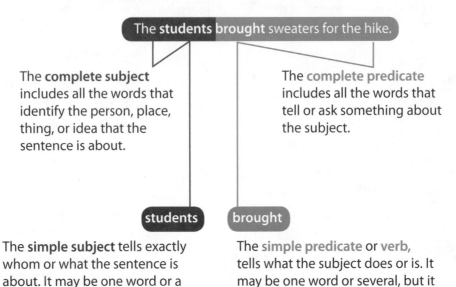

The **students brought** sweaters for the hike.

The **complete subject** includes all the words that identify the person, place, thing, or idea that the sentence is about.

The complete predicate includes all the words that tell or ask something about the subject.

students

brought

The **simple subject** tells exactly whom or what the sentence is about. It may be one word or a group of words, but it does not include modifiers.

The simple predicate or verb, tells what the subject does or is. It may be one word or several, but it does not include modifiers.

Every word in a sentence is part of a complete subject or a complete predicate.

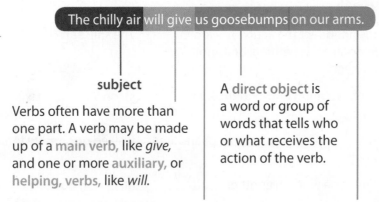

The chilly air will give us goosebumps on our arms.

subject

Verbs often have more than one part. A verb may be made up of a main verb, like *give,* and one or more auxiliary, or helping, verbs, like *will.*

A direct object is a word or group of words that tells who or what receives the action of the verb.

An indirect object is a word or group of words that tells to whom or for whom or to what or for what the verb's action is performed. A sentence can have an indirect object only if it has a direct object. The indirect object always comes before the direct object.

A prepositional phrase consists of a preposition, its object, and any modifiers of the object. In this phrase, *on* is the preposition, *arms* is the object, and *our* modifies *arms.*

Quick Reference: Punctuation

Mark	Function	Examples
End Marks period, question mark, exclamation point	ends a sentence	We can start now**.** When would you like to leave**?** What a fantastic hit**!**
period	follows an initial or abbreviation **Exception**: postal abbreviations of states	Mrs**.** Dorothy Parker, Apple Inc**.**, C**.** P**.** Cavafy, P.M**.**, lb**.**, oz**.**, Blvd**.**, Dr**.**, NE (Nebraska), NV (Nevada)

period	follows a number or letter in an outline or a list	I**.** Volcanoes
		  A**.** Central-vent
		    1**.** Shield

Comma	separates parts of a compound sentence	I had never disliked poetry**,** but now I really love it.
	separates items in a series	She is brave**,** loyal**,** and kind.
	separates adjectives of equal rank that modify the same noun	The slow**,** easy route is best.
	sets off a term of address	Maria**,** how can I help you? You must do something**,** soldier.
	sets off a parenthetical expression	Hard workers**,** as you know**,** don't quit. I'm not a quitter**,** believe me.
	sets off an introductory word, phrase, or dependent clause	Yes**,** I forgot my key. At the beginning of the day**,** I feel fresh. While she was out**,** I was here. Having finished my chores**,** I went out.
	sets off a nonessential phrase or clause	Ed Pawn**,** the captain of the chess team**,** won. Ed Pawn**,** who is the captain**,** won. The two leading runners**,** sprinting toward the finish line**,** finished in a tie.
	sets off parts of dates and addresses	Mail it by May 14**,** 2010**,** to the Hauptman Company**,** 321 Market Street**,** Memphis**,** Tennessee.
	separates words to avoid confusion	By noon**,** time had run out. What the minister does**,** does matter. While cooking**,** Jim burned his hand.

continued

Mark	Function	Examples
Semicolon	separates items in a series that contain commas	We spent the first week of summer vacation in Chicago, Illinois; the second week in St. Louis, Missouri; and the third week in Albany, New York.
	separates parts of a compound sentence that are not joined by a coordinating conjunction	The last shall be first; the first shall be last. I read the Bible; however, I have not memorized it.
	separates parts of a compound sentence when the parts contain commas	After I ran out of money, I called my parents; but only my sister was home, unfortunately.
Colon	introduces a list	The names we wrote were the following: Dana, John, and Will.
	introduces a long quotation	Abraham Lincoln wrote: "Four score and seven years ago, our fathers brought forth on this continent a new nation. . . ."
	follows the salutation of a business letter	To Whom It May Concern: Dear Leonard Atole:
	separates certain numbers	1:28 P.M., Genesis 2:5
Dash	indicates an abrupt break in thought	I was thinking of my mother—who is arriving tomorrow— just as you walked in.
Parentheses	enclose less important material	It was so unlike him (John is always on time) that I began to worry. The last World Series game (did you see it?) was fun.
Ellipses	replace material omitted from a quotation	"Early one morning, Mrs. Bunnin wobbled into the classroom lugging a large cardboard box. . . . Robert was at his desk scribbling a ball-point tattoo . . . on the tops of his knuckles."
Italics	indicate the title of a book, a play, a magazine, a long poem, an opera, a film, or a TV series, or the name of a ship	*Colin Powell: Military Leader, The Prince and the Pauper, Time, After the Hurricane, The Marriage of Figaro, Hatchet, American Idol, Titanic*

continued

Mark	Function	Examples
Hyphen	joins parts of a compound adjective before a noun	That's a not-so-happy face.
	joins parts of a compound with *all-*, *ex-*, *self-*, or *-elect*	The ex-firefighter helped rescue him. Our president-elect is self-conscious.
	joins parts of a compound number (to ninety-nine)	My bicycle wheel has twenty-six spokes.
	joins parts of a fraction	My cup is one-third full.
	joins a prefix to a word beginning with a capital letter	Were your grandparents born post-World War II? The mid-April snowstorm surprised everyone.
	indicates that a word is divided at the end of a line	How could you have any reasonable expectations of getting a new computer?

©Pamela Moore/iStockphoto.com

Quick Reference: Capitalization

Category	Examples
People and Titles	
Names and initials of people	Maya Angelou, **W.E.B.** DuBois
Titles used before a name	Mrs. Price, Scoutmaster Brenkman
Deities and members of religious groups	Jesus, Allah, Buddha, Zeus, Baptists
Names of ethnic and national groups	Hispanics, Jews, African Americans
Geographical Names	
Cities, states, countries, continents	Philadelphia, Kansas, Japan, Europe
Regions, bodies of water, mountains	the South, Lake Baikal, Mount Everest
Geographic features, parks	Great Basin, Yellowstone National Park
Streets and roads, planets	318 East Sutton Drive, Charles Court, Jupiter, Mars
Organizations, Events, Etc.	
Companies, organizations, teams	Ford Motor Company, Boy Scouts of America, St. Louis Cardinals
Buildings, bridges, monuments	Empire State Building, Eads Bridge, Washington Monument
Documents, awards	Declaration of Independence, Stanley Cup
Special named events	Mardi Gras, World Series
Government bodies, historical periods and events	U.S. Senate, House of Representatives, Middle Ages, Vietnam War
Days and months, holidays	Thursday, March, Thanksgiving, Labor Day
Specific cars, boats, trains, planes	Porsche, *Carpathia*, *Southwest Chief*, Concorde
Proper Adjectives	
Adjectives formed from proper nouns	French cooking, Spanish omelet, Edwardian age

continued

First Words and the Pronoun *I*	
First word in a sentence or quotation	**T**his is it. **H**e said, "**L**et's go." **I** have it.
First word of a sentence in parentheses that is not within another sentence	The spelling rules are covered in another section. (**C**onsult that section for more information.)
First words in the salutation and closing of a letter	**D**ear Madam, **V**ery truly yours,
First word, last word, and all important words in a title	"**A**lone in the **N**ets," *Under the Royal Palms*

©GlobalStock/iStockphoto.com

Grammar Handbook

1 Nouns

A **noun** is a word used to name a person, a place, a thing, an idea, a quality, or an action. Nouns can be classified in several ways.

For more information on different types of nouns, see **Quick Reference: Parts of Speech**, page R2.

1.1 COMMON NOUNS

Common nouns are general names, common to entire groups.

1.2 PROPER NOUNS

Proper nouns name specific, one-of-a-kind people, places, and things.

Common	Proper
volcano, student, country, president	Mount Vesuvius, June, China, President Cleveland

For more information, see **Quick Reference: Capitalization**, page R8.

1.3 SINGULAR AND PLURAL NOUNS

A noun may take a singular or a plural form, depending on whether it names a single person, place, thing, or idea or more than one. Make sure you use appropriate spellings when forming plurals.

Singular	Plural
walrus, bully, lagoon, goose	walruses, bullies, lagoons, geese

For more information, see **Forming Plural Nouns**, page R68.

1.4 POSSESSIVE NOUNS

A **possessive noun** shows who or what owns something.

For more information, see **Forming Possessives,** page R69.

2 Pronouns

A **pronoun** is a word that is used in place of a noun or another pronoun. The word or word group to which the pronoun refers is called its **antecedent.**

2.1 PERSONAL PRONOUNS

Personal pronouns change their form to express person, number, gender, and case. The forms of these pronouns are shown in the following chart.

	Nominative	Objective	Possessive
Singular			
First Person	I	me	my, mine
Second Person	you	you	your, yours
Third Person	she, he, it	her, him, it	her, hers, his, its
Plural			
First Person	we	us	our, ours
Second Person	you	you	your, yours
Third Person	they	them	their, theirs

2.2 AGREEMENT WITH ANTECEDENT

Pronouns should agree with their antecedents in number, gender, and person.

If an antecedent is singular, use a singular pronoun.

EXAMPLE: *That **poem** was fun to read. It rhymed.*

If an antecedent is plural, use a plural pronoun.

EXAMPLES: ***Poets** choose their words carefully. I like **poems**, but Mischa doesn't care for them.*

The gender of a pronoun must be the same as the gender of its antecedent.

EXAMPLE: ***Eve Merriam's** creativity makes her poems easy to remember.*

The person of the pronoun must be the same as the person of its antecedent. As the chart in Section 2.1 shows, a pronoun can be in first-person, second-person, or third-person form.

EXAMPLES: ***We** each have our favorite poets.*

Grammar Practice

Rewrite each sentence so that the underlined pronoun agrees with its antecedent.

1. The speaker in Maya Angelou's poem "Life Doesn't Frighten Me" talks about <u>their</u> fears.
2. When I read this poem, <u>we</u> felt braver already.
3. Scary things lose <u>its</u> power.
4. Even frogs and snakes don't seem as bad as <u>you</u> usually do.
5. I want to know how to be unafraid in <u>her</u> life.

2.3 PRONOUN FORMS

Personal pronouns change form to show how they function in sentences. The three forms are the subject form, the object form, and the possessive form. For examples of these pronouns, see the chart in Section 2.1.

A **subject pronoun** is used as a subject in a sentence.

EXAMPLES: *Steven is my brother. He is the best player on the team.*

Also use the subject form when the pronoun follows a linking verb.

EXAMPLE: *The girl in the closet was she.*

An **object pronoun** is used as a direct object, an indirect object, or the object of a preposition.

SUBJECT   OBJECT

They locked her in it.

OBJECT OF PREPOSITION

A **possessive pronoun** shows ownership. The pronouns *mine, yours, hers, his, its, ours,* and *theirs* can be used in place of nouns.

EXAMPLE: *The cat is mine.*

The pronouns *my, your, her, his, its, our,* and *their* are used before nouns.

EXAMPLE: *I found her keys on the floor.*

WATCH OUT! Many spelling errors can be avoided if you watch out for *its* and *their.* Don't confuse the possessive pronoun *its* with the contraction *it's,* meaning "it is" or "it has." The homonyms *they're* (a contraction of *they are*) and *there* ("in that place") are often mistakenly used for *their.*

TIP To decide which pronoun to use in a comparison, such as "He tells better tales than (*I* or *me*)," fill in the missing word(s): *He tells better tales than I tell.*

Grammar Practice

Write the correct pronoun form to complete each sentence.

1. When (he, him) is done with the book, I will give it to you.
2. Mary is going to invite (her, she) to go rollerskating.
3. My friends have lost (their, they) tickets.
4. (We, Us) can cook vegetables on the grill tonight, or we can make a salad.
5. (I, Me) sent an e-mail earlier today to my aunt.

2.4 REFLEXIVE AND INTENSIVE PRONOUNS

These pronouns are formed by adding *-self* or *-selves* to certain personal pronouns. Their forms are the same, and they differ only in how they are used.

A **reflexive pronoun** follows a verb or preposition and reflects back on an earlier noun or pronoun.

EXAMPLES: *He likes himself too much. She is now herself again.*

Intensive pronouns intensify or emphasize the nouns or pronouns to which they refer.

EXAMPLES: *They themselves will educate their children.*

You yourself did it.

WATCH OUT! Avoid using *himself* or *theirselves.* Standard English does not include these forms.

NONSTANDARD: *The children congratulated theirselves.*

STANDARD: *The children congratulated themselves.*

2.5 DEMONSTRATIVE PRONOUNS

Demonstrative pronouns point out things and persons near and far.

	Singular	Plural
Near	this	these
Far	that	those

2.6 INDEFINITE PRONOUNS

Indefinite pronouns do not refer to specific persons or things and usually have no antecedents. The chart shows some commonly used indefinite pronouns.

Singular	Plural	Singular or Plural	
another	both	all	none
anybody	few	any	some
no one	many	more	most
neither			

TIP Indefinite pronouns that end in *one, body,* or *thing* are always singular.

INCORRECT: *Did everybody play their part well?*

If the indefinite pronoun might refer to either a male or a female, *his or her* may be used to refer to it, or the sentence may be rewritten.

CORRECT: *Did everybody play his or her part well? Did all the students play their parts well?*

2.7 INTERROGATIVE PRONOUNS

An **interrogative pronoun** tells a reader or listener that a question is coming. The interrogative pronouns are *who, whom, whose, which,* and *what.*

EXAMPLES: *Who is going to rehearse with you? From whom did you receive the script?*

TIP *Who* is used as a subject; *whom* is used as an object. To find out which pronoun you need to use in a question, change the question to a statement.

QUESTION: *(Who/Whom) did you meet there?*

STATEMENT: *You met (?) there.*

Since the verb has a subject (*you*), the needed word must be the object form, *whom.*

EXAMPLE: *Whom did you meet there?*

WATCH OUT! A special problem arises when you use an interrupter, such as *do you think,* within a question.

EXAMPLE: *(Who/Whom) do you think will win?*

If you eliminate the interrupter, it is clear that the word you need is *who.*

2.8 RELATIVE PRONOUNS

Relative pronouns relate, or connect, adjective clauses to the words they modify in sentences. The noun or pronoun that a relative clause modifies is the antecedent of the relative pronoun. Here are the relative pronouns and their uses.

	Subject	Object	Possessive
Person	who	whom	whose
Thing	which	which	whose
Thing/Person	that	that	whose

Often, short sentences with related ideas can be combined by using a relative pronoun to create a more effective sentence.

SHORT SENTENCE: *Lucy is an accountant.*

RELATED SENTENCE: *She helped us do our taxes.*

COMBINED SENTENCE: *Lucy is an accountant who helped us do our taxes.*

Grammar Practice

Write the correct form of each incorrect pronoun.

1. John is a car salesman whom helped me buy a new automobile.
2. The pitcher threw the ball to I.
3. To who should I address this letter?
4. Us love the sea.
5. Betty is as smart as her is.

2.9 PRONOUN REFERENCE PROBLEMS

You should always be able to identify the word a pronoun refers to. Avoid problems by rewriting sentences.

An **indefinite reference** occurs when the pronoun *it, you,* or *they* does not clearly refer to a specific antecedent.

UNCLEAR: *They told me how the story ended, and it was annoying.*

CLEAR: *They told me how the story ended, and I was annoyed.*

A **general reference** occurs when the pronoun *it, this, that, which,* or *such* is used to refer to a general idea rather than a specific antecedent.

UNCLEAR: *I'd rather not know what happens. That keeps me interested.*

CLEAR: *I'd rather not know what happens. Not knowing keeps me interested.*

Ambiguous means "having more than one possible meaning." An **ambiguous reference** occurs when a pronoun could refer to two or more antecedents.

UNCLEAR: *Jan told Danielle that she would read her story aloud.*

CLEAR: *Jan told Danielle that she would read Danielle's story aloud.*

Grammar Practice

Rewrite the following sentences to correct indefinite, ambiguous, and general pronoun references.

1. The teacher was speaking to Maggie, and she looked unhappy.
2. High winds developed. This trapped mountain climbers in their tents.
3. Although Matt likes working at a donut shop, he doesn't eat them.
4. The pitcher was set on the glass-topped table and it broke.
5. They unloaded the clothes from the boxes and then threw them away.

3 Verbs

A **verb** is a word that expresses an action, a condition, or a state of being.

For more information, see **Quick Reference: Parts of Speech,** page R2.

3.1 ACTION VERBS

Action verbs express mental or physical activity.

EXAMPLE: *Lucy ran several miles every day.*

3.2 LINKING VERBS

Linking verbs join subjects with words or phrases that rename or describe them.

EXAMPLE: *After a few months, her shoes were worn out.*

3.3 PRINCIPAL PARTS

Action and linking verbs typically have four principal parts, which are used to form verb tenses. The principal parts are the **present,** the **present participle,** the **past,** and the **past participle.**

Action verbs and some linking verbs also fall into two categories: regular and irregular.

A **regular verb** is a verb that forms its past and past participle by adding *-ed* or *-d* to the present form.

Present	Present Participle	Past	Past Participle
jump	(is) jumping	jumped	(has) jumped
solve	(is) solving	solved	(has) solved
grab	(is) grabbing	grabbed	(has) grabbed
carry	(is) carrying	carried	(has) carried

An **irregular verb** is a verb that forms its past and past participle in some other way than by adding *–ed* or *–d* to the present form.

Present	Present Participle	Past	Past Participle
begin	(is) beginning	began	(has) begun
break	(is) breaking	broke	(has) broken
go	(is) going	went	(has) gone

3.4 VERB TENSE

The **tense** of a verb indicates the time of the action or the state of being. An action or state of being can occur in the present, the past, or the future. There are six tenses, each expressing a different range of time.

The **present tense** expresses an action or state that is happening at the present time, occurs regularly, or is constant or generally true. Use the present part.

NOW: *This apple is rotten.*

REGULAR: *I eat an apple every day.*

GENERAL: *Apples are round.*

The **past tense** expresses an action that began and ended in the past. Use the past part.

EXAMPLE: *They settled the argument.*

The **future tense** expresses an action or state that will occur. Use *shall* or *will* with the present part.

EXAMPLE: *You will understand someday.*

The **present perfect tense** expresses an action or state that (1) was completed at an indefinite time in the past or (2) began in the past and continues into the present. Use *have* or *has* with the past participle.

EXAMPLE: *These buildings have existed for centuries.*

The **past perfect tense** expresses an action in the past that came before another action in the past. Use *had* with the past participle.

EXAMPLE: *I had told you, but you forgot.*

The **future perfect tense** expresses an action in the future that will be completed before another action in the future. Use **shall have** or **will have** with the past participle.

EXAMPLE: *She will have found the note by the time I get home.*

TIP A past-tense form of an irregular verb is not used with an auxiliary, or helping, verb, but a past-participle main irregular verb is always used with an auxiliary verb.

INCORRECT: *He has did that too many times.* (*Did* is the past-tense form of an irregular verb and shouldn't be used with *has*.)

INCORRECT: *He done that too many times.* (*Done* is the past participle of an irregular verb and shouldn't be used without an auxiliary verb.)

CORRECT: *He has done that too many times.*

3.5 PROGRESSIVE FORMS

The progressive forms of the six tenses show ongoing actions. Use forms of **be** with the present participles of verbs.

PRESENT PROGRESSIVE: *Angelo is taking the test.*

PAST PROGRESSIVE: *Angelo was taking the test.*

FUTURE PROGRESSIVE: *Angelo will be taking the test.*

PRESENT PERFECT PROGRESSIVE: *Angelo has been taking the test.*

PAST PERFECT PROGRESSIVE: *Angelo had been taking the test.*

FUTURE PERFECT PROGRESSIVE: *Angelo will have been taking the test.*

WATCH OUT! Do not shift from tense to tense needlessly. Watch out for these special cases:

- In most compound sentences and in sentences with compound predicates, keep the tenses the same.

    INCORRECT: *She smiled and shake his hand.*

    CORRECT: *She smiled and shook his hand.*

- If one past action happens before another, do shift tenses.

INCORRECT: *He remembered what he studied.*
CORRECT: *He remembered what he had studied.*

Grammar Practice

Rewrite each sentence using a form of the verb(s) in parentheses. Identify each form that you use.

1. Helen Keller (become) blind and deaf before she (be) two.
2. A wonderful teacher (change) her life.
3. Anne Sullivan (be) almost blind before she (have) an operation.
4. Even now, Keller (be) an inspiration to everyone with a disability.
5. People (remember) both Helen and her teacher for years to come.

Rewrite each sentence to correct an error in tense.

1. Helen Keller writes a book about her life.
2. She described how she learns to understand language.
3. She felt like she knew it once and forgotten it.
4. Anne Sullivan was a determined teacher and does not give up.
5. Helen had began a life of learning.

3.6 ACTIVE AND PASSIVE VOICE

The voice of a verb tells whether its subject performs or receives the action expressed by the verb. When the subject performs the action, the verb is in the **active voice.** When the subject is the receiver of the action, the verb is in the **passive voice.**

Compare these two sentences:

ACTIVE: *Nancy Wood wrote "Animal Wisdom."*

PASSIVE: *"Animal Wisdom" was written by Nancy Wood.*

To form the passive voice, use a form of **be** with the past participle of the verb.

WATCH OUT! Use the passive voice sparingly. It can make writing awkward and less direct.

AWKWARD: *"Animal Wisdom" is a poem that was written by Nancy Wood.*

BETTER: *Nancy Wood wrote the poem "Animal Wisdom."*

There are occasions when you will choose to use the passive voice because:

- you want to emphasize the receiver: *The king was shot.*
- the doer is unknown: *My books were stolen.*
- the doer is unimportant: *French is spoken here.*

4 Modifiers

Modifiers are words or groups of words that change or limit the meanings of other words. Adjectives and adverbs are common modifiers.

4.1 ADJECTIVES

Adjectives modify nouns and pronouns by telling which one, what kind, how many, or how much.

WHICH ONE: *this, that, these, those*

EXAMPLE: *This poem moves along quickly.*

WHAT KIND: *square, dirty, fast, regular*

EXAMPLE: *Fast runners make baseball exciting.*

HOW MANY: *some, few, both, thousands*

EXAMPLE: *Thousands of fans cheer in the stands.*

HOW MUCH: *more, less, enough, as much*

EXAMPLE: *I had more fun watching the game than I expected.*

4.2 PREDICATE ADJECTIVES

Most adjectives come before the nouns they modify, as in the examples above. A **predicate adjective,** however, follows a linking verb and describes the subject.

EXAMPLE: *Baseball players are strong.*

Be especially careful to use adjectives (not adverbs) after such linking verbs as *look, feel, grow, taste,* and *smell.*

EXAMPLE: *Exercising feels good.*

4.3 ADVERBS

Adverbs modify verbs, adjectives, and other adverbs by telling where, when, how, or to what extent.

WHERE: *The children played outside.*

WHEN: *The author spoke yesterday.*

HOW: *We walked slowly behind the leader.*

TO WHAT EXTENT: *He worked very hard.*

Adverbs may occur in many places in sentences, both before and after the words they modify.

EXAMPLE: *Suddenly the wind shifted.*

The wind suddenly shifted.

The wind shifted suddenly.

4.4 ADJECTIVE OR ADVERB?

Many adverbs are formed by adding *–ly* to adjectives.

EXAMPLES: *sweet, sweetly; gentle, gently*

However, *–ly* added to a noun will usually yield an adjective.

EXAMPLES: *friend, friendly; woman, womanly*

4.5 COMPARISON OF MODIFIERS

Modifiers can be used to compare two or more things. The form of a modifier shows the degree of comparison. Both adjectives and adverbs have **comparative** and **superlative forms.**

The **comparative form** is used to compare two things, groups, or actions.

EXAMPLES: *Today's weather is hotter than yesterday's.*

The boy got tired more quickly than his sister did.

The **superlative form** is used to compare more than two things, groups, or actions.

EXAMPLES: *This has been the hottest month ever recorded.*

Older people were most affected by the heat.

4.6 REGULAR COMPARISONS

Most one-syllable and some two-syllable adjectives and adverbs have comparatives and superlatives formed by adding *-er* and *-est*. All three-syllable and most two-syllable modifiers have comparatives and superlatives formed with **more** or **most.**

Modifier	Comparative	Superlative
messy	messier	messiest
quick	quicker	quickest
wild	wilder	wildest
tired	more tired	most tired
often	more often	most often

WATCH OUT! Note that spelling changes must sometimes be made to form the comparatives and superlatives of modifiers.

AWKWARD: *friendly, friendlier* (Change *y* to *i* and add the ending.)

sad, sadder (Double the final consonant and add the ending.)

4.7 IRREGULAR COMPARISONS

Some commonly used modifiers have irregular comparative and superlative forms. They are listed in the following chart. You may wish to memorize them.

Modifier	Comparative	Superlative
good	better	best
bad	worse	more
far	farther *or* further	farthest *or* furthest
little	less *or* lesser	least
many	more	most
well	better	best
much	more	most

4.8 PROBLEMS WITH MODIFIERS

Study the tips that follow to avoid common mistakes.

Farther* and *Further Use *farther* for distances; use *further* for everything else.

Double Comparisons Make a comparison by using *-er/-est* or by using **more/most.** Using *-er* with **more** or using *-est* with **most** is incorrect.

INCORRECT: *I like her more better than she likes me.*

CORRECT: *I like her better than she likes me.*

Illogical Comparisons An illogical or confusing comparison occurs when two unrelated things are compared or when something is compared with itself. The word **other** or the word **else** should be used when comparing an individual member to the rest of a group.

ILLOGICAL: *I like "A Voice" more than any poem.* (implies that "A Voice" isn't a poem)

LOGICAL: *I like "A Voice" more than any other poem.*
(identifies that "A Voice" is a poem)

Bad* vs. *Badly *Bad,* always an adjective, is used before a noun or after a linking verb. *Badly,* always an adverb, never modifies a noun. Be sure to use the right form after a linking verb.

INCORRECT: *I felt badly that I missed the game.*

CORRECT: *I felt bad that I missed the game.*

Good vs. Well *Good* is always an adjective. It is used before a noun or after a linking verb. *Well* is often an adverb meaning "expertly" or "properly." *Well* can also be used as an adjective after a linking verb when it means "in good health."

INCORRECT: *I wrote my essay good.*

CORRECT: *I wrote my essay well.*

CORRECT: *I didn't feel well when I wrote it, though.*

Double Negatives If you add a negative word to a sentence that is already negative, the result will be an error known as a double negative. When using *not* or *-n't* with a verb, use *any-* words, such as *anybody* or *anything,* rather than *no-* words, such as *nobody* or *nothing,* later in the sentence.

INCORRECT: *The teacher didn't like nobody's paper.*

CORRECT: *The teacher didn't like anybody's paper.*

Using *hardly, barely,* or *scarcely* after a negative word is also incorrect.

INCORRECT: *My friends couldn't hardly catch up.*

CORRECT: *My friends could hardly catch up.*

Misplaced Modifiers Sometimes a modifier is placed so far away from the word it modifies that the intended meaning of the sentence is unclear. Prepositional phrases and participial phrases are often misplaced. Place modifiers as close as possible to the words they modify.

MISPLACED: *We found the child in the park who was missing.*

CLEARER: *We found the child who was missing in the park.* (The child was missing, not the park.)

Dangling Modifiers Sometimes a modifier doesn't appear to modify any word in a sentence. Most dangling modifiers are participial phrases or infinitive phrases.

DANGLING: *Looking out the window, his brother was seen driving by.*

CLEARER: *Looking out the window, Josh saw his brother driving by.*

Grammar Practice

Choose the correct word from each pair in parentheses.

1. According to my neighbor, squirrels are a (bad, badly) problem in the area.
2. The (worst, worse) time of the year to go to India is in the summer.
3. The boy didn't have (any, no) interest in playing baseball.
4. Molly sings really (good, well), though.
5. Tom was (more, most) daring than any other boy scout on the trip.

Grammar Practice

Rewrite each sentence that contains a misplaced or dangling modifier. Write "correct" if the sentence is written correctly.

1. Coyotes know how to survive in the wild.
2. Hunting their prey, we have seen them in the forest.
3. Looking out the window, a coyote was seen in the yard.
4. My brother and I found books about coyotes at the library.
5. We learned that wolves are their natural enemies reading about them.

5 The Sentence and Its Parts

A **sentence** is a group of words used to express a complete thought. A complete sentence has a subject and a predicate.

For more information, see **Quick Reference: The Sentence and Its Parts,** page R4.

5.1 KINDS OF SENTENCES

There are four basic types of sentences.

Type	Definition	Example
Declarative	states a fact, a wish, an intent, or a feeling	Salisbury writes about young people.
Interrogative	asks a question	Have you read "The Ravine"?
Imperative	gives a command or direction	Find a copy.
Exclamatory	expresses strong feeling or excitement	It's really suspenseful!

5.2 COMPOUND SUBJECTS AND PREDICATES

A compound subject consists of two or more subjects that share the same verb. They are typically joined by the coordinating conjunction *and* or *or.*

EXAMPLE: *A short story or novel will keep you interested.*

A compound predicate consists of two or more predicates that share the same subject. They too are usually joined by a coordinating conjunction such as *and, but,* or *or.*

EXAMPLE: *The class finished all the poetry but did not read the short stories.*

5.3 COMPLEMENTS

A **complement** is a word or group of words that completes the meaning of a sentence. Some sentences contain only a subject and a verb. Most sentences, however, require additional words placed after the verb to complete the meaning of the sentence. There are three kinds of complements: direct objects, indirect objects, and subject complements.

Direct objects are words or word groups that receive the action of action verbs. A direct object answers the question *what* or *who.*

EXAMPLES: *Daria caught the ball.* (Caught what?)
She tagged the runner. (Tagged who?)

Indirect objects tell to whom or what or for whom or what the actions of verbs are performed. Indirect objects come before direct objects. In the examples that follow, the indirect objects are highlighted.

EXAMPLES: *The audience gave us a standing ovation.* (Gave to whom?)
We offered the newspaper an interview.
(Offered to what?)

Subject complements come after linking verbs and identify or describe the subjects. A subject complement that names or identifies a subject is called a **predicate nominative.** Predicate nominatives include **predicate nouns** and **predicate pronouns.**

EXAMPLES: *The students were happy campers.*
The best actor in the play is he.

A subject complement that describes a subject is called a **predicate adjective.**

EXAMPLE: *The coach seemed thrilled.*

6 Phrases

A **phrase** is a group of related words that does not contain a subject and a predicate but functions in a sentence as a single part of speech.

6.1 PREPOSITIONAL PHRASES

A **prepositional phrase** is a phrase that consists of a preposition, its object, and any modifiers of the object. Prepositional phrases that modify nouns or pronouns are called **adjective phrases.** Prepositional phrases that modify verbs, adjectives, or adverbs are **adverb phrases.**

ADJECTIVE PHRASE: *The central character of the story is a villain.*

ADVERB PHRASE: *He reveals his nature in the first scene.*

6.2 APPOSITIVES AND APPOSITIVE PHRASES

An **appositive** is a noun or pronoun that identifies or renames another noun or pronoun. An **appositive phrase** includes an appositive and modifiers of it. An appositive usually follows the noun or pronoun it identifies.

An appositive can be either **essential** or **nonessential.** An **essential appositive** provides information that is needed to identify what is referred to by the preceding noun or pronoun.

> EXAMPLE: *Longfellow's poem is about the American patriot Paul Revere.*

A **nonessential appositive** adds extra information about a noun or pronoun whose meaning is already clear. Nonessential appositives and appositive phrases are set off with commas.

> EXAMPLE: *The story, a poem, has historical inaccuracies.*

7 Verbals and Verbal Phrases

A **verbal** is a verb form that is used as a noun, an adjective, or an adverb. A **verbal phrase** consists of a verbal along with its modifiers and complements. There are three kinds of verbals: infinitives, participles, and gerunds.

7.1 INFINITIVES AND INFINITIVE PHRASES

An **infinitive** is a verb form that usually begins with *to* and functions as a noun, an adjective, or an adverb. An **infinitive phrase** consists of an infinitive plus its modifiers and complements.

> NOUN: *To be happy is not easy.* (subject) *I want to have fun.* (direct object)

My hope is to enjoy every day. (predicate nominative)

ADJECTIVE: *That's a goal to be proud of.* (adjective modifying goal)

ADVERB: *I'll work to achieve it.* (adverb modifying work)

Because *to,* the sign of the infinitive, precedes infinitives, it is usually easy to recognize them. However, sometimes *to* may be omitted.

> EXAMPLE: *No one can help me [to] achieve my goal.*

7.2 PARTICIPLES AND PARTICIPIAL PHRASES

A **participle** is a verb form that functions as an adjective. Like adjectives, participles modify nouns and pronouns. Most participles are present-participle forms ending in *-ing,* or past-participle forms ending in *-ed* or *-en.* In the examples below, the participles are highlighted.

> MODIFYING A NOUN: *The waxed floor was sticky.*

> MODIFYING A PRONOUN: *Sighing, she mopped up the mess.*

Participial phrases are participles with all their modifiers and complements.

> MODIFYING A NOUN: *The girls working on the project are very energetic.*

> MODIFYING A PRONOUN: *Having finished his work, he took a nap.*

7.3 DANGLING AND MISPLACED PARTICIPLES

A participle or participial phrase should be placed as close as possible to the word that it modifies. Otherwise the meaning of the sentence may not be clear.

> MISPLACED: *The boys were looking for squirrels searching the trees.*

> CLEARER: *The boys searching the trees were looking for squirrels.*

A participle or participial phrase that does not clearly modify anything in a sentence is called a **dangling participle.** A dangling participle causes confusion because it appears to modify a word that it cannot sensibly modify. Correct a dangling participle by providing a word for the participle to modify.

DANGLING: *Waiting for the show to start, the phone rang.* (The phone wasn't waiting.)

CLEARER: *Waiting for the show to start, I heard the phone ring.*

7.4 GERUNDS AND GERUND PHRASES

A **gerund** is a verb form ending in *-ing* that functions as a noun. Gerunds may perform any function nouns perform.

SUBJECT: *Cooking is a good way to relax.*

DIRECT OBJECT: *I enjoy cooking.*

INDIRECT OBJECT: *They should give cooking a chance.*

SUBJECT COMPLEMENT: *My favorite pastime is cooking.*

OBJECT OF PREPOSITION: *A love of cooking runs in the family.*

Gerund phrases are gerunds with all their modifiers and complements.

SUBJECT: *Depending on luck never got me far.*

OBJECT OF PREPOSITION: *I will finish before leaving the office.*

APPOSITIVE: *Her hobby, training horses, finally led to a career.*

Grammar Practice

Rewrite each sentence, adding the type of phrase shown in parentheses.

1. "Fine?" is by Margaret Peterson Haddix. (appositive phrase)
2. Bailey suffered from a migraine headache. (infinitive phrase)
3. Bailey had an MRI. (prepositional phrase)
4. The pediatric wing is full. (gerund phrase)
5. Bailey's mom leaves the hospital. (participial phrase)

---

8 Clauses

A **clause** is a group of words that contains a subject and a predicate. A sentence may contain one clause or more than one. The sentence in the following example contains two clauses. The subject and verb in each clause are highlighted.

EXAMPLE: *Some students like to play sports, but others prefer to play music.*

There are two kinds of clauses: independent clauses and subordinate clauses.

8.1 INDEPENDENT AND SUBORDINATE CLAUSES

An independent clause expresses a complete thought and can stand alone as a sentence.

INDEPENDENT CLAUSE: *I read "The Banana Tree."*

A sentence may contain more than one independent clause.

EXAMPLE: *I read it once, and I liked it.*

In the preceding example, the coordinating conjunction *and* joins two independent clauses.

For more information, see **Coordinating Conjunctions,** page R3.

A **subordinate (dependent) clause** cannot stand alone as a sentence because it does not express a complete thought. By itself, a subordinate clause is a sentence fragment. It needs an independent clause to complete its meaning. Most subordinate clauses are introduced by words such as *after, although, because, if, that, when,* and *while.*

SUBORDINATE CLAUSE: *Because they worked hard.*

A subordinate clause can be joined to an independent clause to make a sentence that expresses a complete thought. In the following example, the subordinate clause explains why the students did well on the test.

EXAMPLE: *The students did well on the test because they worked hard.*

9 The Structure of Sentences

When classified by their structure, there are four kinds of sentences: simple, compound, complex, and compound-complex.

9.1 SIMPLE SENTENCES

A **simple sentence** is a sentence that has one independent clause and no subordinate clauses. Even a simple sentence can include many details.

> EXAMPLES: *Chloe looked for the train.*
> *Seth drove to the station in an old red pickup truck.*

A simple sentence may contain a compound subject or a compound verb. A compound subject is made up of two or more subjects that share the same verb. A compound verb is made up of two or more verbs that have the same subject.

> EXAMPLES: *Seth and Chloe drove to the station.* (compound subject)
> *They waved and shouted as the train pulled in.* (compound verb)

9.2 COMPOUND SENTENCES

A **compound sentence** consists of two or more independent clauses. The clauses in compound sentences are joined with commas and coordinating conjunctions (*and, but, or, nor, yet, for, so*) or with semicolons. Like simple sentences, compound sentences do not contain any subordinate clauses.

> EXAMPLES: *We all get older, but not everyone gets wiser.*
> *Some young people don't want to grow up; others grow up too quickly.*

WATCH OUT! Do not confuse compound sentences with simple sentences that have compound parts.

> EXAMPLE: *Books and clothes were scattered all over her room.*

Here, the conjunction *and* is used to join the parts of a compound subject, not the clauses in a compound sentence.

9.3 COMPLEX SENTENCES

A **complex sentence** consists of one independent clause and one or more subordinate clauses. Most subordinate clauses start with words such as *when, until, who, where, because,* and *so that.*

EXAMPLES: *While I eat my breakfast, I often wonder what I'll be like in ten years. When I think about the future, I see a canvas that has nothing on it.*

Write these sentences on a sheet of paper. Underline each independent clause once and each subordinate clause twice.

1. Although the Foster Grandparent Program is more than 40 years old, many people do not know about it.
2. This program was established so that children with special needs could get extra attention.
3. Anyone can volunteer who is at least 60 years old and meets other requirements.
4. After a volunteer is trained, he or she works 15 to 40 hours a week.
5. Foster grandparents often help with homework so that the children can improve in school.
6. Since this program was founded in 1965, there have been foster grandparent projects in all 50 states.

9.4 COMPOUND-COMPLEX SENTENCES

A **compound-complex** sentence contains two or more independent clauses and one or more subordinate clauses. Compound-complex sentences are both compound and complex. If you start with a compound sentence, all you need to do to form a compound-complex sentence is add a subordinate clause.

COMPOUND: *All the students knew the answer, yet they were too shy to volunteer.*

COMPOUND–COMPLEX: *All the students knew the answer that their teacher expected, yet they were too shy to volunteer.*

Identify each sentence as compound (*CD*), complex (*C*), or compound-complex (*CC*).

1. In 1998, a hurricane swept through Central America, where it hit Honduras and Nicaragua especially hard.
2. Hurricane Mitch was one of the strongest storms ever in this region; it caused great destruction.
3. People on the coast tried to flee to higher ground, but flooding and mudslides made escape difficult.
4. More than 9,000 people were killed, and crops and roads were wiped out.
5. TV images of homeless and hungry people touched many Americans, who responded generously.
6. They donated money and supplies, which were flown to the region.
7. Volunteers helped clear roads so that supplies could get to villages that needed them.
8. Charity groups distributed food and safe drinking water, and they handed out sleeping bags and mosquito nets, which were needed in the tropical climate.
9. Medical volunteers treated people who desperately needed care.
10. Other volunteers rebuilt homes, and they helped restore the farm economy so that people could earn a living again.

10 Writing Complete Sentences

Remember, a sentence is a group of words that expresses a complete thought. In writing that you wish to share with a reader, try to avoid both sentence fragments and run-on sentences.

10.1 CORRECTING FRAGMENTS

A **sentence fragment** is a group of words that is only part of a sentence. It does not express a complete thought and may be confusing to a reader or listener. A sentence fragment may be lacking a subject, a predicate, or both.

FRAGMENT: *Didn't care about sports.* (no subject)

CORRECTED: *The lawyer didn't care about sports.*

FRAGMENT: *Her middle-school son.* (no predicate)

CORRECTED: *Her middle-school son played on the soccer team.*

FRAGMENT: *Before every game.* (neither subject nor predicate)

CORRECTED: *Before every game, he tried to teach his mom the rules.*

In your writing, fragments may be a result of haste or incorrect punctuation. Sometimes fixing a fragment will be a matter of attaching it to a preceding or following sentence.

FRAGMENT: *She made an effort. But just couldn't make sense of the game.*

CORRECTED: *She made an effort but just couldn't make sense of the game.*

10.2 CORRECTING RUN-ON SENTENCES

A **run-on sentence** is made up of two or more sentences written as though they were one. Some run-ons have no punctuation within them. Others may have only commas where conjunctions or stronger punctuation marks are necessary. Use your judgment in correcting run-on sentences, as you have choices. You can change a run-on to two sentences if the thoughts are not closely connected. If the thoughts are closely related, you can keep the run-on as one sentence by adding a semicolon or a conjunction.

RUN–ON: *Most parents watched the game his mother read a book instead.*

MAKE TWO SENTENCES: *Most parents watched the game. His mother read a book instead.*

RUN–ON: *Most parents watched the game they played sports themselves.*

USE A SEMICOLON: *Most parents watched the game; they played sports themselves.*

ADD A CONJUNCTION: *Most parents watched the game since they played sports themselves.*

WATCH OUT! When you form compound sentences, make sure you use appropriate punctuation: a comma before a coordinating conjunction, a semicolon when there is no coordinating conjunction. A very common mistake is to use a comma without a conjunction or instead of a semicolon. This error is called a **comma splice.**

INCORRECT: *He finished the job, he left the village.*

CORRECT: *He finished the job, and he left the village.*

11 Subject-Verb Agreement

The subject and verb in a clause must agree in number. Agreement means that if the subject is singular, the verb is also singular, and if the subject is plural, the verb is also plural.

11.1 BASIC AGREEMENT

Fortunately, agreement between subjects and verbs in English is simple. Most verbs show the difference between singular and plural only in the third person of the present tense. In the present tense, the third-person singular form ends in **-s.**

Present-Tense Verb Forms	
Singular	**Plural**
I sleep	we sleep
you sleep	you sleep
she, he, it sleeps	they sleep

11.2 AGREEMENT WITH *BE*

The verb *be* presents special problems in agreement, because this verb does not follow the usual verb patterns.

Forms of *Be*			
Present Tense		**Past Tense**	
Singular	**Plural**	**Singular**	**Plural**
I am	we are	I was	we were
you are	you are	you were	you were
she, he, it is	they are	she, he, it was	they were

11.3 WORDS BETWEEN SUBJECT AND VERB

A verb agrees only with its subject. When words come between a subject and a verb, ignore them when considering proper agreement. Identify the subject and make sure the verb agrees with it.

EXAMPLES: *The poem I read describes a moose. The moose in the poem searches for a place where he belongs.*

11.4 AGREEMENT WITH COMPOUND SUBJECTS

Use plural verbs with most compound subjects joined by the word *and.*

EXAMPLE: *My father and his friends play chess every day.*

To confirm that you need a plural verb, you could substitute the plural pronoun *they* for *my father and his friends.*

If a compound subject is thought of as a unit, use a singular verb. Test this by substituting the singular pronoun *it.*

EXAMPLE: *A bagel and cream cheese [it] is my usual breakfast.*

Use a singular verb with a compound subject that is preceded by *each, every,* or *many a.*

EXAMPLES: *Each novel and short story seems grounded in personal experience.*

When the parts of a compound subject are joined by *or, nor,* or the correlative conjunctions *either . . . or* or *neither . . . nor,* make the verb agree with the noun or pronoun nearest the verb.

EXAMPLES: *Cookies or ice cream is my favorite dessert.*
Either Cheryl or her parents are being invited.
Neither ice storms nor snow is predicted today.

11.5 PERSONAL PRONOUNS AS SUBJECTS

When using a personal pronoun as a subject, make sure to match it with the correct form of the verb *be.* (See the chart in Section 11.2.) Note especially that the pronoun *you* takes the forms *are* and *were,* regardless of whether it is singular or plural.

WATCH OUT! *You is* and *you was* are nonstandard forms and should be avoided in writing and speaking. *We was* and *they was* are also forms to be avoided.

INCORRECT: *You was a good student.*

CORRECT: *You were a good student.*

INCORRECT: *They was starting a new school.*

CORRECT: *They were starting a new school.*

11.6 INDEFINITE PRONOUNS AS SUBJECTS

Some indefinite pronouns are always singular; some are always plural.

Singular Indefinite Pronouns			
another	either	neither	one
anybody	every-body	nobody	somebody
anyone	everyone	no one	someone
anything	every-thing	nothing	something
each	much		

EXAMPLES: *Each of the writers was given an award.*
Somebody in the room upstairs is sleeping.

Plural Indefinite Pronouns			
both	few	many	several

EXAMPLES: *Many of the books in our library are not in circulation.*
Few have been returned recently.

Still other indefinite pronouns may be either singular or plural.

Singular or Plural Indefinite Pronouns		
all	more	none
any	most	some

The number of the indefinite pronoun *any* or *none* often depends on the intended meaning.

EXAMPLES: *Any of these stories has an important message.* (any one story)
Any of these stories have important messages. (all of the many stories)

The indefinite pronouns *all, some, more, most,* and *none* are singular when they refer to quantities or parts of things. They are plural when they refer to numbers of individual things. Context will usually give a clue.

EXAMPLES: *All of the flour is gone.* (referring to a quantity)
All of the flowers are gone. (referring to individual items)

11.7 INVERTED SENTENCES

A sentence in which the subject follows the verb is called an **inverted sentence.** A subject can follow a verb or part of a verb phrase in a question; a sentence beginning with **here** or **there**; or a sentence in which an adjective, an adverb, or a phrase is placed first.

EXAMPLES: *Here comes the scariest part. There goes the hero with a flashlight.*
Then, into the room rushes a big black cat!

TIP To check subject-verb agreement in some inverted sentences, place the subject before the verb. For example, change **There are many people** to **Many people are there.**

11.8 SENTENCES WITH PREDICATE NOMINATIVES

In a sentence containing a predicate noun (nominative), the verb should agree with the subject, not the predicate noun.

EXAMPLES: *Josh's jokes are a source of laughter.* (*Jokes* is the subject—not *source*—and it takes the plural verb *are.*)
One source of laughter is Josh's jokes. (The subject is *source*—not *jokes*—and it takes the singular verb *is.*)

11.9 *DON'T* AND *DOESN'T* AS AUXILIARY VERBS

The auxiliary verb **doesn't** is used with singular subjects and with the personal pronouns **she, he,** and **it.** The auxiliary verb **don't** is used with plural subjects and with the personal pronouns **I, we, you,** and **they.**

SINGULAR: *The humor doesn't escape us. Doesn't the limerick about Dougal MacDougal make you laugh?*

PLURAL: *We don't usually forget such funny images.*
Don't people like to recite limericks?

11.10 COLLECTIVE NOUNS AS SUBJECTS

Collective nouns are singular nouns that name groups of persons or things. *Team,* for example, is a collective name of a group of individuals. A collective noun takes a singular verb when the group acts as a single unit. It takes a plural verb when the members of the group act separately.

EXAMPLES: *The class creates a bulletin board of limericks.* (The class as a whole creates the board.)
The faculty enjoy teaching poetry. (The individual members enjoy teaching poetry.)

11.11 RELATIVE PRONOUNS AS SUBJECTS

When the relative pronoun *who, which,* or *that* is used as a subject in an adjective clause, the verb in the clause must agree in number with the antecedent of the pronoun.

SINGULAR: *The* **myth** *from ancient Greece* **that** *interests me most is "The Apple of Discord I."*

The antecedent of the relative pronoun *that* is the singular *myth*; therefore, *that* is singular and must take the singular verb *interests.*

PLURAL: *James Berry and Sandra Cisneros are writers who publish short stories.*

The antecedent of the relative pronoun *who* is the plural subject *writers.* Therefore *who* is plural, and it takes the plural verb *publish.*

Grammar Practice

Locate the subject of each verb in parentheses in the sentences below. Then choose the correct verb form.

1. George Graham Vest's "Tribute to a Dog" (describes, describe) the friendship and loyalty canines show humans.
2. Stories about a dog (is, are) touching.
3. Besides dogs, few animals (has, have) an innate desire to please humans.
4. Many traits specific to dogs (bring, brings) their owners happiness.
5. No matter if the owner is rich or poor, a dog, and all canines for that matter, (acts, act) with love and devotion.
6. There (is, are) countless reasons to own a dog.
7. A dog's unselfishness (endears, endear) it to its owner.
8. (Doesn't, Don't) a dog offer its owner constant affection and guardianship?
9. A man's dog (stands, stand) by him in prosperity and in poverty.
10. A dog (guards, guard) his master as if the owner was a prince.

Vocabulary and Spelling

The key to becoming an independent reader is to develop a tool kit of vocabulary strategies. By learning and practicing the strategies, you'll know what to do when you encounter unfamiliar words while reading. You'll also know how to refine the words you use for different situations—personal, school, and work.

Being a good speller is important when communicating your ideas in writing. Learning basic spelling rules and checking your spelling in a dictionary will help you spell words that you may not use frequently.

1 Using Context Clues

The context of a word is made up of the punctuation marks, words, sentences, and paragraphs that surround the word. A word's context can give you important clues about its meaning.

1.1 GENERAL CONTEXT

Sometimes you need to determine the meaning of an unfamiliar word by reading all the information in a passage.

> *Kevin set out the broom, a dustpan, and three trash bags before beginning the monumental task of cleaning his room.*

You can figure out from the context that *monumental* means "huge."

1.2 SPECIFIC CONTEXT CLUES

Sometimes writers help you understand the meanings of words by providing specific clues such as those shown in the chart. When reading content area materials, use word, sentence, and paragraph clues to help you figure out meanings.

1.3 IDIOMS, SLANG, AND FIGURATIVE LANGUAGE

Use context clues to figure out the meanings of idioms, slang, and figurative language.

An **idiom** is an expression whose overall meaning differs from the meaning of the individual words.

> *The mosquitos drove us crazy on our hike.* (Drove us crazy means "irritated.")

Slang is informal language that features made-up words and ordinary words that are used to mean something different from their meanings in formal English.

> *That's a really cool backpack you're wearing.* (Cool means "excellent.")

Figurative language is language that communicates meaning beyond the literal meaning of the words.

> *Like a plunging horse, my car kicked up dirt, moved ahead quickly, and made a loud noise when I hit the gas.* (Kicked up dirt, moved ahead, and made a loud noise describe a plunging horse.)

Specific Context Clues		
Type of Clue	**Key Words/ Phrases**	**Example**
Definition or restatement of the meaning of the word	or, which is, that is, in other words, also known as, also called	In 1909, a French inventor flew a *monoplane*, or a **single-winged plane.**

continued

Type of Clue	Key Words/ Phrases	Example
Example following an unfamiliar word	such as, like, as if, for example, especially, including	The stunt pilot performed *acrobatics,* such as **dives and wingwalking.**
Comparison with a more familiar word or concept	as, like, also, similar to, in the same way, likewise	The doctor prescribed a *bland* diet, similar to the **rice and potatoes** he was already eating.
Contrast with a familiar word or experience	unlike, but, however, although, on the other hand, on the contrary	The moon will *diminish* at the end of the month; however it will **grow** during the first part of the month.
Cause-and-effect relationship in which one term is familiar	because, since, when, consequently, as a result, therefore	Because their general was *valiant,* the soldiers **showed courage** in battle.

2 Analyzing Word Structure

Many words can be broken into smaller parts. These word parts include base words, roots, prefixes, and suffixes.

2.1 BASE WORDS

A **base word** is a word part that by itself is also a word. Other words or word parts can be added to base words to form new words.

2.2 ROOTS

A **root** is a word part that contains the core meaning of the word. Many English words contain roots that come from older languages such as Greek and Latin. Knowing the meanings of a word's root can help you determine the word's meaning.

Root	Meaning	Example
auto (Greek)	self, same	**auto**mobile
hydr (Greek)	water	**hydr**ant
cent (Latin)	hundred	**cent**ury
circ (Latin)	ring	**circ**le
port (Latin)	carry	**port**able

2.3 PREFIXES

A **prefix** is a word part attached to the beginning of a word. Most prefixes come from Greek, Latin, or Old English (OE).

Prefix	Meaning	Example
dis- (Latin)	not	**dis**honest
auto- (Greek)	self, same	**auto**biography
un- (OE)	the opposite of, not	**un**happy
re- (Latin)	carry, back	**re**pay

2.4 SUFFIXES

A **suffix** is a word part that appears at the end of a root or base word to form a new word.

Some suffixes do not change word meaning. These suffixes are:

- added to nouns to change the number of persons or objects
- added to verbs to change the tense
- added to modifiers to change the degree of comparison

Suffix	Meaning	Example
-s, -es	to change the number of a noun	lock + s = locks
-d, -ed, -ing	to change verb tense	stew + ed = stewed
-er, -est	to indicate comparison in modifiers	mild + er = milder soft + est = softest

Other suffixes can be added to the root or base to change the word's meaning. These suffixes can also determine a word's part of speech.

Suffix	Meaning	Example
-ion (Latin)	process of	operation
-able (Latin)	capable of	readable
-ize (Greek)	to cause or become	legalize

Strategies for Understanding New Words

- If you recognize elements—prefix, suffix, root, or base—of a word, you may be able to guess its meaning by analyzing one or two elements.
- Think about the way the word is used in the sentence. Use the context and the word parts to make a logical guess about the word's meaning.
- Look in a dictionary to see if you are correct.

3 Understanding Word Origins

3.1 ETYMOLOGIES

Etymologies show the origin and historical development of a word. When you study a word's history and origin, you can find out when, where, and how the word came to be.

em·per·or (ĕm′pər-ər) n. **1.** The male ruler of an empire. **2a.** The emperor butterfly. **b.** The emperor moth. [Middle English emperour, from Old French empereor, from Latin imperātor, from imperāre, to command: in-, in; see EN–[1] + parāre, to prepare.]

3.2 WORD FAMILIES

Words that have the same root make up a word family and have related meanings. The following chart shows a common Greek root and a common Latin root. Notice how the meanings of the example words are related to the meanings of their roots.

Latin Root	*man:* "hand"
English	**manual** by hand **manage** handle **manuscript** document written by hand
Greek Root	*phon:* "sound"
English	**telephone** an instrument that transmits sound **phonograph** machine that reproduces sound **phonetic** representing sounds of speech

3.3 FOREIGN WORDS IN ENGLISH

The English language includes words from other languages, such as French, Dutch, Spanish, Italian, and Chinese. Many words have stayed the way they were in their original language.

French	Dutch	Spanish	Italian
ballet	boss	canyon	diva
vague	caboose	rodeo	cupola
mirage	dock	bronco	spaghetti

Practice and Apply

Look up the origin and meaning of each word listed in the preceding chart. Then use each word in a sentence.

4 Synonyms and Antonyms

4.1 SYNONYMS

A **synonym** is a word with a meaning similar to that of another word. You can find synonyms in a thesaurus or a dictionary. In a dictionary, synonyms are often given as part of the definition of a word. The following word pairs are synonyms:

satisfy/please   occasionally/sometimes

rob/steal   schedule/agenda

4.2 ANTONYMS

An **antonym** is a word with a meaning opposite that of another word. The following word pairs are antonyms.

accurate/incorrect   similar/different

fresh/stale   unusual/ordinary

5 Denotation and Connotation

5.1 DENOTATION

A word's dictionary meaning is called its **denotation.** For example, the denotation of the word *thin* is "having little flesh; spare; lean."

5.2 CONNOTATION

The images or feelings you connect to a word add a finer shade of meaning, called **connotation.** The connation of a word goes beyond its basic dictionary definition. Writers use connotations of words to communicate positive or negative feelings.

Positive	Negative
slender	scrawny
thrifty	cheap
young	immature

Make sure you understand the denotation and connotation of a word when you read it or use it in your writing.

6 Analogies

An **analogy** is a comparison between two things that are similar in some way but are otherwise not alike. Analogies are sometimes used in writing when unfamiliar subjects or ideas are explained in terms of familiar ones. Analogies often appear on tests as well. In an analogy problem, the analogy is expressed using two groups of words. The relationship between the first pair of words is the same as the relationship between the second pair of words. Some analogy problems are expressed like this:

in love : hate :: war : _____

a. soldier **b.** peace **c.** battle **d.** argument

Follow these steps to determine the correct answer:

- Read the problem as "*Love* is to *hate* as *war* is to . . . ."
- Ask yourself how the words *love* and *hate* are related. (*Love* and *hate* are antonyms.)
- Ask yourself which answer choice is an antonym of *war*. (*Peace* is an antonym of *war*, therefore *peace* is the best answer.)

7 Homonyms, Homographs, and Homophones

7.1 HOMONYMS

Homonyms are words that have the same spelling and sound but have different meanings.

> The snake shed its skin in the shed behind the house.

Shed can mean "to lose by natural process," but an identically spelled word means "a small structure."

Sometimes only one of the meanings of a homonym may be familiar to you. Use context clues to help you figure out the meaning of an unfamiliar word.

7.2 HOMOGRAPHS

Homographs are words that are spelled the same but have different meanings and origins. Some are also pronounced differently, as in these examples:

> Please close the door. (klōz)
>
> That was a close call. (klōs)

If you see a word used in a way that is unfamiliar to you, check a dictionary to see if it is a homograph.

7.3 HOMOPHONES

Homophones are words that sound alike but have different meanings and spellings. The following homophones are frequently misused:

it's/its   they're/their/there

to/too/two   stationary/stationery

Many misused homophones are pronouns and contractions. Whenever you are unsure whether to write *your* or *you're* and *who's* or *whose,* ask yourself if you mean *you are* and *who is/has.* If you do, write the contraction. For other homophones, such as *fair* and *fare,* use the meaning of the word to help you decide which one to use.

8 Words with Multiple Meanings

Over time, some words have acquired additional meanings that are based on the original meaning.

> I had to be replaced in the cast of the play because of the cast on my arm.

These two uses of cast have different meanings, but both of them have the same origin. You will find all the meanings of cast listed in one entry in the dictionary. Context can also help you figure out the meaning of the word.

9 Specialized Vocabulary

Specialized vocabulary is a group of terms suited to a particular field of study or work. For example, science, mathematics, and history all have their own technical or specialized vocabularies. To figure out specialized terms, you can use context clues and reference sources, such as dictionaries on specific subjects, atlases, or manuals.

10 Using Reference Sources

10.1 DICTIONARIES

A **general dictionary** will tell you not only a word's definitions but also its pronunciation, syllabication, parts of speech, history, and origin.

tan·gi·ble (tăn´jə-bəl) *adj.*
1a. Discernible by the touch; palpable. **b.** Possible to touch. **c.** Possible to be treated as fact; real or concrete. **2.** Possible to understand or realize. **3.** *Law* That can be valued monetarily. [Late Latin *tangibilis*, from Latin *tangere*, to touch.]

1. Entry word syllabication
2. Pronunciation
3. Part of speech
4. Definitions
5. Etymology

A **specialized dictionary** focuses on terms related to a particular field of study or work. Use a dictionary to check the spelling of any word you are unsure of in your reading.

10.2 THESAURI

A **thesaurus** (plural, *thesauri*) is a dictionary of synonyms. A thesaurus can be especially helpful when you find yourself using the same modifiers over and over again.

10.3 SYNONYM FINDERS

A **synonym finder** is often included in wordprocessing software. It enables you to highlight a word and be shown a display of its synonyms.

10.4 GLOSSARIES

A **glossary** is a list of specialized terms and their definitions. It is often found in the back of a book and sometimes includes pronunciations. Many textbooks contain glossaries. In fact, this textbook has three glossaries: the **Glossary of Literary and Informational Terms,** the **Glossary of Academic Vocabulary,** and the **Glossary of Critical Vocabulary.** Use these glossaries to help you understand how terms are used in this textbook.

11 Spelling Rules

11.1 WORDS ENDING IN A SILENT *E*

Before adding a suffix beginning with a vowel or *y* to a word ending in a silent *e,* drop the *e* (with some exceptions).

> amaze + -ing = amazing
> love + -able = lovable
> create + -ed = created
> nerve + -ous = nervous

Exceptions: *change + -able = changeable; courage + -ous = courageous*

When adding a suffix beginning with a consonant to a word ending in a silent *e,* keep the *e* (with some exceptions).

> late + -ly = lately
> spite + -ful = spiteful
> noise + -less = noiseless
> state + -ment = statement

Exceptions: *truly, argument, ninth, wholly, awful,* and *others*

When a suffix beginning with *a* or *o* is added to a word with a final silent *e,* the final *e* is usually retained if it is preceded by a soft *c* or a soft *g.*

> bridge + -able = bridgeable
> peace + -able = peaceable
> outrage + -ous = outrageous
> advantage + -ous = advantageous

When a suffix beginning with a vowel is added to words ending in *ee* or *oe,* the final, silent *e* is retained.

> agree + -ing = agreeing
> free + -ing = freeing
> hoe + -ing = hoeing
> see + -ing = seeing

11.2 WORDS ENDING IN *Y*

Before adding most suffixes to a word that ends in *y* preceded by a consonant, change the *y* to *i.*

> easy + -est = easiest

crazy + -est = craziest
silly + -ness = silliness
marry + -age = marriage

Exceptions: *dryness, shyness,* and *slyness*

However, when you add **-ing,** the **y** does not change.

empty + -ed = emptied   but
empty + -ing = emptying

When adding a suffix to a word that ends in **y** preceded by a vowel, the **y** usually does not change.

play + -er = player
employ + -ed = employed
coy + -ness = coyness
pay + -able = payable

11.3 WORDS ENDING IN A CONSONANT

In one-syllable words that end in one consonant preceded by one short vowel, double the final consonant before adding a suffix beginning with a vowel, such as **-ed** or **-ing.** These are sometimes called 1+1+1 words.

dip + -ed = dipped
set + -ing = setting
slim + -est = slimmest
fit + -er = fitter

The rule does not apply to words of one syllable that end in a consonant preceded by two vowels.

feel + -ing = feeling
peel + -ed = peeled
reap + -ed = reaped
loot + -ed = looted

In words of more than one syllable, double the final consonant when (1) the word ends with one consonant preceded by one vowel and (2) when the word is accented on the last syllable.

be•gin´   per•mit´   re•fer´

In the following examples, note that in the new words formed with suffixes, the accent remains on the same syllable.

be•gin´ + -ing = be•gin´ning = beginning

per•mit´ + -ed = per•mit´ted = permitted

Exceptions: In some words with more than one syllable, though the accent remains on the same syllable when a suffix is added, the final consonant is nevertheless not doubled, as in the following examples.

tra´vel + er = tra´vel•er = traveler
mar´ket + er = mar´ket•er = marketer

In the following examples, the accent does not remain on the same syllable; thus, the final consonant is not doubled:

re•fer´ + -ence = ref´er•ence = reference
con•fer´ + -ence = con´fer•ence = conference

11.4 PREFIXES AND SUFFIXES

When adding a prefix to a word, do not change the spelling of the base word. When a prefix creates a double letter, keep both letters.

dis- + approve = disapprove
re- + build = rebuild
ir- + regular = irregular
mis- + spell = misspell
anti- + trust = antitrust
il- + logical = illogical

When adding **-ly** to a word ending in **l,** keep both **l's.** When adding **-ness** to a word ending in **n,** keep both **n's.**

careful + -ly = carefully
sudden + -ness = suddenness
final + -ly = finally
thin + -ness = thinness

11.5 FORMING PLURAL NOUNS

To form the plural of most nouns, just add **-s.**

prizes   dreams   circles   stations

For most singular nouns ending in **o,** add **-s.**

solos   halos   studios   photos   pianos

For a few nouns ending in **o,** add **-es.**

heroes   tomatoes   potatoes   echoes

When a singular noun ends in **s, sh, ch, x,** or **z,** add **-es.**

waitresses   brushes   ditches
axes   buzzes

When a singular noun ends in **y** with a consonant before it, change the **y** to **i** and add **-es.**

> army—armies candy—candies
> baby—babies diary—diaries
> ferry—ferries conspiracy—conspiracies

When a vowel (**a, e, i, o, u**) comes before the **y,** just add **-s.**

> boy—boys way—ways
> array—arrays alloy—alloys
> weekday—weekdays jockey—jockeys

For most nouns ending in **f** or **fe,** change the **f** to **v** and add **-es** or **-s.**

> life—lives loaf—loaves
> calf—calves knife—knives
> thief—thieves shelf—shelves

For some nouns ending in **f,** add **-s** to make the plural.

> roofs chiefs reefs beliefs

Some nouns have the same form for both singular and plural.

> deer sheep moose salmon trout

For some nouns, the plural is formed in a special way.

> man—men goose—geese
> ox—oxen woman—women
> mouse—mice child—children

For a compound noun written as one word, form the plural by changing the last word in the compound to its plural form.

> stepchild—stepchildren firefly—fireflies

If a compound noun is written as a hyphenated word or as two separate words, change the most important word to the plural form.

> brother-in-law—brothers-in-law
> life jacket—life jackets

11.6 FORMING POSSESSIVES

If a noun is singular, add **'s.**

> mother—my mother's car
> Ross—Ross's desk

Exception: An apostrophe alone is used to indicate the possessive case with the names Jesus and Moses and with certain names in classical mythology (such as Zeus).

If a noun is plural and ends with **s,** add an apostrophe.

> parents—my parents' car
> the Santinis—the Santinis' house

If a noun is plural but does not end in **s,** add **'s.**

> people—the people's choice
> women—the women's coats

11.7 SPECIAL SPELLING PROBLEMS

Only one English word ends in **-sede:** supersede. Three words end in **-ceed: exceed, proceed,** and **succeed.** All other verbs ending in the sound "seed" are spelled with **-cede.**

> concede precede recede secede

In words with **ie** or **ei,** when the sound is long **e** (as in **she**), the word is spelled **ie** except after **c** (with some exceptions).

i before **e**	thief	relieve	field
piece	grieve	pier	
except	conceit	perceive	ceiling
after c	receive	receipt	
Exceptions:	either	neither	weird
leisure	seize		

11.8 USING A SPELL CHECKER

Most computer word processing programs have spell checkers to catch misspellings. Most computer spell checkers do not correct errors automatically. Instead, they stop at a word and highlight it. Sometimes the highlighted word may not be misspelled; it may be that the program's dictionary does not include the word. Keep in mind that spell checkers will identify only misspelled words, not misused words. For example, if you used **their** when you meant to use **there,** a spelling checker will not catch the error.

12 Commonly Confused Words

Words	Definitions	Examples
accept/ except	The verb *accept* means "to receive" or "to believe." *Except* is usually a preposition meaning "excluding."	Did the teacher **accept** your report? Everyone smiled for the photographer **except** Jody.
advice/advise	*Advise* is a verb. *Advice* is a noun naming that which an *adviser* gives.	I **advise** you to take that job. Whom should I ask for **advice**?
affect/effect	As a verb, *affect* means "to influence." *Effect* as a verb means "to cause." If you want a noun, you will almost always want *effect*.	How deeply did the news **affect** him? The students tried to **effect** a change in school policy. What **effect** did the acidic soil produce in the plants?
all ready/ already	*All ready* is an adjective meaning "fully ready." *Already* is an adverb meaning "before" or "by this time."	He was **all ready** to go at noon. I have **already** seen that movie.
desert/ dessert	*Desert* (dĕz´ərt) means "a dry, sandy, barren region." *Desert* (dĭ-zûrt´) means "to abandon." *Dessert* (dĭ-zûrt´) is a sweet, such as cake.	The Sahara, in North Africa, is the world's largest **desert**. The night guard did not **desert** his post. Alison's favorite **dessert** is chocolate cake.
among/ between	*Between* is used when you are speaking of only two things. *Among* is used for three or more.	**Between** ice cream and sherbet, I prefer the latter. Gary Soto is **among** my favorite authors.
bring/take	*Bring* is used to denote motion toward a speaker or place. *Take* is used to denote motion away from such a person or place.	**Bring** the books over here, and I will **take** them to the library.
fewer/less	*Fewer* refers to the number of separate, countable units. *Less* refers to bulk quantity.	We have **less** literature and **fewer** selections in this year's curriculum.

contined

Words	Definitions	Examples
leave/let	*Leave* means "to allow something to remain behind." *Let* means "to permit."	The librarian will **leave** some books on display but will not **let** us borrow any.
lie/lay	To *lie* is "to rest or recline." It does not take an object. *Lay* always takes an object.	Rover loves to **lie** in the sun. We always **lay** some bones next to him.
loose/lose	*Loose* (lo͞os) means "free, not restrained." *Lose* (lo͞oz) means "to misplace" or "to fail to find."	Who turned the horses **loose**? I hope we won't **lose** any of them.
passed/past	*Passed* is the past tense of *pass* and means "went by." *Past* is an adjective that means "of a former time." *Past* is also a noun that means "time gone by."	We **passed** through the Florida Keys during our vacation. My **past** experiences have taught me to set my alarm. Ebenezer Scrooge is a character who relives his **past**.
than/then	Use *than* in making comparisons. Use *then* on all other occasions.	Ramon is stronger **than** Mark. Cut the grass and **then** trim the hedges.
two/too/to	*Two* is the number. *Too* is an adverb meaning "also" or "very." Use *to* before a verb or as a preposition.	Meg had **to** go **to** town, **too**. We had **too** much reading **to** do. **Two** chapters is **too** many.
their/there/they're	*Their* means "belonging to them." *There* means "in that place." *They're* is the contraction for "they are."	**There** is a movie playing at 9 P.M. **They're** going to see it with me. Sakara and Jessica drove away in **their** car after the movie.

Using the Glossary

This glossary is an alphabetical list of vocabulary words found in the selections in this book. Use this glossary just as you would a dictionary— to determine the meanings, parts of speech, pronunciation, and syllabication of words. (Some technical, foreign, and more obscure words in this book are not listed here but are defined for you in the footnotes that accompany many of the selections.)

Many words in the English language have more than one meaning. This glossary gives the meanings that apply to the words as they are used in the selections in this book. Words closely related in form and meaning are listed together in one entry (for instance, *consumption* and *consume*), and the definition is given for the first form.

The following abbreviations are used to identify parts of speech of words:

adj. adjective *adv.* adverb *n.* noun *v.* verb

Each word's pronunciation is given in parentheses. A guide to the pronunciation symbols appears in the Pronunciation Key below. The stress marks in the Pronunciation Key are used to indicate the force given to each syllable in a word. They can also help you determine where words are divided into syllables.

For more information about the words in this glossary or for information about words not listed here, consult a dictionary.

Pronunciation Key

Symbol	Examples	Symbol	Examples	Symbol	Examples	Sounds in Foreign Words	
ă	pat	l	lid, needle* (nĕd'l)	sh	ship, dish	KH	German i**ch**, a**ch**; Scottish lo**ch**
ā	pay			t	tight, stopped		
ä	father	m	mum	th	thin	N	French, bon (bôn)
âr	care	n	no, sudden* (sud'n)	th	this	œ	French feu, œuf; German schön
b	bib			ŭ	cut		
ch	church	ng	thing	ûr	urge, term, firm, word, heard	ü	French tu; German uber
d	deed, milled	ŏ	pot				
ĕ	pet	ō	toe	v	valve		
ē	bee	ô	caught, paw	w	with		
f	fife, phase, rough	oi	noise	y	yes		
g	gag	ŏŏ	took	z	zebra, xylem		
h	hat	ōō	boot	zh	vision, pleasure, garage		
hw	which	ŏŏr	lure				
ĭ	pit	ôr	core	ə	about, item, edible, gallop, circus		
ī	pie, by	ou	out				
îr	pier	p	pop	ər	butter		
j	judge	r	roar				
k	kick, cat, pique	s	sauce				

*In English the consonants *l* and *n* often constitute complete syllables by themselves.

Stress Marks

The relevant emphasis with which the syllables of a word or phrase are spoken, called stress, is indicated in three different ways. The strongest, or primary, stress is marked with a bold mark ('). An intermediate, or secondary, level of stress is marked with a similar but lighter mark ('). The weakest stress is unmarked. Words of one syllable show no stress mark.

Glossary of Literary and Informational Terms

Act An act is a major division within a play, similar to a chapter in a book. Each act may be further divided into smaller sections, called scenes. Plays can have as many as five acts, or as few as one.

Adventure Story An adventure story is a literary work in which action is the main element. An **adventure novel** usually focuses on a main character who is on a mission and faces many challenges and choices.

Alliteration Alliteration is the repetition of consonant sounds at the beginning of words. Note the repetition of the **d** sound in this line: The **d**aring boy **d**ove into the **d**eep sea.

Allusion An allusion is a reference to a famous person, place, event, or work of literature.

Almanac *See* Reference Works.

Analogy An analogy is a comparison between two things that are alike in some way. Often, writers use analogies to explain unfamiliar subjects or ideas in terms of familiar ones.
See also **Metaphor; Simile.**

Anecdote An anecdote is a short account of an event that is usually intended to entertain or make a point.

Antagonist The antagonist is a force working against the protagonist, or main character, in a story, play, or novel. The antagonist is usually another character but can be a force of nature, society itself, or an internal force within the main character.
See also Protagonist.

Appeal to Authority An appeal to authority is an attempt to persuade an audience by making reference to people who are experts on a subject.

Argument An argument is speaking or writing that expresses a position on a problem and supports it with reasons and evidence. An argument often anticipates and answers objections that opponents might raise.
See also Claim; Counterargument; Evidence.

Assonance Assonance is the repetition of vowel sounds within nonrhyming words. An example of assonance is the repetition of the o͞o sound in the following line: Do you like blue?

Assumption An assumption is an opinion or belief that is taken for granted. It can be about a specific situation, a person, or the world in general. Assumptions are often unstated.

Audience The audience of a piece of writing is the group of readers that the writer is addressing. A writer considers his or her audience when deciding on a subject, a purpose, a tone, and a style in which to write.

Author's Message An author's message is the main idea or theme of a particular work.
See also Main Idea; Theme.

Author's Perspective An author's perspective is the combination of ideas, values, feelings, and beliefs that influences the way the writer looks at a topic. **Tone,** or attitude, often reveals an author's perspective.
See also Author's Purpose; Tone.

Author's Position An author's position is his or her opinion on an issue or topic.
See also Claim.

Author's Purpose A writer usually writes for one or more of these purposes: to express thoughts or feelings, to inform or explain, to persuade, or to entertain.
See also Author's Perspective.

Autobiography An autobiography is a writer's account of his or her own life. In almost every case, it is told from the first-person point of view. An autobiography focuses on the most important events and people in the writer's life over a period of time.
See also Memoir; Personal Narrative.

Ballad A ballad is a type of narrative poem that tells a story and was originally meant to be sung or recited. Because it tells a story, a ballad has a setting, a plot, and characters. **Folk ballads** were composed orally and handed down by word of mouth from generation to generation.

Bias In a piece of writing, the author's bias is the side of an issue that he or she favors. Words with extremely positive or negative connotations are often a signal of an author's bias.

Bibliography A bibliography is a list of related books and other materials used to write a text. Bibliographies can be good sources for further study on a subject.
See also Works Consulted.

Biography A biography is the true account of a person's life, written by another person. As such, biographies are usually told from a third-person point of view. The writer of a biography—a **biographer**—usually researches his or her subject in order to present accurate information. The best biographers strive for honesty and balance in their accounts of their subjects' lives.

Business Correspondence Business correspondence is written business communications such as business letters, e-mails, and memos. In general, business correspondence is brief, to the point, clear, courteous, and professional.

Cast of Characters In the script of a play, a cast of characters is a list of all the characters in the play, usually in order of appearance. It may include a brief description of each character.

Cause and Effect Two events are related by cause and effect when one event brings about, or causes, the other. The event that happens first is the **cause**; the one that follows is the **effect.** Cause and effect is also a way of organizing an entire piece of writing. It helps writers show the relationships between events or ideas.

Character Characters are the people, animals, or imaginary creatures who take part in the action of a work of literature. Like real people, characters display certain qualities, or **character traits,** that develop and change over time, and they usually have **motivations,** or reasons, for their behaviors.

Main character: Main characters are the most important characters in literary works. Generally, the plot of a short story focuses on one main character, but a novel may have several main characters.

Minor characters: The less important characters in a literary work are known as minor characters. The story is not centered on them, but they help carry out the action of the story and help the reader learn more about the main character.

Dynamic character: A dynamic character is one who undergoes important changes as a plot unfolds. The changes occur because of the character's actions and experiences in the story. The changes are usually internal and may be good or bad. Main characters are usually, though not always, dynamic.

Static character: A static character is one who remains the same throughout a story. The character may experience events and interact with other characters, but he or she is not changed because of them.

See also Characterization; Character Traits.

Character Development Characters that change during a story are said to undergo character development. Any character can change, but main characters usually develop the most.

See also Character: Dynamic Character.

Characterization The way a writer creates and develops characters is known as characterization. There are four basic methods of characterization.

- The writer may make direct comments about a character through the voice of the narrator.
- The writer may describe the character's physical appearance.
- The writer may present the character's own thoughts, speech, and actions.
- The writer may present the thoughts, speech, and actions of other characters.

See also Character; Character Traits.

Character Traits Character traits are the qualities shown by a character. Traits may be physical (tall) or expressions of personality (confidence). Writers reveal the traits of their characters through methods of characterization. Sometimes writers directly state a character's traits, but more often readers need to infer traits from a character's words, actions, thoughts, appearance, and relationships. Examples of words that describe traits include **brave, considerate,** and **rude.**

Chronological Order Chronological order is the arrangement of events in their order of occurrence. This type of organization is used in fictional narratives and in historical writing, biography, and autobiography.

Claim In an argument, a claim is the writer's position on an issue or problem. Although an argument focuses on supporting one claim, a writer may make more than one claim in a text.

Clarify Clarifying is a reading strategy that helps readers understand or make clear what they are reading. Readers usually clarify by rereading, reading aloud, or discussing.

Classification Classification is a pattern of organization in which objects, ideas, and/or information are presented in groups, or classes, based on common characteristics.

Cliché A cliché is an overused expression. "Better late than never" and "hard as nails" are common examples. Good writers generally avoid clichés unless they are using them in dialogue to indicate something about a character's personality.

Climax The climax stage is the point of greatest interest in a story or play. The climax usually occurs toward the end of a story, after the reader has understood the **conflict** and become emotionally involved with the characters. At the climax, the conflict is resolved and the outcome of the plot usually becomes clear.

See also Plot.

Comedy A comedy is a dramatic work that is light and often humorous in tone, usually ending happily with a peaceful resolution of the main conflict.

Compare and Contrast To compare and contrast is to identify the similarities and differences of two or more subjects. Compare and contrast is also a pattern of organizing an entire piece of writing.

See also Pattern of Organization.

Conclusion A conclusion is a statement of belief based on evidence, experience, and reasoning. A valid conclusion is one that logically follows from the facts or statements upon which it is based.

Conflict A conflict is a struggle between opposing forces. Almost every story has a main conflict—a conflict that is the story's focus. An **external conflict** involves a character who struggles against a force outside him- or herself, such as nature, a physical obstacle, or another character. An **internal conflict** is one that occurs within a character. For example, a character with an internal conflict might struggle with fear.

See also Plot.

Connect Connecting is a reader's process of relating the content of a text to his or her own knowledge and experience.

Connotation A word's connotations are the ideas and feelings associated with the word, as opposed to its dictionary definition. For example, the word *bread,* in addition to its basic meaning ("a baked food made from flour and other ingredients"), has connotations of life and general nourishment.

See also Denotation.

Consumer Documents Consumer documents are printed materials that accompany products and services. They usually provide information about the use, care, operation, or assembly of the product or service they accompany. Some common consumer documents are applications, contracts, warranties, manuals, instructions, labels, brochures, and schedules.

Context Clues When you encounter an unfamiliar word, you can often use context clues to understand it. Context clues are the words or phrases surrounding the word that provide hints about the word's meaning.

Counterargument A counterargument is an argument made to oppose another argument. A good argument anticipates opposing viewpoints and provides counterarguments to disprove them.

Couplet A couplet is a rhymed pair of lines. A couplet may be written in any rhythmic pattern. For example, Follow your heart's desire/And good things may transpire.

See also Rhyme; Stanza.

Credibility Credibility is the believability or trustworthiness of a source and the information it provides.

Critical Essay *See* Essay.

Critical Review A critical review is an evaluation or critique by a reviewer, or critic. Types of reviews include film reviews, book reviews, music reviews, and art show reviews.

Cultural Values Cultural values are the behaviors that a society expects from its people.

Database A database is a collection of information that can be quickly and easily accessed and searched and from which information can be easily retrieved. It is frequently presented in an electronic format.

Debate A debate is an organized exchange of opinions on an issue. In school settings, debate is usually a formal contest in which two opposing teams defend and attack a proposition.

See also Argument.

Deductive Reasoning Deductive reasoning is a way of thinking that begins with a generalization, presents a specific situation, and then moves forward with facts and evidence toward a logical conclusion. The following passage has a deductive argument embedded in it: "All students in the math class must take the quiz on Friday. Since Lana is in the class, she had better show up." This deductive argument can be broken down as follows: generalization—All students in the math class must take the quiz on Friday; specific situation—Lana is a student in the math class; conclusion—Therefore, Lana must take the math quiz.

Denotation A word's denotation is its dictionary definition.

See also **Connotation.**

Description Description is writing that helps a reader to picture events, objects, and characters. To create descriptions, writers often use **imagery**—words and phrases that appeal to the reader's senses.

Dialect A dialect is a form of a language that is spoken in a particular place or by a particular group of people. Dialects may feature unique pronunciations, vocabulary, and grammar.

Dialogue Dialogue is written conversation between two or more characters. Writers use dialogue to bring characters to life and to give readers insights into the characters' qualities, traits, and reactions to other characters. In fiction, dialogue is usually set off with quotation marks. In drama, stories are told primarily through dialogue.

Diary A diary is a daily record of a writer's thoughts, experiences, and feelings. As such, it is a type of autobiographical writing. A **journal** is another term for a diary.

Dictionary *See* **Reference Works.**

Drama A drama, or play, is a form of literature meant to be performed by actors in front of an audience. In a drama, the characters' dialogue and actions tell the story. The written form of a drama is called a script. A script usually includes dialogue, a cast of characters, and stage directions that give instructions about performing the drama. The person who writes the drama is known as the playwright or dramatist.

Draw Conclusions To draw a conclusion is to make a judgment or arrive at a belief based on evidence, experience, and reasoning.

Editorial An editorial is an opinion piece that usually appears on the editorial page of a newspaper or as part of a news broadcast. The editorial section of the newspaper presents opinions rather than objective news reports.

See also Op/Ed Piece.

Either/Or Fallacy An either/or fallacy is a statement that suggests that there are only two choices available in a situation when in fact there are more than two.

Emotional Appeal An emotional appeal is a message that creates strong feelings in order to make a point.

An appeal to fear is a message that taps into people's fear of losing their safety or security. An appeal to pity is a message that taps into people's sympathy and compassion for others to build support for an idea, a cause, or a proposed action. An appeal to vanity is a message that attempts to persuade by tapping into people's desire to feel good about themselves.

Encyclopedia *See* Reference Works.

Epic Poem An epic poem is a long narrative poem about the adventures of a hero whose actions reflect the ideals and values of a nation or a group of people.

Essay An essay is a short work of nonfiction that deals with a single subject. There are many types of essays. An **expository essay** presents or explains information and ideas. A **persuasive essay** attempts to convince the reader to adopt a certain viewpoint. A **critical essay** evaluates a situation or a work of art. A **personal essay** usually reflects the writer's experiences, feelings, and personality.

Ethical Appeal In an ethical appeal, a writer links a claim to a widely accepted value in order to gain moral support for the claim. The appeal also creates an image of the writer as a trustworthy, moral person.

Evaluate To evaluate is to examine something carefully and to judge its value or worth. A reader can evaluate the actions of a particular character, for example. A reader can also form opinions about the value of an entire work.

Evidence Evidence is a specific piece of information that supports a claim. Evidence can take the form of a fact, a quotation, an example, a statistic, or a personal experience, among other things.

Exaggeration An extreme overstatement of an idea is called an exaggeration. It is often used for purposes of emphasis or humor.

Exposition Exposition is the first stage of a typical story plot. The exposition provides important background information and introduces the setting and the important characters. The conflict the characters face may also be introduced in the exposition, or it may be introduced later, in the rising action.

See also Plot.

Expository Essay *See* Essay.

External Conflict *See* Conflict.

Fable A fable is a brief tale told to illustrate a moral or teach a lesson. Often the moral of a fable appears in a distinct and memorable statement near the tale's beginning or end.

See also Moral.

Fact Versus Opinion A **fact** is a statement that can be proved, or verified. An opinion, on the other hand, is a statement that cannot be proved because it expresses a person's beliefs, feelings, or thoughts.

See also Generalization; Inference.

Fallacious Reasoning Reasoning that includes errors in logic or fallacies.

Fallacy A fallacy is an error of reasoning. Typically, a fallacy is based on an incorrect inference or a misuse of evidence.

See also Either/Or Fallacy; Logical Appeal; Overgeneralization.

Falling Action The falling action is the stage of the plot in which the story begins to draw to a close. The falling action comes after the **climax** and before the **resolution,** also called denouement. Events in the falling action show the results of the important decision or action that happened at the climax. Tension eases as the falling action begins; however, the final outcome of the story is not yet fully worked out at this stage.

See also Climax; Plot.

Fantasy Fantasy is a type of fiction that is highly imaginative and portrays events, settings, or characters that are unrealistic. The setting might be a nonexistent world, the plot might involve magic or the supernatural, and the characters might have superhuman powers.

Faulty Reasoning *See* Fallacy.

Feature Article A feature article is an article in a newspaper or magazine about a topic of human interest or lifestyles.

Fiction Fiction is prose writing that tells an imaginary story. The writer of a short story or novel might invent all the events and characters or might base parts of the story on real people and events. The basic elements of fiction are plot, character, setting, and theme. Different types of fiction include realistic fiction, historical fiction, science fiction, and fantasy.

See also Novel; Novella; Short Story.

Figurative Language In figurative language, words are used in an imaginative way to express ideas that are not literally true. "Megan has a bee in her bonnet" is an example of figurative language. The sentence does not mean that Megan is wearing a bonnet, nor that there is an actual bee in it. Instead, it means that Megan is angry or upset about something. Figurative language is used for comparison, emphasis, and emotional effect.

See also Metaphor; Onomatopoeia; Personification; Simile.

First-Person Point of View *See* **Point of View.**

Flashback In a literary work, a flashback is an interruption of the action to present events that took place at an earlier time. A flashback provides information that can help a reader better understand a character's current situation.

Folklore The traditions, customs, and stories that are passed down within a culture are known as its folklore. Folklore includes various types of literature, such as legends, folk tales, myths, trickster tales, and fables.

See also Fable; Folk Tale; Myth.

Folk Tale A folk tale is a story that has been passed down from generation to generation by word of mouth. Folk tales may be set in the distant past and involve supernatural events. The characters in them may be animals, people, or superhuman beings.

Foreshadowing Foreshadowing occurs when a writer provides hints that suggest future events in a story. Foreshadowing creates suspense and makes readers eager to find out what will happen.

Form The structure or organization of a written work is often called its form. The form of a poem includes the arrangement of its words and lines on the page.

Free Verse Poetry without regular patterns of rhyme and rhythm is called free verse. Some poets use free verse to capture the sounds and rhythms of ordinary speech.

See also Rhyme, Rhythm.

Generalization A generalization is a broad statement about a class or category of people, ideas, or things based on a study of, or a belief about, only some of its members.

See also Overgeneralization; Stereotyping.

Genre The term *genre* refers to a category in which a work of literature is classified. The major genres in literature are fiction, nonfiction, poetry, and drama.

Government Publications Government publications are documents produced by government organizations. Pamphlets, brochures, and reports are just some of the many forms these publications take. Government publications can be good resources for a wide variety of topics.

Graphic Aid A graphic aid is a visual tool that is printed, handwritten, or drawn. Charts, diagrams, graphs, photographs, and maps are examples of graphic aids.

Graphic Organizer A graphic organizer is a "word picture"—a visual illustration of a verbal statement—that helps a reader understand a text. Charts, tables, webs, and diagrams can all be graphic organizers. Graphic organizers and graphic aids can look the same. However, graphic organizers and graphic aids do differ in how they are used. Graphic aids help deliver important information to students using a text. Graphic organizers are actually created by students themselves. They help students understand the text or organize information.

Haiku Haiku is a form of Japanese poetry in which 17 syllables are arranged in three lines of 5, 7, and 5 syllables. The rules of haiku are strict. In addition to following the syllabic count, the poet must create a clear picture that will evoke a strong emotional response in the reader. Nature is a particularly important source of inspiration for Japanese haiku poets, and details from nature are often the subjects of their poems.

Hero A hero is a main character or protagonist in a story. They are typically courageous, strong, honorable, and intelligent. They are protectors of society who hold back the forces of evil and fight to make the world a better place. In modern literature, a hero may simply be the most important character in a story. Such a hero is often an ordinary person with ordinary problems.

Historical Document Historical documents are writings that have played a significant role in human events. The Declaration of Independence, for example, is a historical document.

Historical Fiction A short story or a novel can be called historical fiction when it is set in the past and includes real places and real events of historical importance.

How-To Book A how-to book explains how to do something—usually an activity, a sport, or a household project.

Humor Humor is a quality that provokes laughter or amusement. Writers create humor through exaggeration, amusing descriptions, irony, and witty and insightful dialogue.

Idiom An idiom is an expression that has a meaning different from the meaning of its individual words.

For example, "to let the cat out of the bag" is an idiom meaning "to reveal a secret or surprise."

Imagery Imagery consists of words and phrases that appeal to a reader's five senses. Writers use sensory details to help the reader imagine how things look, feel, smell, sound, and taste.

Implied Main Idea *See* Main Idea.

Index The index of a book is an alphabetized list of important topics covered in the book and the page numbers on which they can be found. An index can be used to quickly find specific information about a topic.

Inductive Reasoning Inductive reasoning is the process of logical reasoning that starts with observations, examples, and facts and moves on to a general conclusion or principle.

Inference An inference is a logical guess that is made based on facts and one's own knowledge and experience.

Informational Text Informational text is writing that provides factual information. Examples include news reports, a science textbook, and lab reports. Informational text also includes literary nonfiction, such as personal essays, opinion pieces, speeches, biographies, and historical accounts.

Internal Conflict *See* Conflict.

Internet The Internet is a global, interconnected system of computer networks that allows for communication through e-mail, listservs, and the World Wide Web. The Internet connects computers and computer users throughout the world.

Interview An interview is a conversation conducted by a writer or reporter in which facts or statements are elicited from another person, recorded, and then broadcast or published.

Irony Irony is a contrast between what is expected and what actually exists or happens. Exaggeration and sarcasm are techniques writers use to express irony.

Journal A journal is a periodical publication used by legal, medical, and other professional organizations. The term may also be used to refer to a diary or daily record. *See* **Diary.**

Legend A legend is a story handed down from the past about a specific person, usually someone of heroic accomplishments. Legends usually have some basis in historical fact.

Limerick A limerick is a short, humorous poem made up of five lines. It usually has the rhyme scheme **aabba,** created by two rhyming couplets followed by a fifth line that rhymes with the first couplet. A limerick typically has a sing-song rhythm.

Literary Nonfiction *See* Narrative Nonfiction.

Loaded Language Loaded language consists of words with strongly positive or negative connotations intended to influence a reader's or listener's attitude.

Logical Appeal A logical appeal is a way of writing or speaking that relies on logic and facts. It appeals to people's reasoning or intellect rather than to their values or emotions. Flawed logical appeals—that is, errors in reasoning—are called logical fallacies.

See also **Fallacy.**

Logical Argument A logical argument is an argument in which the logical relationship between the support and claim is sound.

Lyric Poetry Lyric poetry is poetry that presents the personal thoughts and feelings of a single speaker. Most poems, other than narrative poems, are lyric poems. Lyric poetry can be in a variety of forms and cover many subjects, from love and death to everyday experiences.

Main Character *See* Character.

Main Idea The main idea, or central idea, is the most important idea about a topic that a writer or speaker conveys. It can be the central idea of an entire work or of just a paragraph. Often, the main idea of a paragraph is expressed in a topic sentence. However, a main idea may just be implied, or suggested, by details. A main idea is typically supported by details.

Make Inferences *See* **Inference.**

Memoir A memoir is a form of autobiographical writing in which a writer shares his or her personal experiences and observations of important events or people. Often informal in tone, memoirs usually give readers information about a particular person or period of time in the writer's life. In contrast, autobiographies focus on many important people and events in the writer's life over a long period of time.

See also Autobiography; Personal Narrative.

Metaphor A metaphor is a comparison of two things that are basically unlike but have some qualities in common. Unlike a simile, a metaphor does not contain the words **like** or **as.**

See also Figurative Language; Simile.

Meter In poetry, meter is the regular pattern of stressed (ˊ) and unstressed (˘) syllables. Although poems have rhythm, not all poems have regular meter. Each unit of meter is known as a **foot** and is made up of one stressed syllable and one or two unstressed syllables.

See also Rhythm.

Minor Character *See* **Character.**

Monitor Monitoring is the strategy of checking your comprehension as you read and modifying the strategies you are using to suit your needs. Monitoring often includes the following strategies: questioning, clarifying, visualizing, predicting, connecting, and rereading.

Mood Mood is the feeling or atmosphere that a writer creates for the reader. Descriptive words, imagery, and figurative language all influence the mood of a work.

Moral A moral is a lesson that a story teaches. A moral is often stated at the end of a fable.

See also Fable.

Motivation Motivation is the reason why a character acts, feels, or thinks in a certain way. A character may have more than one motivation for his or her actions. Understanding these motivations helps readers get to know the character.

Myth A myth is a traditional story that attempts to answer basic questions about human nature, origins of the world, mysteries of nature, and social customs.

Narrative Writing that tells a story is called a narrative. The events in a narrative may be real or imagined. Autobiographies and biographies are narratives that deal with real people or events. Fictional narratives include short stories, fables, myths, and novels. A narrative may also be in the form of a poem.

See also Autobiography; Biography; Personal Narrative.

Narrative Nonfiction Narrative nonfiction is writing that reads much like fiction, except that the characters, setting, and plot are real rather than imaginary. Narrative nonfiction includes autobiographies, biographies, and memoirs.

Narrative Poetry Poetry that tells a story is called narrative poetry. Like fiction, a narrative poem contains characters, a setting, and a plot. It might also contain such elements of poetry as rhyme, rhythm, imagery, and figurative language.

Narrator The narrator is the voice that tells a story. Sometimes the narrator is a character in the story. At other times, the narrator is an outside voice created by the writer. The narrator is not the same as the writer.

See also Point of View.

News Article A news article is writing that reports on a recent event. In newspapers, news articles are usually brief and to the point, presenting the most important facts first, followed by more detailed information.

Nonfiction Nonfiction is writing that tells about real people, places, and events. Unlike fiction, nonfiction is mainly written to convey factual information. Nonfiction includes a wide range of writing—newspaper articles, letters, essays, biographies, movie reviews, speeches, true-life adventure stories, advertising, and more.

Novel A novel is a long work of fiction. Like a short story, a novel is the product of a writer's imagination. Because a novel is considerably longer than a short story, a novelist can develop the characters and story line more thoroughly.

See also Fiction.

Novella A novella is a work of fiction that is longer than a short story but shorter than a novel. Due to its shorter length, a novella generally includes fewer characters and a less complex plot than a novel.

See also Fiction; Novel; Short Story.

Ode An ode is a type of lyric poem that deals with serious themes, such as justice, truth, or beauty.

Onomatopoeia Onomatopoeia is the use of words whose sounds echo their meanings, such as *buzz, whisper, gargle,* and *murmur.*

Op/Ed Piece An op/ed piece is an opinion piece that typically appears opposite ("op") the editorial page of a newspaper. Unlike editorials, op/ed pieces are written and submitted by readers.

Oral Literature Oral literature, or the oral tradition, consists of stories that have been passed down by word of mouth from generation to generation. Oral literature includes folk tales, legends, and myths. In more recent times, some examples of oral literature have been written down or recorded so that the stories can be preserved.

Organization *See* Pattern of Organization.

Overgeneralization An overgeneralization is a statement that is too broad to be accurate. You can often recognize overgeneralizations by the appearance of words and phrases such as *all, everyone, every time, any, anything, no one,* or *none.* An example is

"None of the city's workers really cares about keeping the environment clean." In all probability, there are many exceptions. The writer can't possibly know the feelings of every city worker.

Overview An overview is a short summary of a story, a speech, or an essay.

Paraphrase Paraphrasing is the restating of information in one's own words.

See also **Summarize.**

Parody A parody is a humorous imitation of another writer's work. Parodies can take the form of fiction, drama, or poetry. Jon Scieszka's "The True Story of the Three Little Pigs" is an example of a parody.

Pattern of Organization The term *pattern of organization* refers to the way ideas and information are arranged and organized. Patterns of organization include cause and effect, chronological, compare and contrast, classification, and problem-solution, among others.

See also Cause and Effect; Chronological Order; Classification; Compare and Contrast; Problem-Solution Order; Sequential Order.

Periodical A periodical is a magazine or another type of publication that is issued on a regular basis.

Personal Narrative A short essay told as a story in the first-person point of view. A personal narrative usually reflects the writer's experiences, feelings, and personality.

See also Autobiography; Memoir.

Personification The giving of human qualities to an animal, object, or idea is known as personification.

See also Figurative Language.

Persuasion Persuasion is the art of swaying others' feelings, beliefs, or actions. Persuasion normally appeals to both the mind and the emotions of readers.

See also Appeal to Authority; Emotional Appeal; Ethical Appeal; Loaded Language; Logical Appeal.

Persuasive Essay *See* Essay.

Play *See* Drama.

Playwright *See* Drama.

Plot The series of events in a story is called the plot. The plot usually centers on a **conflict,** or struggle, faced by the main character. The action that the characters take to solve the problem builds toward a **climax** in the story. At this point, or shortly afterward, the problem is solved and the story ends. Most story plots have five stages: exposition, rising action, climax, falling action, and resolution.

See also Climax; Conflict; Exposition; Falling Action; Rising Action.

Poetry Poetry is a type of literature in which words are carefully chosen and arranged to create certain effects. Poets use a variety of sound devices, imagery, and figurative language to express emotions and ideas.

See also Alliteration; Assonance; Ballad; Free Verse; Imagery; Meter; Narrative Poetry; Rhyme; Rhythm; Stanza.

Point of View Point of view refers to how a writer chooses to narrate a story. When a story is told from the **first-person** point of view, the narrator is a character in the story and uses first-person pronouns, such as *I, me,* and *we.* In a story told from the **third-person** point of view, the narrator is not a character in the story. A writer's choice of narrator affects the information readers receive.

See also Narrator.

Predict Predicting is a reading strategy that involves using text clues to make a reasonable guess about what will happen next in a story.

Primary Source *See* Sources.

Prior Knowledge Prior knowledge is the knowledge a reader already possesses about a topic. This information might come from personal experiences, expert accounts, books, films, or other sources.

Problem-Solution Order Problem-solution order is a pattern of organization in which a problem is stated and analyzed and then one or more solutions are proposed and examined.

Prop The word *prop,* originally an abbreviation of the word *property,* refers to any physical object that is used in a drama.

Propaganda Propaganda is any form of communication that is so distorted that it conveys false or misleading information to advance a specific belief or cause.

Prose The word *prose* refers to all forms of writing that are not in verse form. The term may be used to describe very different forms of writing, such as short stories and essays.

Protagonist A protagonist is the main character in a story, play, or novel. The protagonist is involved in the main conflict of the story. Usually, the protagonist undergoes changes as the plot runs its course.

Public Document Public documents are documents that were written for the public to provide information that is of public interest or concern. They include government documents, speeches, signs, and rules and regulations.

See also Government Publications.

Pun A pun is a play on words based on similar senses of two or more words, or on various meanings of the same word. A pun is usually made for humorous effect. For example, the fisherman was fired for playing hooky.

Radio Play A radio play is a drama that is written specifically to be broadcast over the radio. Because the audience is not meant to see a radio play, sound effects are often used to help listeners imagine the setting and the action. The stage directions in the play's script indicate the sound effects.

Realistic Fiction Realistic fiction is fiction that is set in the real, modern world. The characters behave like real people and use human abilities to cope with modern life's problems and conflicts.

Recurring Theme *See* Theme.

Reference Work Reference works are sources that contain facts and background information on a wide range of subjects. Most reference works are good sources of reliable information because they have been reviewed by experts. The following are some common reference works: encyclopedias, dictionaries, thesauri, almanacs, atlases, and directories.

Refrain A refrain is one or more lines repeated in each stanza of a poem.

Repetition Repetition is a technique in which a sound, word, phrase, or line is repeated for emphasis or unity. Repetition often helps to reinforce meaning and create an appealing rhythm.

See also Alliteration; Refrain; Sound Devices.

Resolution *See* Falling Action.

Review *See* Critical Review.

Rhetorical Question Rhetorical questions are those that have such obvious answers that they do not require a reply. Writers often use them to suggest that their claim is so obvious that everyone should agree with it.

Rhyme Rhyme is the repetition of sounds at the end of words. Words rhyme when their accented vowels and the letters that follow have identical sounds. *Pig* and *dig* rhyme, as do *reaching* and *teaching.* The most common type of rhyme in poetry is called **end**

rhyme, in which rhyming words come at the ends of lines. Rhyme that occurs within a line of poetry is called **internal rhyme.**

Rhyme Scheme A rhyme scheme is a pattern of end rhymes in a poem. A rhyme scheme is noted by assigning a letter of the alphabet, beginning with *a,* to each line. Lines that rhyme are given the same letter.

Rhythm Rhythm is the musical quality created by the alternation of stressed and unstressed syllables in a line of poetry. Poets use rhythm to emphasize ideas and to create moods. Devices such as alliteration, rhyme, and assonance often contribute to creating rhythm.

See also Meter.

Rising Action The rising action is the stage of the plot that develops the **conflict,** or struggle. During this stage, events occur that make the conflict more complicated. The events in the rising action build toward a **climax,** or turning point.

See also Plot.

Scanning Scanning is the process used to search through a text for a particular fact or piece of information. When you scan, you sweep your eyes across a page, looking for key words that may lead you to the information you want.

Scene In drama, the action is often divided into acts and scenes. Each scene presents an episode of the play's plot and typically occurs at a single place and time.

See also Act.

Scenery Scenery is a painted backdrop or other structures used to create the setting for a play.

Science Fiction Science fiction is fiction in which a writer explores unexpected possibilities of the past or the future, combining scientific information with his or her creative imagination. Most science fiction writers create believable worlds, although some create fantasy worlds that have familiar elements.

See also Fantasy.

Scope Scope refers to a work's focus. For example, an article about Austin, Texas, that focuses on the city's history, economy, and residents has a broad scope. An article that focuses only on the restaurants in Austin has a narrower scope.

Script The text of a play, film, or broadcast is called a script.

Secondary Source *See* Source.

Sensory Details Sensory details are words and phrases that appeal to the reader's senses of sight, hearing, touch, smell, and taste.

See also Imagery.

Sequential Order Sequential order is a pattern of organization that shows the order of steps or stages in a process.

Setting The setting of a story, poem, or play is the time and place of the action. Sometimes the setting is clear and well-defined. At other times, it is left to the reader's imagination. Elements of setting include geographic location, historical period (past, present, or future), season, time of day, and culture.

Setting a Purpose The process of establishing specific reasons for reading a text is called setting a purpose. Readers can look at a text's title, headings, and illustrations to guess what it might be about. They can then use these guesses to figure out what they want to learn from reading the text.

Short Story A short story is a work of fiction that centers on a single idea and can be read in one sitting. Generally, a short story has one main conflict that involves the characters and keeps the story moving.

See also Fiction.

Sidebar A sidebar is additional information set in a box alongside or within a news or feature article. Popular magazines often make use of sidebars.

Signal Words In a text, signal words are words and phrases that help show how events or ideas are related. Some common examples of signal words are ***and, but, however, nevertheless, therefore,*** and ***in addition.***

Simile A simile is a figure of speech that makes a comparison between two unlike things using the words ***like*** or ***as.***

See also Figurative Language; Metaphor.

Sound Devices Sound devices are ways of using words for the sound qualities they create. Sound devices can help convey meaning and mood in a writer's work. Some common sound devices include **alliteration, assonance, meter, onomatopoeia, repetition, rhyme,** and **rhythm.**

See also Alliteration; Assonance; Meter; Onomatopoeia; Repetition; Rhyme; Rhythm.

Source A source is anything that supplies information. **Primary sources** are materials created by people who witnessed or took part in the event they supply information about. Letters, diaries, autobiographies, and eyewitness accounts are primary sources. **Secondary sources** are those made by people who were not directly involved in the event or even present when it occurred. Encyclopedias, textbooks, biographies, and most news articles are secondary sources.

Speaker In poetry the speaker is the voice that "talks" to the reader, similar to the narrator in fiction. The speaker is not necessarily the poet.

Speech A speech is a talk or public address. The purpose of a speech may be to entertain, to explain, to persuade, to inspire, or any combination of these purposes.

Stage Directions In the script of a play, the instructions to the actors, director, and stage crew are called the stage directions. Stage directions might suggest scenery, lighting, sound effects, and ways for actors to move and speak. Stage directions often appear in parentheses and in italic type.

Stanza A stanza is a group of two or more lines that form a unit in a poem. Each stanza may have the same number of lines, or the number of lines may vary.

See also Couplet; Form; Poetry.

Stereotype In literature, characters who are defined by a single trait are known as stereotypes. Such characters do not usually demonstrate the complexities of real people. Familiar stereotypes in popular literature include the absent-minded professor and the busybody.

Stereotyping Stereotyping is a dangerous type of overgeneralization. It can lead to unfair judgments of people based on their ethnic background, beliefs, practices, or physical appearance.

Structure The structure of a work of literature is the way in which it is put together. In poetry, structure involves the arrangement of words and lines to produce a desired effect. One structural unit in poetry is the stanza. In prose, structure involves the arrangement of such elements as sentences, paragraphs, and events. **Sentence structure** refers to the length and types of sentences used in a work.

Style A style is a manner of writing. It involves how something is said rather than what is said.

Subject The subject of a literary work is its focus or topic. In an autobiography, for example, the subject is the life of the person telling the story. Subject differs from

theme in that theme is a deeper meaning, whereas the subject is the main situation or set of facts described by the text.

Summarize To summarize is to briefly retell the main ideas of a piece of writing in one's own words.

See also Paraphrase.

Support Support is any information that helps to prove a claim.

Supporting Detail *See* Main Idea.

Surprise Ending A surprise ending is an unexpected plot twist at the end of a story. The surprise may be a sudden turn in the action or a piece of information that gives a different perspective to the entire story.

Suspense Suspense is a feeling of growing tension and excitement experienced by a reader. Suspense makes a reader curious about the outcome of a story or an event within a story. A writer creates suspense by raising questions in the reader's mind. The use of **foreshadowing** is one way that writers create suspense.

See also Foreshadowing.

Symbol A symbol is a person, a place, an object, an animal, or an activity that stands for something beyond itself. For example, a flag is a colored piece of cloth that stands for a country. A white dove is a bird that represents peace.

Synthesize To synthesize information means to take individual pieces of information and combine them in order to gain a better understanding of a subject.

Tall Tale A tall tale is a humorously exaggerated story about impossible events, often involving the supernatural abilities of the main character. Stories about folk heroes such as Pecos Bill and Paul Bunyan are typical tall tales.

Teleplay A teleplay is a play written for television. In a teleplay, scenes can change quickly and dramatically. The camera can focus the viewer's attention on specific actions. The camera directions in teleplays are much like the stage directions in stage plays.

Text Feature Text features are elements of a text, such as boldface type, headings, and subheadings, that help organize and call attention to important information. Italic type, bulleted or numbered lists, sidebars, and graphic aids such as charts, tables, timelines, illustrations, and photographs are also considered text features.

Theme A theme is a message about life or human nature that the writer shares with the reader. In many cases, readers must infer the writer's message. One way to infer a theme is to note the lessons learned by the main characters.

> **Recurring themes:** Themes found in a variety of works. For example, authors from different backgrounds might express similar themes having to do with the importance of family values.

> **Universal themes:** Themes that are found throughout the literature of all time periods. For example, Cinderella stories contain a universal theme relating to goodness being rewarded.

See also Moral.

Thesaurus *See* Reference Works.

Thesis Statement A thesis statement, or controlling idea, is the main proposition that a writer attempts to support in a piece of writing.

Third-Person Point of View *See* Point of View.

Title The title of a piece of writing is the name that is attached to it. A title often refers to an important aspect of the work.

Tone The tone of a literary work expresses the writer's attitude toward his or her subject. Words such as ***angry, sad,*** and ***humorous*** can be used to describe different tones.

See also Author's Perspective.

Topic Sentence The topic sentence of a paragraph states the paragraph's main idea. All other sentences in the paragraph provide supporting details.

Tragedy A tragedy is a dramatic work that presents the downfall of a character or characters. The events in a tragic plot are set in motion by a decision that is often an error in judgment on the part of the hero. Events are linked in a cause-and-effect relationship and lead to a disastrous conclusion, usually death.

Traits *See* Character.

Treatment The way a topic is handled in a work is referred to as its treatment. Treatment includes the form the writing takes as well as the writer's purpose and tone.

Turning Point *See* Climax.

Universal Theme *See* Theme.

Unsupported Inference A guess that may seem logical but that is not supported by facts.

Visualize Visualizing is the process of forming a mental picture based on written or spoken information.

Voice The term ***voice*** refers to a writer's unique use of language that allows a reader to "hear" a human personality in the writer's work. Elements of style that contribute to a writer's voice can reveal much about the author's personality, beliefs, and attitudes.

Website A website is a collection of "pages" on the World Wide Web that usually covers a specific subject. Linked pages are accessed by clicking hyperlinks or menus, which send the user from page to page within a website. Websites are created by companies, organizations, educational institutions, government agencies, the military, and individuals.

Word Choice The success of any writing depends on the writer's choice of words. Words not only communicate ideas but also help describe events, characters, settings, and so on. Word choice can make a writer's work sound formal or informal, serious or humorous. A writer must choose words carefully depending on the goal of the piece of writing. For example, a writer working on a science article would probably use technical, formal words; a writer trying to establish the setting in a short story would probably use more descriptive words. Word choice is sometimes referred to as diction.

See also Style.

Workplace Document Workplace documents are materials that are produced or used within a work setting, usually to aid in the functioning of the workplace. They include job applications, office memos, training manuals, job descriptions, and sales reports.

Works Cited The term ***works cited*** refers to a list of all the works a writer has referred to in his or her text. This list often includes not only books and articles but also Internet sources.

Works Consulted The term ***works consulted*** refers to a list of all the works a writer consulted in order to create his or her text. It is not limited just to those works cited in the text.

See also Bibliography.

Glossary of Academic Vocabulary

accompany (ə-kŭm´pə-nē, ə-kŭmp´nē) *v.* to play music behind; to go somewhere with

alert (ə-lûrt´) *adj.* watching carefully and ready to act; *v.* to warn someone of something

assist (ə-sĭst´) *v.* to help someone

awe (ô) *n.* a feeling of amazement

captured (kăp´chərd) *v.* caught and held prisoner; described or shown well

comfort (kŭm´fərt) *v.* to make someone feel better; *n.* the feeling of being relaxed and without pain

condition (kən-dĭsh´ən) *n.* the state that something is in; a sickness or other medical problem

confidence (kŏn´fĭ-dəns) *n.* a feeling of trust

convey (kən-vā´) *v.* to share ideas or feelings

critics (krĭt´ĭks) *n.* people who find something wrong with what they see; people whose job is to tell what they like and don't like about a book, movie, etc.

deserve (dĭ-zûrv´) *v.* to have a right to

display (dĭ-splā´) *v.* to put something where people can see it; *n.* a group of things that are set up for people to look at

effort (ĕf´ərt) *n.* energy used to do something; the act of trying hard

entertaining (ĕn´tər-tā´nĭng) *adj.* interesting and fun

extraordinary (ĭk-strôr´dn-ĕr´ē, ĕk´strə- ôr´-) *adj.* unusual and extremely good

habitats (hăb´ĭ-tăts´) *n.* places where particular plants and animals live and grow

independent (ĭn´dĭ-pĕn´dənt) *adj.* not controlled by another person, country, etc.

informed (ĭn-fôrmd´) *adj.* having information, aware

introduce (ĭn´trə-dōōs´, -dyōōs´) *v.* to present someone to someone else; to tell people what they are about to see; to show or offer for the first time

memorable (mĕm´ər-ə-bəl) *adj.* special or unusual and easy to remember

mood (mōōd) *n.* the way someone feels; the feeling a writer creates by choosing certain words

overcome (ō´vər-kŭm´) *v.* to defeat or deal with something; to be strongly affected

performs (pər-fôrmz´) *v.* puts on a show in front of people; does or carries out an action

positive (pŏz´ĭ-tĭv) *adj.* certain that something is true; good or useful

progress (prŏg´rĕs´, -rəs, prō´grĕs´) *v.* move forward or improve; *n.* movement forward or improvement

rapidly (răp´ĭd-lē) *adv.* quickly

scarce (skârs) *adj.* small in number

species (spē´shēz, -sēz) *n.* groups of living things that share traits

variety (və-rī´ĭ-tē) *n.* many different kinds or types; a certain kind of person or thing

vast (văst) *adj.* very large

Index of Titles and Authors

Acknowledgments

Balto's Story by Dina McClellan. Copyright © 2014 by Escletxa. Reprinted by permission of Escletxa.

Black Beauty retold by Escletxa. Copyright © 2014 by Escletxa. Reprinted by permission of Escletxa.

"Disorientation" excerpted and titled from *The Magic Trap* by Jacqueline Davies. Text copyright © 2014 by Jacqueline Davies. Reprinted by permission of Adams Literary and Houghton Mifflin Harcourt Publishing Company.

"The King" excerpted and titled from *Le Petit Prince*. Originally published by Harcourt, Inc. in English as *The Little Prince* by Antoine de Saint-Exupéry, translated by Richard Howard, illustrated by Antoine de Saint-Exupéry. Copyright © 1943 by Antoine de Saint-Exupéry. Copyright renewed © 1971 by Consuelo de Saint-Exupéry. Translation copyright © 2000 by Richard Howard. Reprinted by permission of Editions Gallimard and Houghton Mifflin Harcourt Publishing Company.

The Lion's Whisker by Mercedes Roffé. Copyright © 2014 by Escletxa. Reprinted by permission of Escletxa.

"Mama Goose and Jonathan" excerpted and titled from *A Bear Named Trouble* by Marion Dane Bauer. Text copyright © 2005 by Marion Dane Bauer. Reprinted by permission of Houghton Mifflin Harcourt Publishing Company.

Excerpt from *Mr. Popper's Penguins* by Richard and Florence Atwater. Text copyright © 1938 by Richard and Florence Atwater, renewed 1966 by Florence Atwater, Doris Atwater, and Carroll Atwater Bishop. Reprinted by permission of Little, Brown and Company, a division of Hachette Book Group, Inc.

Nelson Mandela by Jessica Cohn. Copyright © 2014 by Escletxa. Reprinted by permission of Escletxa.

The Prince and the Pauper retold by Mercedes Roffé. Copyright © 2014 by Escletxa. Reprinted by permission of Escletxa.

20,000 Leagues Under the Sea retold by Meredith Mann. Copyright © 2014 by Escletxa. Reprinted by permission of Escletxa.

Excerpts from *The Wild Book* by Margarita Engle. Text copyright © 2012 by Margarita Engle. Reprinted by permission of Houghton Mifflin Harcourt Publishing Company.

Excerpt from *The Year of the Dog* by Grace Lin. Text copyright © 2006 by Grace Lin. Reprinted by permission of Little, Brown and Company, a division of Hachette Book Group, Inc.

Podcast Acknowledgments

"Alex and Me" by Irene Pepperburg. Used by permission of Irene Pepperburg and The Moth.

NPR *Morning Edition* news report "Crocodile Meets Godzilla - A Swimming Dino Bigger than T-Rex," September 11, 2014. © 2014 by National Public Radio, Inc. Used by permission of NPR. Any unauthorized duplication is strictly prohibited.